The Great Crash

The Great Crash

How the Stock Market Crash of 1929
Plunged the World into Depression

Selwyn Parker

PIATKUS

PIATKUS

First published in Great Britain in 2008 by Piatkus Books

Copyright © 2008 Selwyn Parker

The moral right of the author has been asserted

Mary Brooksbank poem, pg. 150, from MS 103/3/8, courtesy of University of Dundee Archive Services.

A CIP catalogue record for this book
is available from the British Library

ISBN 978-0-7499-0987-1

Edited by Daniel Balado
Typeset in Scala by
Action Publishing Technology Ltd, Gloucester
Printed and bound in Great Britain by
MPG Books, Bodmin, Cornwall

Piatkus Books
An imprint of
Little, Brown Book Group
100 Victoria Embankment
London EC4Y 0DY

An Hachette Livre UK Company
www.hachettelivre.co.uk

To the great narrative historians who can tell the story

Contents

Acknowledgements

My sincere thanks to my publisher Alan Brooke, who was kind enough to risk giving me the project and then left me to it, and to my agent Andrew Lownie, who is a great enthusiast and judge of narrative history.

Prologue

Jack Pierpont Morgan and his wife Jessie followed the same routine whenever they came to Britain. They crossed the Atlantic aboard the elegant British-built *Mauretania*, or the newer *Aquitania* with its four racy-looking, angled smokestacks, or the *Corsair*, Morgan's private ocean-going vessel. After berthing at Southampton, they were chauffeured to their stately home in the tiny village of Aldenham in leafy Hertfordshire where they generally settled in for a long stay.

Wall Hall was a grandiose home befitting the world's best-known banker, and probably its richest man. Dating from the early 1800s, it was a late-model castle built in the Gothic revival style complete with a castellated façade and other medieval cues. Appropriately enough, the original occupant of Wall Hall was another prosperous banker, one George Woodford Thelluson, who achieved immortality as a character in Charles Dickens' novel of the French revolution *A Tale of Two Cities*. Tellson, as Dickens chose to call him, owned a bank in Temple Bar that functioned as 'a kind of high exchange' to which aristocrats, mainly refugees from the revolution, entrusted their wealth.

In 1929, Jack, as his friends knew him, or J. P. Morgan Jr as the papers usually described him, could hardly wait to get away from New York and take up residence in Hertfordshire. Having lived in London for several years before returning to New York to take over the parent bank from his father, the fabled Junius Pierpont, he had bought Wall Hall in 1908 after he and his wife fell in love with it. For

Boston-educated Jessie, herself the daughter of a banker, the English countryside provided a respite from the teeming streets of the big city; for her husband, it served to lighten the load of the onerous responsibilities that had fallen by inheritance on his shoulders. And at Wall Hall he could become an English gentleman, albeit with an American accent. The residence's panelled dining room regularly hosted the upper strata of English society: members of the royal family including Elizabeth, the future Queen Mother, representatives of the aristocracy, leading Churchmen, politicians and bankers. They formed a circle natural to a man who possessed seemingly unlimited wealth and enviable influence in the highest levels of government around the world.

Proud of Wall Hall and its immediate environs, Jack Morgan lavished considerable expense on the estate, and on the village that sat practically on its doorstep. Indeed he was very much the lord of Aldenham, his wife the lady. Jessie threw herself into activities at the local Women's Institute, which met regularly in an old brick building barely five minutes' walk from the castle. The couple sometimes worshipped in the seven-hundred-year-old Church of St John the Baptist, and occasionally joined locals for a beer at the Three Compasses pub nearby. The local schools regularly benefited from the banker's largesse. And although he knew little about the game, he was an enthusiastic and generous patron of Wall Hall's resident cricket team.

Jack Morgan was in some ways a reluctant banker. Much of his affection for Aldenham derived from the freedom it gave him to pursue non-business interests. At Wall Hall, he set aside a natural history room for his microscope and his cherished specimens. He created a darkroom where he played around with the new miracle of colour photography. He took a city boy's delight in the farming of the estate, partly to provide a livelihood for the people who worked on it but also to earn a satisfactory return on the investment: the financial disciplines he had inherited from his formidable father would not permit him to sink money into any venture that did not produce a profit. 'I think now that within a year or so we shall be really producing here enough of milk and pigs and eggs to keep the whole place and all the people on it and [who] work for it going well on a paying basis,' he enthusiastically noted in his diaries. 'Though what rate of interest we shall earn on the investment remains to be seen. If we don't earn a fair rate, one year with another, it will mean that we have not been successful.' Thus wool from the estate's Southdown sheep was sold for conversion into cloth for suits that went on sale in London. Still, profitable or not, he was invariably delighted when the farm won prizes at agricultural shows.

Wall Hall also served as a launching point for motoring escapades around the countryside, and for extended grouse-shooting trips to Gannochy in Scotland, where Jack socialised with the flower of English society. In a typical season he would blaze away over the heather-covered Highlands with the likes of the Duke and Duchess of Beaufort, the Earl of Dalkeith, the Duke of Roxburghe (a later Viceroy of India) and the Marquis of Linlithgow, Viscount Lewisham. 'My mind is singing a little song of joy in the back of my head all the time at the thought of the delights of that month up there!' he confided to his diary.

In 1929, J. P. Morgan Jr was 61 years old and at the zenith of an illustrious career. Honoured in Britain for having arranged the finance for much of the 1914–18 war effort (albeit at a return of some $30 million in fees to his banking empire), a confidant of the world's central bankers – in part for helping to solve the German reparations crisis – and the undisputed head of the world's greatest bank with fabulous deposits of nearly $500 million, he was an essential presence around the table in most major international negotiations involving finance. It was Jack Morgan who was instrumental in stabilising the tottering French franc in 1924 by arranging a credit of $100 million – a stupendous sum at the time. In that year he also underwrote a massive German loan to shore up the German currency. A year later, as the financial agents of Benito Mussolini's fascist government, J. P. Morgan & Co raised another $100 million to save the lira. Shortly after that, another J. P. Morgan-syndicated loan stabilised the Spanish currency. Jack Morgan's power, reputation and influence had been of vital importance in rescuing Europe's economies from the ravages of war.

The parent bank, J. P. Morgan & Co, dominated Wall Street, and the London branch of the bank, Morgan, Grenfell & Co, held an assured position in the City as a trusted name and a leading issuer of sovereign bonds for governments. Edward Grenfell, senior partner of the London branch, was one of Jack Morgan's closest friends. As banking was a business based on trust, Jack liked to associate with people he considered to be of impeccable reputation, and Grenfell certainly fulfilled that criterion. Son of a former governor of the Bank of England, educated at Harrow and Trinity College, Cambridge, he was a director of the Bank of England, a financial agent for the Treasury and a Member of Parliament.

Jack Morgan had his enemies in the City, among them Lord Revelstoke, the head of Barings, who resented an American house pirating the City's long-established business, especially the prestigious and lucrative syndicating of sovereign loans to governments. As far as Revelstoke was concerned, Morgan money was ill-gotten, 'insolent wealth' acquired through Britain's 'loss of blood and treasure' in the First World War. They were 'the greatest profiteers the world has ever seen', he once wrote in a fit of spleen. But bankers generally profited by financing the reconstruction that inevitably followed war; Barings itself had turned to good account similar business in the wake of earlier wars.

As the 1920s drew to a close, however, the head of J. P. Morgan & Co could afford to be philosophical about criticism. Never an instinctive dealmaker like his father, he was steadily withdrawing from the firm. He felt he had done enough. Also, his beloved wife Jessie had died in 1925 at the early age of 57 after contracting sleeping sickness (encephalitis lethargica), for which there was no cure. A grief-stricken Morgan gave $200,000 for the study and treatment of the disease – enough to equip and maintain an entire floor of the neurological institute in Manhattan.

From that point he began to devote himself to extra-curricular interests: his photography and specimens, his valued New York library of old books, cruises in company aboard *Corsair*, his many charities, and the further development of Wall Hall, probably the favourite of his three residences. In short, he was looking forward to twilight years free from the rigours of financial diplomacy, with his wealth and reputation seemingly impregnable.

Then, almost overnight, Jack Morgan's world began to crumble.

Song of the Stock Ticker

The Western Union stock ticker was a marvel of modern technology. Clacking away in most of the western world's stock exchanges, it combined an advanced knowledge of several sciences and technologies: electricity, electromagnets, mechanical devices and production engineering. Generally known as the self-winder, it incorporated several breakthroughs that enabled it to punch out the stock prices considerably faster than any of its numerous predecessors, each of them equally impressive in their time.

Typed in at the stock exchange end, dozens of quotations were printed out every minute on a three-quarter-inch-wide length of tape that rolled into thousands of offices in America and beyond. And with the volume of share-dealing rising by the week, especially in Wall Street and other exchanges in the United States, speed was of the essence. Bankers, brokers, manufacturers, businesspeople, professional investors, anybody trading on a daily basis – they all owned, rented or had regular access to the self-winder or plain 'ticker'. By the late 1920s the ticker had become the symbol of the sharemarket boom, the only price-issuing technology that could match the furious pace of the exchanges. The noise it made, like that of a hyperactive clock, became the theme music of the boom, inspiring songs such as the sardonic 'A Tale of a Ticker', composed by two musicians from Ohio, Frank Crumit and Frank O'Brien:

And here is the song they sing the whole day long:
'Oh! The market's not so good today.
Your stocks look kind of sick.
In fact they all dropped down a point a time the ticker's tick.'

The heritage of the self-winder says much about America's growing infatuation with the stockmarket throughout the roaring twenties. For half a century the competition to produce the fastest stock price-printing machine was almost as frantic as the pursuit of the stocks and shares. Indeed for many, the two were inseparable. Had not broker and banker Horace L. Hotchkiss, a founder of manufacturer Gold & Stock which would later produce the self-winder, once declared that it was 'through the instant dissemination of the quotations made on [the stock exchange] floor that the active and continuous interest in the markets is sustained'?

The first machine to sustain this 'active and continuous interest' was the gold indicator in 1867, a mechanical device that cleverly spun three barrels to display the latest prices from Wall Street's Gold Exchange. Over the ensuing years a series of constantly improved printers appeared: the popular Calahan, which the London Stock Exchange installed in 1872, the Edison and Pope, the Phelps, and, in the mid-1870s, Thomas Alva Edison's robust Universal, which put the great inventor on the scientific map. Gradually, the machines came to replace foot-borne quotations conveyed by sweating 'runners' who sprinted up and down the steps of banks and broking houses, pausing only long enough to shout the latest prices before heading off, chests heaving, to the next location.

As volumes of business continued to build, the participants in the market demanded ever more timely quotations and the quest for faster tickers never let up. Around 1910, manufacturer Stock Quotation Telegraph produced the Burry machine that was not only lighter than existing models but also offered a limited self-winding capability. But it was Western Union, the offspring of Gold & Stock, that achieved the breakthrough that came closest to satisfying the rampant appetite for share-dealing. Its machine was smaller than the Burry, achieved in part by locating the escapement magnet and adjustment screws in the frame of the device. More importantly, it was faster. At first burdened with the title the Scott-Phelps-Barclay-Page Ticker, it soon became known around the world as the Western Union self-winder, and it cornered the market. No fewer than sixteen thousand self-winders left the factories in the 1920s, and many were exported. Now everybody could keep up with the markets, buying and selling at the same speed as Wall Street.

The decade finally had the stock quotation machine it needed. But, as Hotchkiss had observed, the Western Union was more than a mere machine. By churning out quotes at ever-increasing speeds, the ticker actually helped feed the sharemarket boom. As we shall see, much of the information it delivered with such reliability proved to be of dubious value, but that only bothered the more astute traders. However, even this marvel of technology would soon experience difficulties when it came to keeping up with the markets.

The epicentre of the sharemarket boom, both worldwide and in the United States, was the New York Stock Exchange. A noble-looking building of neo-classic design located at 18 Broad Street, it featured an elaborate marble sculpture above a grand façade supported by six Corinthian pillars. Called 'Integrity Protecting the Works of Man', the sculpture portrayed the benign presence of a Greek goddess presiding over toiling individuals. The implicit message of John Quincy Adams Ward's work was that the exchange was there to ensure that the production of the people was converted into greater wealth for the general good.

This was certainly the ethic the exchange had steadily assumed for itself in the 137 years since it was founded under a buttonwood tree outside 68 Wall Street. The people who governed the exchange in 1929 were the grandees of the market and, like their predecessors, ran it with complete independence from government. Indeed they had done so since its establishment, a state of affairs with which Washington was reasonably content. Not everybody liked the arrangement, however. From time to time the exchange's freedom from independent supervision came under attack, one critic denouncing 'the carnival – I would almost say orgy – of corruption and swindling that has marked its history'.

However, as long as the economy prospered, as it was assuredly doing in the 1920s, President Calvin Coolidge saw no reason to regulate the nation's premier palace of investment. The United States was in the middle of what was known as the Coolidge bull market, and the famously taciturn president, by 1929 into his seventh and final year in office, was the hero of a business community very much in the ascendant. New industries were prospering, automobile manufacturing and radio in particular, and corporate profits were rising. The stockmarket was the beneficiary of this surge in prosperity; indeed, during the Coolidge bull market the dividends paid to investors had risen by more than 100 per cent.

Foreign money had flooded into the United States during the decade, looking for a high-earning home. This was partly the result of the 1914–18 war, which had left Britain and Europe economically devastated and heavily indebted, in particular to the United States. About 15 per cent of Britain's overseas investments, and especially those in America, had been sold off to help fight the war. Thus America emerged from the conflict as a creditor nation owning vast assets abroad. The proceeds of these assets in the form of dividends, interest and profits – in short, capital – were making the country cash-rich.

By contrast, lenders in the City of London had been hamstrung by the Bank of England, which was so worried about the weakness of the British pound that it placed tight limits on the amount of capital that could be loaned abroad. This slowed the business in which London's bankers had long considered themselves world leaders – the provision of capital for overseas development. Although the City could still claim a reputation as the true centre of banking expertise – most London bankers regarded their counterparts across the Atlantic as buccaneers – it was undoubtedly New York that had most of the money.

In the late 1920s, as the stockmarket boom showed no sign of slowing, some in the government began to fear the economy was overheating. 'Silent Cal' was not one of them. Ignoring the warnings of Commerce Secretary Herbert Hoover, who feared the boom was unsustainable and would end in tears, Coolidge continued to relax business regulations in the conviction that commerce could be trusted to behave sensibly, decently and honestly without Washington becoming its conscience. Thus he made sure that the numerous supervisory authorities under the control of federal government were stacked with pro-business appointees only too happy to let the boom run. Unlike some of his predecessors – such as trust-busting William Howard Taft, who sought to curb the power of big business, for instance by forcing the break-up of all-powerful companies such as Rockefeller's Standard Oil, American Tobacco and railway giant Northern Securities; or Taft's immediate successor Woodrow Wilson, who moved to prevent companies from colluding to rig prices – Coolidge had a benign faith in the inherent goodness of America's captains of industry. About the only law passed during his laissez-faire administration that could be described as anti-business was one outlawing corruption – hardly something a president could oppose. Indeed, Coolidge liked to mix with the titans of commerce. In their final month in office, the presidential couple were guests of honour at a cabinet dinner attended by Henry Ford and his wife, among other leaders of the commercial community. Essentially, Coolidge believed in the decency of individuals, whether employers or employees, and in letting them get on with their industrious lives without excessive interference. 'All growth depends upon activity,' he observed in one of his radio speeches. 'There is no development physically or intellectually without effort, and effort means work.'

Thus, under his minimalist stewardship, commercial monopolies multiplied and America's mighty economic engine fell into the hands of fewer and fewer people. By 1929, one half of all America's corporate wealth was controlled by just two hundred companies.

Not that anybody was worried. Coolidge had complete faith that the profits of business would eventually flow into the pockets of the general population. More than that, he was convinced that business was the people's hope for an ever-rising material future. In 1925, as the decade was starting to roar, he once lectured the American Society of Newspaper Editors on the importance of reporting commerce more conscientiously: 'It is probable that a press which maintains an intimate touch with the business currents of the nation is likely to be more reliable than it would be if it were a stranger to these influences. After all, the chief business of the American people is business. They are profoundly concerned with buying, selling, investing and prospering in the world.'

Ever the farm boy, Coolidge was a thrifty president. He set great store on the federal budgeting process, which had only been initiated two years before he took office, and under his watchful eye government spending stuck remarkably closely to the preliminary estimates. In his final budget statement, Coolidge fired his usual shot across the bows of Congress, warning them to disburse taxpayers' money with prudence and astuteness. 'Our splendid Treasury is not a bottomless, automatically replenishing fountain of fiscal supply, and its outflow must be eternally watched and carefully and wisely directed into proper channels,' he warned. Coolidge prided himself on the surpluses the government accounts usually showed after the money had been disbursed on the business of the nation.

In Andrew Mellon, he had a like-minded treasury secretary. A champion of big business who had built his own industrial empire in oil, steel, ship-building and construction, Mellon was the epitome of the American dream, the son of immigrants from Northern Ireland who had parlayed his father's social and financial success into enormous wealth (Mellon senior was a banker and a judge in an era when it was by no means considered incompatible to be both). One of the most successful of self-made men, the younger Mellon believed in America, self-help, hard work and a government that did not intrude. 'Any man of energy and initiative in this country can get what he wants out of life,' he wrote. 'But when initiative is crippled by legislation or by a tax system which denies him the right to receive a reasonable share of his earnings, then he will no longer exert himself and the country will be deprived of the energy on which its continued greatness depends.'

Mellon had been secretary of the treasury since 1921, reforming the tax system in a way that in general favoured the wealthy but which also encouraged honest toil. He put it elegantly in a 1924 book called *Taxation: The People's Business*: 'The fairness of taxing more lightly income from wages, salaries or from investments is beyond question. In the first case, the income is uncertain and limited in duration; sickness or death destroys it and old age diminishes it ... Surely we can afford to make a distinction between the people whose only capital is their mental and physical energy and the people whose income is derived from instruments.' And in his eleven-year reign as treasury secretary,

Mellon behaved as he preached. He halved (from 40 per cent to 20 per cent) the maximum tax payable on earnings and, even better for the rich, halved estate tax. A stickler for prudence in government finance, he also reduced the public debt by nearly 40 per cent. By 1929, Mellon had a legendary reputation as a sure hand at the helm of America's finances.

So as the boom accelerated, Coolidge saw no reason to discourage it. After all, was not the welfare of the people synonymous with the profits of commerce? In January 1929, two months before he left office, it was difficult to gainsay him. Factories were sprouting up everywhere – 22,800 new ones in Coolidge's final four-year term.

For all this output Coolidge could thank, at least in part, a management revolution inspired by Frederick Winslow Taylor. The founder of a genuinely new way of organising production that enormously boosted industrial profits and reduced the price of consumer goods, Taylor was the scion of a wealthy Quaker family. His system dismantled the entire manufacturing process into its individual components and subjected them to minute analysis. Having done that, it devised ways of doing each one of them better, meaning faster and more cheaply. Finally, it reassembled the discrete parts into a much more efficient and coherent whole.

Deeply resented by the unions because 'Taylorism' took little or no account of workers' welfare and even less of their own experience and insights into the manufacturing process, scientific management did little for employees' morale. 'It is only through *enforced* standardisation of methods, *enforced* adaptation of the best implements and working conditions, and *enforced* cooperation that this faster work can be assured,' the uncompromising Taylor wrote (the italics are his). 'And the duty of enforcing the adaptation of standards and enforcing this cooperation rests with management alone.' This essential enforcement process was executed by a team of bosses who constantly monitored workers for speed, efficiency, discipline, conformity to instructions, costs and repairs, among various other measurements.

Taylor died in 1915, long before Coolidge took office, but his methods had steadily gained momentum in the United States with impressive results. Between 1921 and 1928, the Federal Reserve's index of industrial production shot up from 67 to 110, and it would continue to accelerate deep into 1929. Taylorism was also gaining traction in France, Switzerland, Britain, and even in the USSR, where Lenin and, later, Stalin saw the system as a way of turning post-revolutionary Russia into an economic powerhouse.

So as Coolidge's final term drew to a close, Americans had every reason to feel optimistic. In general they were getting richer, although at unconscionably different rates, and the price of goods was falling relative to income. Factory workers might not have been enamoured of Taylorism but its undoubted benefit was more affordable consumer goods such as fridges – one of the luxuries of the inter-war years – automobiles, radios and other thrilling products. Thanks to rampant production, the stores were full of goods that just a few years earlier were priced beyond the average person's reach. Even if they weren't rich in the same sense as an Andrew Mellon or a Jack Morgan, many Americans *felt* prosperous. They had disposable income for the first time and were acquiring more possessions than ever before. And in a virtuous circle, because Americans were spending, factories were working overtime.

Every year promised to be better than the previous one. A nationwide business survey conducted in January by a Manhattan advertising agency (and duly delivered to a delighted Coolidge) concluded that all the signs 'pointed to a prosperous 1929'. In his final State of the Union address that year, Coolidge congratulated himself on 'the highest record of prosperity in years' and declared that no other Congress 'has met with a more pleasing prospect than that which appears at the present time. In the domestic field there is tranquillity and contentment.' In short, what could possibly go wrong?

In statistical terms, the total real (after inflation) income of Americans had increased by an average 3.4 per cent a year for most of Coolidge's period in office. As economist Harold Bierman Jr noted, 'The 1920s were in fact a period of real growth and prosperity.' Although richer Americans had done much better than the average American, and the richest had done far better than everybody else, most of the nation was sharing to a greater or lesser extent in the benefits of economic growth.

None of those benefits was considered more desirable than the automobile, the acknowledged symbol of prosperity. In 1929 Americans bought, usually on credit, 4.45 million passenger cars at an average retail price of around $876. No fewer than 21.6 million automobiles and 3.1 million trucks were registered by 1928, giving Americans 78 per cent of the world's total stock of automobiles. Predictably, the biggest-selling models were the cheaper ones like Ford's Model A, General Motors' Chevrolet and Durant Motors' Star, but the increasingly affluent were fast trading up to the mid-line Princetons, Packards, Chryslers and Cadillacs, while the wealthiest travelled in eight-cylinder monsters such as the Cadillac Locomobile Stearns-Knight, one of the luxury speedsters. There was such a strong market for these top-of-the-line models that Manhattan's National Automobile Show of January 1929 set aside a specially carpeted area of the exhibition building where, as *Time* magazine reported, 'soft-voiced salesmen, in tuxedos, point out the glories of the Auburn Jordan Peerless, Black Hawk La Salle Fierce-Arrow, Stutz's Lincoln Reo, Franklin Moon Stutz, Gardner Packard'. Faced with such chrome-bedecked, low-slung wonders, ticket-holders did not know quite what to make of the stubby little British cars (Austin and Vauxhall were now owned by General Motors after a deal brokered in London by Morgan, Grenfell) which were displayed in a less prestigious corner of the exhibition. Although designed for a country of narrower roads and more expensive petrol, the cars from the other side of the Atlantic were still snapped up to fill a spare space in American garages. Cheaper models were popular with the wealthy as 'an auxiliary gadabout' to complement the luxury vehicles that dominated Wall Street. Yes, the American automobile industry had travelled a long way since just before the turn of the century when, after a bad experience, an unimpressed Rudyard Kipling described the highly unreliable steam-engined version of the Locomobile as a 'nickel-plated fraud'.

As automobiles were the aspirational symbol of this highly acquisitive, unworried decade, one magnate of the industry decided to commission a building to pay them homage – more specifically, homage to his own particular brand. Having bought a plot of land in lower Manhattan, Walter P. Chrysler hired architect William van Alen to produce a suitably triumphant edifice that would serve as a totem for the roaring twenties. Like so many American industrialists, Chrysler came from humble origins, which did nothing to deter his sense of ambition. Quite the reverse, in fact. Unlike Britain and many other western European nations with their highly stratified societies, humble birth was not considered a handicap in America. Indeed, men like Chrysler almost revelled in their dirt-poor backgrounds.

Son of a railway engineer, he had grown up in Ellis, a railroad shop town in Kansas, and started working life as a dollar-a-day sweeper in the local Union Pacific yards. Yet, 'mad with curiosity' about machines, as he put it, he became a brilliant, largely self-taught engineer who cut his teeth designing entire locomotives. He was also mad about cars: he once bought a $5000 Locomobile on credit just to pull it apart to see how it all worked. Very much a product of the industrial boom, Chrysler launched out on his own as soon as he could find financial backers, of which there was almost a surfeit in the United States (this was also very different from Britain). By the late 1920s, Chrysler had carved himself a reputation for imaginatively marketed, mechanically innovative vehicles. The company's four main brands – Chrysler, Plymouth, Dodge and DeSoto – were so successful that they became a thorn in the side of giants Ford and GM. The latest DeSoto was on the way to selling over 81,000 models in the first twelve months of production at a base price of $845 – a record for a new model that would not be beaten for more than thirty years. Walter Chrysler was even rivalling Ford in export sales: his cars could be found in the showrooms of 3800 dealerships around the world. Chrysler had a global vision for the automobile, particularly his own models, that was almost missionary. 'It devolves upon the United States to help to motorize the world. Road building is taking root in Australia, vast Africa, Spain, South America. Every new development, highway, railroad, steamship line, building operation, whether it be a drainage project in old Greece or a new water system in Peru, means an added use of the automobile.' He confidently predicted the United States would export a million automobiles in 1930. This toweringly ambitious automobile magnate saw no reason why he could not one day challenge both giants of the industry for supremacy.

With his company's models soaring in popularity, Chrysler desired an appropriate architectural statement – 'a bold structure' as he described it to van Alen. He was determined that it should typify the unstoppable ambition that animated the streets below, and that it should be the tallest building in the world, even if only briefly. He knew the Empire State Building, another expression of American industrial might that was under construction nearby, would be taller than his Chrysler Building, but he also knew it would not be completed until 1931. He ordered van Alen to proceed at all speed.

Despite the blame that has been heaped on it, the investing community of the roaring twenties was not entirely reprehensible. True, there was plenty of chicanery, greed and irrational exuberance, as we shall see. In the five-year run-up to the Crash, gullible investors borrowed wildly to get into the markets, and many were systematically duped by Wall Street and the stockmarket fraternity at large. The prevailing mood was summed up by poems like this sardonic lullaby which appeared in the *Saturday Evening Post*:

> *O hush thee, my babe, granny's bought some more shares*
> *Daddy's gone to play with the bulls and the bears*
> *Mother's buying on tips and she simply can't lose*
> *And baby shall have some expensive new shoes.*

An expert in the Department of Commerce would shortly establish that about half of the $50 billion worth of securities sold in the United States during the roaring twenties were 'undesirable or worthless'. But that means the other half was more or less bona fide paper offering investors a stake in sectors of the economy that were producing genuine profits. These securities allowed the investor to participate in the growth of businesses in glamour sectors such as aviation, retailing, telephone and telegraph, oil and power, radio – the building blocks of huge future industries. Americans saw themselves as sharing in the unstoppable power of the US economy. Although in many cases the prices of the shares outstripped the underlying earnings of the companies issuing them, most of these companies were showing real growth.

One of the bellwethers of the market was mighty US Steel, its share price up $241 by late autumn 1929; another was pioneering phone company AT&T, sky-high at $304. General Electric tripled in value over the eighteen months to early September to an almost unafford-able $396 a share. Some of the most glamorous stocks were those in aviation, among them Wright Aeronautics, whose main shareholders were the Wright brothers, and Boeing, which was flying mail across America in its two-passenger 40As and had just unveiled a four-seater flying boat for private buyers. Highly acquisitive, Boeing had swal-lowed up nine other competitors including Pratt & Whitney Aircraft, Northrop Aircraft and Sikorsky Aviation. Another popular stock was that of a fledgling escalator and elevator manufacturer named Otis.

Automobile stocks were particularly fashionable. As Walter Chrysler pointed out in a booklet, anybody who bought a $100 block of shares in his company in 1923 was now $1353 richer – a gain by a factor of over thirteen. Averaged out over six years, that represented an annual return of over 200 per cent, or at least twenty times what would be considered a handsome reward in more normal circumstances. GM's stock had done even better: a $10,000 investment in 'The Gen-eral's' shares in 1920 would have produced $1,490,000 by 1929.

The runaway returns of the shares of Radio Corporation of Amer-ica, popularly known as Radio, provide another illustration of the furious pace of the market. Under the guidance of a tenacious Russian-born Jew named David Sarnoff, who was one of the first to foresee the future of popular broadcasting, Radio did it all. It manu-factured sets, made commercial programmes which it transmitted through its own stations, and produced phonograph records as RCA-Victor. Even then, the far-sighted Sarnoff was quietly funding the development of all-electronic television. Radio was seen as an icon of the market, emblematic of America's world-beating technological growth. It never paid a cent in dividends, but that did not stop its share price rising from a paltry $1.50 in 1921 to a high of $570 in April 1929 – and that was after the stock was split, a multiplication of the shares available designed to make them more affordable.

By the late 1920s the majority of investors had almost come to expect such incredible gains, and the 1928 presidential election cam-paign to find a replacement for Coolidge did nothing to talk this expectation down. Indeed, when Hoover, the former commerce secre-tary who was the Republican candidate, took to the hustings, he sometimes sounded like Coolidge. 'We shall soon, with the help of God, be in sight of the day when poverty will be banished from this nation,' he roared. Both the Republicans and Democrats did their best to win votes by feeding voters' optimism. The campaign manager for Al Smith, Hoover's opponent, was General Motors executive John J. Raskob, author of an article entitled 'Everybody Ought to be Rich'. Raskob argued that eternal wealth was more or less inevitable: 'Prosperity is in the nature of an endless chain and we can break it only by refusing to see what it is.'

Given such encouragement, it is understandable that many Americans truly believed the secret of wealth had been discovered. Just like their automobiles, the mighty economy would drive them ever onwards. Little wonder that Irving Berlin's 'Blue Skies' became the hit song of 1929 ('Blues skies smiling at me, Nothing but blue skies do I see').

Easily the best known of the nine significant private banking firms in New York, J. P. Morgan & Co was one of the rocks on which this popular boom stood. Its office stood at 23 Wall Street, on the corner of Broad. Jack Morgan's father, Junius Pierpont, could hardly have chosen a more prestigious location. Right opposite on one side was the New York Stock Exchange, on the other the United States Sub-Treasury. Since nobody could enter the building without invitation, there was no need for a sign on the outside. If you did not know where the world's biggest private bank was, you had no place being there. It was known among Wall Streeters as The House on the Corner. Shoeshine boys competed to set up their stalls outside – not just for the tips, which were generous enough if you did a good job on the partners' button-up boots, but also for the inside information. The story went that several shoeshine boys profited mightily on the strength of advice they gleaned from Jack Morgan and others.

The bank's official discretion went further than an absence of signage; its notepaper did not even bother to state its business, just its name. And although J. P. Morgan & Co's influence extended worldwide, it did not feel the need to divulge any details about itself. The institution had never issued a public statement. The only time a partner had gone on record on any matter whatsoever occurred during Junius's unwilling but good-natured appearance (with son Jack lending moral support from the back seats) before the Pujo hearings in 1912 over the 'money trust' issue. Conducted by chairman Arsène Pujo 'to investigate banking and currency in the United States as a basis for remedial legislation', the hearings attempted to uncover the existence of a cabal of bankers – the alleged 'trust' – that controlled the nation's supply of currency. Nothing was proved, but a response was elicited from the elder Morgan, who reportedly displayed 'unusual wit' and 'aroused laughter' during his hours on the stand that inadvertently said much about his bank's power. 'There is no way in which one man could obtain a money monopoly,' he indignantly responded to one question before a fascinated audience of politicians. 'Commercial credit is based primarily on character. Money cannot buy it ... A man I do not trust could not get money from me on all the bonds in Christendom ... I have known men to come into my office and I have given them a check for $1 million when I knew they had not a cent in the world.'

Apart from such rare forced appearances, discretion remained J. P. Morgan & Co's watchword and preference (though it was virtually enforced by law: New York banking regulations made it an offence for a private banker to advertise his services or even to solicit deposits). The bank's concern for confidentiality extended even to its daily partners' conference. For nearly a quarter of a century, as a matter of policy not a single record was kept of these hallowed discussions. Nor was there any chance of a leak because the only people present were the partners.

There were twenty of them in 1929, and they stood at the very heart of the rampant American economy. The partners did not exactly run big business, as is often claimed, but they certainly pulled the financial strings and expected the captains of industry to be answerable to them. Between J. P. Morgan & Co and sister bank Drexel & Company, the partners held twenty directorships in fifteen big bank and trust companies, twelve in ten railroads, nineteen in thirteen power companies, and fifty-eight in thirty-eight industrial companies, all of them big. In total, it later emerged, the partners sat on the boards of eighty-nine corporations with total assets of $20 billion. Certainly other private banks such as Kuhn, Loeb were nearly as powerful, especially in the railroads, but they were not seen to be as truly American as the House of Morgan assuredly was.

Because of its reputation, J. P. Morgan & Co was able to choose its customers. Anybody arriving without a letter of introduction from a trusted referee, no matter how wealthy, did not get inside the door. The bank selected its clients mainly from among the titans of the financial community. Charles E. Mitchell of National City, Seward Prosser of Bankers Trust, Artemus Gates of New York Trust, Charles G. Dawes of Chicago's Central Trust, and similar illustrious names – these were the chosen people who formed the inner clique. 'They are friends of ours, and we know that they are good, sound, straight fellows,' Jack Morgan would tell a subsequent Senate inquiry.

The bank also did favours for the great, the famous and the powerful by distributing securities through what was known in-house as the 'preferred list'. With practically guaranteed profits, given the provenance of the promoter, there was naturally a lot of competition to make the list, but the bank, as its doorkeeper, ensured its gilded nature. In mid-1929 the list included the now former president Coolidge, legendary aviator Charles Lindbergh, various US Navy top brass, senators in both political camps, ambassadors, local politicians, lawyers, bankers, professional investors such as Bernard Baruch, captains of industry, and former members of the cabinet. These were the people with the right credentials, 'good, sound, straight fellows'. As the senior partner, Jack Morgan therefore had unrivalled access to the corridors of power. Indeed, it was at the president's request that he left for Europe to offer his counsel to the reparations committee working on Germany's fines for its role in instigating the 1914–18 war.

In the markets, that kind of weight was worth gold, as the bank's promotion of United Corporation in January 1929 demonstrated. The House on the Corner had long prided itself on staying aloof from what it regarded as the discreditable speculation in stocks. Its main business was the infinitely more respectable (and steady) dealing in bonds, raising loans for industry and government. However, unable to resist the siren song of the boom, J. P. Morgan & Co began to promote common stock which had hitherto been the traffic of lesser houses.

In practice, promoting a stock meant the bank raised the money for the company by wholesaling it, or selling it to major investors. It also took a slice of the action for doing so while generally retaining some stock for itself, which was often considered an indication of the promoter's faith in the underlying business. United Corporation was a holding company, meaning its *raison d'être* was solely to maintain shareholdings in other companies. United Corporation did not actually make or produce anything; it simply invested. However, those investments were extremely substantial and diverse. United owned a number of power utilities, which in turn held stakes in scores of other companies in the same industry. One of them, for example, United Gas Improvement, had no fewer than sixty subsidiaries under its belt. Altogether, through a spider's web of loans and shareholdings in United Corporation, J. P. Morgan & Co held effective control over a swathe of electric power companies spread across the whole of America. (Although this was regarded as perfectly normal and acceptable business practice, the bank's enormous reach over the utility companies was already being closely watched by supporters of an aspiring politician by the name of Franklin Delano Roosevelt.)

The prestige of United Corporation's backers ensured that the stock soared, in particular the 1.7 million perpetual option warrants that J. P. Morgan & Co retained for itself. These $1 warrants gave J. P. Morgan & Co the right to buy common stock (ordinary shares) if the price rose above a certain level. In this case the trigger level for exercising that right was $27.50 a share, which quickly proved a low hurdle given the attractiveness of the paper. Within a few months the warrants were worth $47, and they just kept on going. If the partners had sold out at the peak, they would have banked a fabulous combined profit of $122 million in the space of a single year. Measured by the underlying earnings of United Corporation's businesses, the warrants were not worth anything like that much; but investors saw nothing but blue skies overhead.

Indeed, it was the success of the United Corporation and similar promotions that gave Americans such faith in the markets. Any Cassandras who dared to forewarn of a stockmarket Armageddon were seen as spoiling the party, even as unpatriotic. Yet they insisted on having their say. Statistician and mathematician Professor Roger Babson was one of the most stubborn of these unheeded prophets. He had consistently predicted a collapse pretty much since the start of the bull market, and he was far from a crank; he was in fact a genuine authority on the sharemarket who had been analysing the value of stocks for a quarter of a century, and had written many books on the subject of investment, including *Business Barometers*, which would be reprinted for many years after the Crash. Much more than a stock-picker, he also spent the 1920s trying to apply the laws of physics – specifically Sir Isaac Newton's theory of action and reaction – to the interpretation of business cycles. Despite his baleful forecasts about overheated markets, Babson was certainly not against sharemarket investment. Far from it: he believed the ownership of stocks was an essential element of wealth creation.

By 1929 Professor Babson was not alone in his prophecies of doom. Some of America's best-known businessmen were beginning to deplore Wall Street's injudicious exuberance. Myron C. Taylor, the boss of US Steel, expressed his alarm at 'the folly of the speculative frenzy' driving his firm's share price ever higher, even though US Steel significantly benefited from it. Responsible bankers like Paul Warburg were worried too. He was a partner in the august firm of Kuhn, Loeb, a specialist securities house that had helped bankroll the development of the railroads. In a remarkably prescient speech in March 1929, Warburg tried to talk the market down: 'If orgies of unre-strained speculation are permitted to spread too far, the ultimate collapse is certainly not only to affect the speculators themselves, but also to bring about a general depression involving the entire country.'

But almost nobody was listening. As the firm's distinguished elder partner Otto Kahn, a cultivated banker who had emigrated to America from Germany forty years earlier, would later observe, 'The public was determined that every piece of paper would be worth tomorrow twice what it was today.' Although Kuhn, Loeb behaved with high profes-sionalism during the sharemarket boom, it did little good to the partners' reputations after the boom collapsed. Lumped into an all-embracing category of 'international money lenders', bankers of German origin such as the Kahns, the Warburgs and others would be vilified as 'money Jews' and be given much of the blame.

Several historians of the Crash, especially those writing in the 1960s and 1970s, firmly believed that the market first started to become unhinged from reality in Coolidge's last full year in office. It was in early 1928, as John Kenneth Galbraith famously observed in his *The Great Crash of 1929*, that 'the mass escape into make-believe, so much a part of the true speculative orgy, started in earnest'. Quite suddenly the prevailing sense of euphoria gathered momentum, swamping the rational investors who had hitherto given the markets legitimacy. By early 1929, the value of the New York Stock Exchange's index of common stocks had nearly doubled from three years earlier, surpassing even the wildest predictions. In that year new securities worth a cataclysmic $15 billion were issued. A conviction had taken hold that the exchanges and the general economy were inextricably entwined and that ever-rising prosperity was inevitable. Had not Coolidge and Hoover virtually promised exactly that?

Of all the products of the sharemarket, it was the investment trusts that most completely expressed the mounting fever. Created with the sole purpose of investing in other companies, investment trusts did not produce anything; they merely invested in investments, burrowing deeper and deeper into other trusts, sometimes five to ten layers down. Their success – at least for the promoters – depended on a ready supply of fools to buy the bonds and preferred stock that were thrown out of them, like so much confetti. The attraction of trusts for ordinary investors was the interest and preferred dividends that they paid out. The serious profits, though, were buried in the so-called common stock, which the promoters were careful to retain for themselves.

A typical example was Trading Corporation – a suitably vague name. First launched by Goldman Sachs in 1928, the corporation's principals – that is, Goldman Sachs – issued new blocks of shares at regular intervals. All were massively oversubscribed, so much so that by mid-1929 the stock was worth more than $220, and rising. Along the way, Trading Corporation erected ever more companies on top of this shaky foundation, such as Shenandoah with authorised capital of $102.3 million and, bigger and bolder, Blue Ridge with $142 million. The presence of distinguished directors on the board always helped boost the appeal of investment trusts, and in the case of Trading Corporation the star was John Foster Dulles, a later secretary of state. Very soon, Trading Corporation turned into a pyramid of profit. As Galbraith pointed out, Trading Corporation 'made' $550 million in nine months without actually producing anything. Apart from the securities in which it dealt, Trading Corporation did not even trade.

Goldman Sachs' lucrative creation had many counterparts, like the impressive-sounding US & Foreign Securities Corporation. Established by investment bank Dillon, Read & Co in the mid-1920s, US & Foreign immediately attracted huge sums for its first preferred stock – non-voting paper that entitled the holder to receive dividends at 6 per cent – on nothing more than a sketchy prospectus. The bank's founder was the self-made Clarence Dillon, son of a Pole named Lapowski who ran a general store in San Angelo, Texas, but who was shrewd enough to change his name. A banker called Lapowski would never have prospered in a community dominated by long-established American families who sent their sons, future partners in the business, to the best universities.

Within a few years, US & Foreign was so profitable that Dillon and his partners floated another trust, the even grander-sounding US & International Securities, over the top of the first one. The public, which so far had gained only a modest cashflow from dividends, rushed to buy $50 million of preferred stock. By 1929, US & Foreign's 'common' had soared to $72 a share. Nobody knew it at the time because it was never disclosed – there was no legal requirement to do so – but the partners' return on the original investment was now 28,000 per cent. As the price soared, some of them quietly sold their stock and cashed in the gains. As *Time* magazine would later report, 'stock costing originally US$24,110 was unloaded for US$6,844,000'.

There was of course nothing to stop the public from cashing in for similar returns, but in general they opted not to do so, convinced that their investment would keep rising. Also, US & Foreign was a good dividend-payer, which helped convince shareholders to stay with the stock. It is, however, a comment on the expectations of the times that the public was happy to hold an investment that had already delivered fairytale returns. Nor was US & Foreign's pyramidal structure considered suspect; everybody was doing it. In the first eight months of 1929, $1 billion worth of investment trusts were sold, two and a half times more than for all of the previous year.

Although investment trusts were not illegal, trickery was being deployed to fool the unsuspecting public. One ruse was the 'wash sale' whereby an operator of a pool of stock 'sold' $40 shares to another party at a price of $41. Next day, or shortly afterwards, the first party bought the stock back at the new higher price. What had happened? The first party banked $41 for $40 shares, and although the second party was temporarily exposed, he got his $41 back next day. By then, both parties were square, no better or worse off than before the trade. However, the public did not know that. All they had seen was a rising share price, making it a stock on the move and one to watch. Another deceit was the 'matched sale' whereby one operator sold a stock at $41 under an agreement to buy it back for the same price. Nobody booked a profit, not even a temporary one as in the case of the 'wash', but it had the effect of making the stock look busy – another one to watch. The important point was that none of these trades had anything to do with the underlying value of the stock but everything to do with manipulation. Jiggery-pokery was the order of the day.

When Hoover became president in 1929, he began to see all too clearly where this was heading. Nicknamed the 'great engineer' for his globe-trotting work in mining, Hoover was fiscally astute, a millionaire before he reached thirty. He urged the Federal Reserve, America's equivalent of the Bank of England, to take the heat out of the loan market by lifting the discount rate, a move that would have effectively increased interest rates across the nation. And although he may have agreed with his predecessor that 'the business of America is business', he was not nearly as confident as Coolidge about its good behaviour. Instead of advising newspaper editors to boost business, as Coolidge had done, he urged them to warn of the perils of this epidemic of speculation. He also instructed a reluctant Andrew Mellon to use his powers to promote the purchase of the much safer, if duller, fixed-interest bonds that offered guaranteed if unspectacular returns compared to overheated stocks. And he dispatched an emissary and friend, Los Angeles banker Henry Robinson, on a mission to urge caution on Wall Street. Naturally enough, one of Robinson's first ports of call was The House on the Corner, where Jack Morgan's senior lieutenant, the legendary and fabulously rich Thomas W. Lamont – he usually commuted to Wall Street by private yacht – had no hesitation in rejecting the new president's misgivings. As a partner of twenty years' standing in a business that had long served as an unofficial arm of government – he had repeatedly undertaken missions abroad as a financial emissary – Lamont saw no reason to hide his views.

Thus Wall Street proceeded to frustrate Hoover at every turn. Its bankers controlled the powerful New York branch of the Federal Reserve, meaning they had a significant voice in dictating monetary policy. And nor did Wall Street heed an increasingly worried Senate, which in the spring deplored 'illegitimate and harmful speculation' and threatened to introduce regulation to prevent it.

Hoover next took on the mighty New York Stock Exchange by warning vice-president Richard Whitney, a pillar of the financial establishment and brother of George, one of J. P. Morgan & Co's partners, that he might move to regulate the exchange if it did not help to curb the speculative excesses. Given the exchange's history, this was a serious matter. The NYSE had jealously guarded its total independence since its founding in 1792, repulsing all attempts to change its self-policing constitution, just as it did Hoover's.

As he tried to cool the markets, the president found himself dealing with an unofficial conspiracy. For instance, when federal authorities tightened money supply, banking czars such as Charles E. Mitchell, head of National City Bank, pumped the money back in again by authorising his officers to make available an extra $100 million in loans. In his own way, Mitchell – 'Billion Dollar Charlie' – was as big a figure as Jack Morgan, and National City was the biggest retail bank in America, easily the biggest in New York. It had branches in London, Amsterdam, Geneva and Berlin. Unlike private banks such as J. P. Morgan & Co, it handled enormous volumes of common stocks at the height of the boom. And equipped with a fast-talking sales team, National City peddled bonds like so many betting slips to gullible investors all over America.

One confused customer, Edgar J. Brown, would later testify to a full-scale federal inquiry that, instead of the solid US government bonds he had specified, a National City representative invested his money into a ragbag of bonds issued by Austria, Germany, Greece, Peru, Chile, Hungary and even poverty-stricken Ireland. When these bonds predictably declined in value, National City loaned him $150,000 and urged him to invest his new-found borrowings in stocks. He did so, but as losses mounted a furious Brown marched into a National City branch in Los Angeles and demanded that his entire portfolio be cashed in before the bank lost all his money. He was persuaded that the investments would recover so he left his money with this duplicitous institution.

National City's salesmen could, it seems, sell just about anything. As the inquiry would establish, the salesmen once issued $16.5 million worth of bonds on behalf of the Brazilian state of Minas Gerais, an infamously delinquent borrower. But somehow the salesmen were able, straight-faced, to market the bonds with the following line: 'Prudent and careful administration of the state's finances has been characteristic with successive administrations in Minas Gerais.' By the time the Minas Gerais business was finished, National City, other banks and retailers had booked a combined profit of $600,000 while the public had lost about $13 million.

In a market where practically any piece of paper was quickly worth more than its issue price, National City next latched on to Peru, another notoriously delinquent nation. After dipping its toe in the water by floating a $15 million issue with gratifying ease, the bank waded in deeper with a $50 million issue, having first secured the business through the payment of a $450,000 'fee' to the president's son, and then a third issue for $25 million. In short order, all three issues would collapse into default. Unconstrained by any official obligation to inform the investing public of the risks of these or any other investments – after all, the New York Stock Exchange established its own rules – National City's promotional literature were masterpieces of deceit. They failed to mention political risks, prior lapses in repayments, or anything else that might be interpreted as rendering the investment hazardous. And when the literature proved to be a tissue of lies and investors lost their shirts, those losses were not disclosed lest the news affect the bank's share price. For instance, National City bit its lip after the collapse of $30 million in loans to Cuban sugar companies. As a direct and intended consequence of this deliberately opaque policy, the bank's stock rose stupendously. Issued at a par value of $100, the shares were worth the equivalent of $2925 in mid-1929 after a five for one split.

There were many gullible investors like Edgar J. Brown who borrowed money to invest. The result was that by mid-1929 the sharemarkets were riding a debt-fuelled boom. It was common for brokers to lend even small investors more than two thirds of the face value of shares, as though they were buying houses. Why wouldn't they? As General Motors' John Raskob had written, prosperity was pouring all over America and the sharemarket was its fount. Most of this debt was 'call money' – payable on demand – and their lenders did not hesitate to call it on those few occasions when the sharemarket, or individual stocks, declined in value, albeit briefly before staging a rally. And if the value of a borrower's investments fell below agreed levels relative to the amount of money on loan, he was subject to a margin call that generally required him to borrow more money to restore the agreed ratios.

As the amount of debt grew, one of the most nervous categories of people in America were bank managers. The song 'A Tale of a Ticker' said it all:

> *We'll have to have more margin now,*
> *There isn't any doubt.*
> *So you better dash with a load of cash*
> *Or we'll have to sell you out.*

And the lyrics were hardly an exaggeration. In 1929 alone, Americans borrowed on margin some $9 billion. In favourable circumstances, borrowing on margin could prove highly profitable. If the stock rose in value, the investor did better than those who had not employed debt. For example, if a $100 stock doubled in value to $200 over a period of, say, eighteen months – which was by no means unusual – anybody who had bought it for $25 cash and $75 debt would have increased their original investment by five times. That is, $125 before brokerage fees and interest payments. Of course, the reverse applied too. If the stock halved in value, the original investment was wiped out and the shareholder still owed $75. (The brokers who loaned the money were not, however, as reckless as their clients. Most of them limited the loans to half of the stock price, not the 90 per cent that is routinely cited. All the major brokerage firms would survive the Crash.)

Thus, by the autumn of 1929, just like Walter Chrysler's skyscraper which was rising at the tremendous rate of four storeys a week, the stockmarket was heading for the clouds.

2

Days of Reckoning

Winston Churchill was delighted with the performance of his American investments. The only British politician who could attract an audience on the other side of the Atlantic, he was on a speaking tour across the States in October 1929 and was therefore in a position to keep an eye on his stocks. Although the investments were relatively modest in size, Churchill hoped they would rescue the finances of his usually indebted household. The former Chancellor of the Exchequer always lived beyond his means.

Churchill had turned to making money for himself earlier that year after the Conservative government lost office, having taken most of the blame for the disastrous restoration of Britain to the gold standard in 1925. Although there was hardly a single dissenter at the time – not among politicians, economists, or officials at the Treasury and the Bank of England, all of whom saw the restoration as an affirmation of the pound's return to glory – Churchill became the scapegoat. Since then he had found solace – and income – in writing. He was doing a lot of it, churning out articles for magazines and newspapers and, as he wrote to his wife Clementine, 'making a small fortune'.

Most of that small fortune was banked with Cassel's, the London house that had put him into his first investment, a portfolio of long-term British government securities known as consols. Under its prodigiously successful founder Sir Ernest Cassel, the bank had long been an investor in America; it had helped fund its railways since the

1880s. Cassel's worked closely with the legendary banking house of Kuhn, Loeb, but Churchill shrewdly invested through other channels, for example placing £2000 with Vickers and McGowan. As the markets continued to rise, Churchill entertained high hopes for the proceeds of these stakes in an economy he so much admired. These earnings 'must not be frittered away', he advised his wife.

Anxious not to let these potentially enormous gains go begging, many European and British investors were also investing heavily across the Atlantic. Institutions and individuals plunged into much the same shares and trusts as did Americans, channelling money through bankers and brokers in London, Hamburg, Paris and Amsterdam, among other centres. Many American banks worked through branches or arrangements of some sort in London, including J. P. Morgan, through sister institution Morgan, Grenfell. All these funds were sorely needed at home to restore war-shattered economies. But the voracious appetite of the American stockmarkets for ever-growing investment, like a huge and permanently open maw, also drew dollars back from Europe. In fact, the ebbing of dollars was more significant for Europe, Germany in particular, than the outflow of pounds and European currencies. Channelled through J. P. Morgan & Co, Kuhn, Loeb and other great New York banking houses, these enormous dollar loans had served as lifelines for the half-ruined European economies. Now, however, as the sharemarket began its final and fatal acceleration, the flow had reversed. The outflow of these much-needed dollars from the United States plunged by more than five times, down from $1.09 billion in 1928 to $206 million in 1929.

By late summer, Sir Montagu Norman was already deeply worried. As the governor of the Bank of England, he had made himself the champion of the pound and the defender of the increasingly tarnished edifice of the gold standard. Originally seen as the bedrock of the international monetary system, the gold standard required major currencies to be fixed at a specific value against the yellow metal, with minor currencies often pegged at either the pound or the dollar. Thus, under the gold standard currencies were not exchanged on the basis of what people thought they were worth but on what they were said to be worth. It was a rigid system, but it had the merit of discipline, and that's why Sir Montagu and other central bankers liked it.

Very much the central banker – a fraternity that held enormous sway in the wider world in view of their semi-mystical utterances on the arcane but highly practical subject of the flow of capital and metals – Sir Montagu certainly dressed the part. He favoured elegant bespoke suits made by London tailors, bow ties and, in a dramatic touch, a cloak worn *en bandoulière*. With his neatly brushed goatee beard, he looked 'like a Spanish grandee', a biographer wrote. Sir Montagu had been one of the most enthusiastic backers of the return to the gold standard in 1925, urging it on Churchill, a novice Chancellor in matters of public finance who was much more reluctant than is generally assumed to do the bidding of the experts from the Treasury and the Bank of England.

Because currencies were fixed at certain rates to the metal under the gold standard, this of course also gave them fixed rates to one another. Adherence to the standard meant nations had to maintain certain deposits of gold relative to the amount of notes and coin on issue. If they were not able to do so, it put the value of the national currency under threat. Further, gold being a commodity like anything else, holders of gold made sure to dispatch their holdings to wherever they earned the highest return. 'The extraordinary speculation on Wall Street in past months has driven up the rate of interest to an unprecedented level,' John Maynard Keynes, probably the only British economist to contribute to the popular American press, wrote in the *New York Evening Post*. Attracted by the high interest rates available in New York, gold was pouring out of Britain in such quantities that Sir Montagu feared Britain might be forced off it – an event he regarded as a calamity, as indeed did others.

In America, however, it was business as usual. Stocks continued to rise briskly – proof positive to most Americans that wealth truly was in the process of being democratised through the medium of the sharemarket. After twenty months of the biggest bull market in memory, the standard measure of common stocks in New York had hit 225, up 125 per cent. Professor Roger Babson's doom-laden prophecies had been consigned to the dustbin of irrelevancy. Hardly anybody was listening when he delivered another warning on 5 September, three days after a record volume of shares changed hands. 'Sooner or later a crash is coming, and it may be terrific,' he told a no doubt sceptical business convention. But some investors must have been paying attention because prices wobbled the very next day in what became known as the 'Babson break', finally putting this Cassandra on the map.

As the market went off the boil, the *Wall Street Journal* plundered the writings of Mark Twain, then dead for nearly twenty years, for its Thought of the Day: 'Don't part with your illusions; when they are all gone you may still exist, but you have ceased to live.' The bible of Wall Street failed to see any contradiction in the suggestion that illusions could play a role in investment. Certainly, the messengers of hope still far outnumbered the harbingers of doom. Peering at the tape on his self-winding ticker, economist Irving Fisher could not see anything seriously untoward. 'There may be a recession in stock prices but not anything in the nature of a crash,' he declared. The professor had such faith in his own prophecies that he promptly bought more shares on margin.

The markets were, however, unsettled by the Hatry crash in Britain, which alarmed the fast-dwindling number of rational investors. Clarence Hatry, a British financier who had started his business career as a clerk, had created a commercial empire based on investment trusts and numerous other enterprises including one that owned thousands of slot machines. This was Hatry's second commercial empire; the first was created on the edifice of the Commercial Bank of London, an institution that had collapsed in 1924. Having paid his debts, Hatry started again. The crowning step was the purchase of United Steel, a struggling company deep in debt. If this had been the United States and not Britain, there would have been plenty of institutions willing to stump up the essential lines of credit, but the City rarely muddied its hands with industrial loans of this kind. In any event, the best banking circles, Sir Montagu Norman among them, regarded Hatry with deep suspicion. A big and ostentatious spender, he was not one of their kind, an outsider. Even the target company, United Steel, had its doubts about their acquirer. After Hatry made an offer for United Steel, the chief accountant hurriedly sought the advice of Grenfell, Morgan and solicited an alternative offer from them. When this was not forthcoming, United Steel had no option other than to accept Hatry's bid. Unfortunately, he did not quite have the money. His fund-raising fell £8 million short of what was required and in desperation he tried to bridge the gap by issuing shares his company did not own. Not even these bogus shares raised enough to meet the shortfall, and, unable to meet its enormous financial obligations, the second Hatry empire collapsed on 20 September.

The failure reverberated through the British economy, triggering a flight of gold that at one point threatened the stability of sterling. A furious Sir Montagu Norman was forced to raise the bank rate to $6^{1}/_{2}$ per cent to stem the flow of gold across the Atlantic. It is fair to say the governor of the Bank of England was not unhappy when Hatry, declaring that he was 'irretrievably ruined', was sentenced the following year to fourteen years in jail, two of them with hard labour.

As a purely British event, the Hatry collapse did not have a direct effect on the American stock exchanges, but it did disturb the sangfroid of bankers, brokers and other wiser participants in the markets. At the very least it demonstrated a drying-up of the liquidity that had long fuelled the boom, as well as the vulnerability of the British pound.

But a comment on 2 October by Philip Snowden, Churchill's successor as Chancellor of the Exchequer, did have a direct effect. From his office in Westminster, he saw fit to warn Americans that they had got themselves into a 'speculative orgy' on Wall Street. Much-quoted in the United States, the remark was given considerable credence because of Snowden's seniority in the new Labour government under Prime Minister Ramsay MacDonald and, according to one authority on the Crash, 'is likely to have triggered the October 3 break'. About the same time, Snowden's counterpart Andrew Mellon finally waded into the debate, scolding investors for being starry-eyed. They were acting, he said, 'as if the price of securities would infinitely advance'.

Almost on cue, on Thursday 3 October, an unusual number of shares changed hands in a demonstration of nerves. Next day, the *Washington Post*'s headline read 'Stock prices crash in frantic selling'. Four days later, London's *Financial Times* quoted a worried president of the American Bankers Association: 'Bankers are gravely alarmed

over the mounting volume of credit being employed in carrying security loans, both by brokers and by individuals.' After years of
debt-fuelled speculation, it was a bit late in the day for such a warning,
especially as the association's members continued to ply their customers with credit.

In mid-October there were further signs of nerves, several
favourites of the boom such as General Electric and Westinghouse
suffering sharp declines. The falls sent a message to the markets that
the utilities just might be overpriced (judged by later and much more
accurate calculations, their share prices may have been overvalued by
as much as three times). For the first time, many investors began to
wonder if something was seriously amiss with the bull market. Was
the euphoria finally evaporating?

On Monday 21 October over six million shares changed hands – the
third-biggest volume of transactions in the history of the New York
Stock Exchange. In the turmoil many investors lost money, and many
non-American investors lost their nerve and cashed out of the market.
The irrepressible Professor Irving Fisher stuck his neck out again,
concluding that only the 'lunatic fringe' had suffered, and continued
to put his faith in what he considered to be rational calculations. One
of the earliest of genuine market theorists, he had spent a couple of
decades trying to develop an all-encompassing theory of how it all
worked, how the markets interrelated with the wider economic environment. Thus he threw into the mix such relatively arcane data as the
velocity and volume of currency in circulation, level of taxes, degree of
private consumption, formation of capital, and many other factors,
none of which was properly understood. Fisher was convinced that
practically everything was 'capable of precise formulation, demonstration and statistical verification'. As early as 1906 he had published a
book called *The Nature of Capital and Income*, making him an authority on consumption (and a very early proponent of consumption-based
taxes rather than income-based ones). His fearless enthusiasm for the
bull run was, at least in his view, highly rational and based on years of
analysis. Already wealthy as a result of a card index system he invented
and sold, Fisher continued to buy massively on margin and exhorted
Americans to do the same, almost as a patriotic duty as well as a personal goal. The accumulation of national wealth was so central to

Fisher's philosophy that he supported Prohibition on the grounds it would (he had calculated) boost national production by $6 billion.

But the market no longer seemed to share the professor's optimism. On Wednesday 23 October the total valuation of the market fell by 4.6 per cent in another worrying decline that further frayed the nerves of the investing community.

As it happened, that was the same day Walter Chrysler claimed the title of the owner of the world's tallest building. One of the most elegant of the world's loftiest constructions, the Chrysler skyscraper featured an art deco exterior ornamented with symbols drawn from the automobile industry. Giant steel hubcaps, the eagle-heads that decorated the automobiles' bonnets, and even (on the thirty-first floor) decorative radiator caps – they all adorned the automobile magnate's triumphant edifice, which towered 1046 feet above New York at the intersection of 42nd Street and Lexington Avenue – truly a 'showcase for Chrysler's company and a symbol of America's power and wealth'.

Actually, the building was more a showcase for William van Alen's flair and the constructor's ingenuity. Built around a steel skeleton, the building was composed of an inner and outer core, like a double sleeve. The concrete inner sleeve stabilised the seventy-seven-storey skyscraper and served as a conduit for elevators, stairs and service systems, while the stone outer housed the offices. The walls' only function was to keep the weather out; they did not support the building in any way whatsoever.

To Chrysler's chagrin, the designer of another skyscraper at 40 Wall Street had quietly added a few feet to its height, making it loftier than his own. At his client's instruction, van Alen secretly designed a 125-foot-long spire and had it built within the frame of the building, invisible to outsiders. On 23 October the spire was hoisted to the very top of the Chrysler Building in just ninety minutes – perhaps the engineering feat of the entire project.

Walter Chrysler's celebrations would be short-lived, however. His empire was about to be imperilled, along with those of his fellow titans in the automobile industry.

On 24 October, a Thursday, there was hardly a calm broker, banker, jobber or shareholder in all of America. When the New York Stock Exchange opened, promptly as usual, the nation held its breath. To investors' relief, prices held reasonably firm at first.

Winston Churchill, who had a morning free from his lucrative speaking tour, had decided to go and see for himself how his investments were performing. Despite assurances there was nothing to worry about, he was concerned about all the talk of overheated markets. As a distinguished visitor, he was admitted into the gallery just in time to witness a mass sell-off. Instead of the measured calm he had hoped for, the floor of the exchange was bedlam, with the jobbers caught in the middle. In vain attempts to be heard above the din, they were screaming orders to sell; when that did not work, they hurled their chits at the chalk girls. Pushing and shoving, they fought to get to the front of the line. Others, transfixed by the plummeting share prices, simply stood where they were in an almost catatonic state.

What Churchill was watching was the collapse of the collective nerve of American shareholders. Their faith in the markets had held through minor tremors during the summer, it had been tested in September, and tested again in early October, and now it was failing. Nearly everybody was desperate to sell. By eleven o'clock, the state of panic on the floor of the NYSE had spread to all the nation's exchanges, and across the Canadian border to the exchanges of Toronto and Montreal. As the markets plummeted, not even the latest Western Union tickers could cope, falling further and further behind the prices. Clacking away non-stop, they told a brutally objective tale of lost fortunes, ruined speculators, wealthy people turned into debtors *en masse*.

In New York, brokers and bankers rushed down to the exchange and, finding no room inside, gathered on the steps outside. They spilled on to the road, exchanging few words, stunned by the turn of events. Formally dressed in suits and hats, they waited underneath the marble sculpture that so nobly depicted the role of the markets in harnessing the wealth created by the toil of the people. They stayed there for hours, hoping for a reversal that might save them from ruin. Every scrap of information was passed around, seized on, urgently discussed. Everybody was looking for a ray of light. At one point somebody yelled that the exchanges in Chicago and Buffalo had shut their doors, unable to cope with the avalanche of selling.

Finally, somebody rushed out of the building to shout that the market was steadying. The crowd held their breath. One by one, others emerged from the exchange to convey the news that the panic was subsiding. Still the crowd grew bigger. Even after the markets closed, the throng remained, discussing the events of the day, analysing them for clues that might predict how the markets would run next day.

Hours later, when the tickers finally caught up and stopped, they showed that almost 12.9 million shares had changed hands in a tumultuous day. The tape gave one ray of hope – prices had recovered in the final hours as a few bold buyers emerged, hoping to buy stocks cheaply – but in general it had been a bad day for investors. Even the glamour radio stocks, another bellwether of the markets, were down by a massive 40 per cent.

Next day, struggling for balance, the *New York Times* noted 'rally at close cheers brokers'; stretching credulity, it added that 'bankers [were] optimistic'. In fact things did get better, but not for long. On Monday 28 October, the Times Industrials, a long-standing measure of the state of the markets reached by averaging the price of selected stocks, collapsed by 49 points. Tuesday was even worse: a total of 16.4 million shares changed hands.

Clearly investors were on the run.

Jack Morgan was still at Wall Hall, reading the papers and receiving cables on the situation from New York. He was not booked to sail back home on the *Olympic* until mid-November, so he got his partners to take charge of a rescue mission. As America's senior banker, he drew together a gold-plated consortium comprising Seward Prosser of Bankers Trust, Albert Wiggin of Chase National, William Potter of Guarantee Trust and Charles Mitchell of National City. Between them they pledged $240 million, which they hoped would provide the foundation for a rally. As J. P. Morgan & Co's Thomas Lamont put it, the money was no more than a 'temporary cushion' to be invested in 'certain key securities', meaning blue-chips. And Richard Whitney, as vice-president of the exchange, was authorised to lead the rebound in a public demonstration of faith in the market.

Whitney certainly seemed the man for the job. An imposing and athletic figure, he was regarded as a worthy representative of the markets. A graduate of Harvard, proud of a lineage that could be traced back to the Mayflower Pilgrims, member of the New York Yacht Club – he was, in short, a man of impeccable credentials and good reputation. Also, everybody knew his eponymous brokerage firm was connected to the richest bank in the world. Although he was known as a big spender, often seeking large sums for investment 'on my face' – a phrase meaning to borrow against his honour – Whitney was presumed to be able to afford a lavish lifestyle.

True to the investors' increasingly gloomy expectations, on Wednesday 30 October the markets ran scared again. Once again, the floor of the New York exchange was on the verge of panic, with prices falling rapidly. Then Whitney emerged from his office. Drawing himself up to his full height, he strode on to the floor. As the yelling died down, he calmly proceeded to issue a round of buy orders for a portfolio of blue-chip stocks. Crowding around, the jobbers fell silent and the chalkers looked up in astonishment as Whitney placed a bid for US Steel at $205 a share before moving ostentatiously on to other blue-chips and issuing further buy orders.

This dramatic gesture served its purpose. Within a few minutes of Whitney investing his 'temporary cushion', an orderly market was restored. The selling continued, but it was slower than earlier. At the end of the day the Times Industrials was down by just 12 points, a significant but not catastrophic decline, and Whitney was lauded as the hero of the hour, the man who had saved the markets. From Wall Hall, Jack Morgan fired off a congratulatory telegram to the New York office, telling the partners they had done better than he himself could have managed.

And so the tide seemed to have turned. Hoover weighed in with a presidential statement of support, affirming his confidence in the robust state of American commerce while adding his usual caveat about the damage that had been caused by 'high interest rates induced by stock speculation'. And the papers duly came to the rescue with headlines such as 'Brokers Believe Worst is Over and Recommend Buying of Real Bargains'.

The temporary cushion was, however, soon deflated. Next day, Thursday 31 October, the selling resumed as soon as the markets opened and quickly slid once more into full-scale panic. 'They [the brokers] roared like a lot of lions and tigers,' remembered a guard at the exchange. 'They hollered and screamed, they clawed at one another's collars. It was like a bunch of crazy men. Every once in a while, when Radio or Steel or Auburn would take another tumble, you'd see some poor devil collapse and fall to the floor.' The tickers trailed the market by several hours. When they finally clacked out the final quote of the day, well after eight o'clock, they told a terrible story. On that day, thirty billion dollars' worth of American wealth had disappeared. The bull market was not just over, it was in headlong retreat.

In the early days of November, with the markets still in decline, the full catastrophic details emerged. The value of a total of twenty-nine public utilities – a crucial sector of the market – was in full flight. Companies such as American Superpower, American Power & Light, Long Island Lighting and Niagara Hudson Power were losing between half and three quarters of their value. Radio had lost 75 per cent of its value in October alone. Along with manufacturers of everything from refrigerators to escalators, even automobile companies such as GM, Ford and Chrysler were in rapid retreat. Again, 'A Tale of a Ticker' summed it up:

> I bought an elevator stock
> And thought that I did well,
> And the little bears all ran downstairs
> And rang the basement bell.

Around the world, the collapse was observed with a conflicting mixture of emotions ranging between wonderment, fear and relief. In Britain, *The Economist* weighed in with the view that 'the deflation of the exaggerated balloon of American stock values will be for the good of the world'. And in better-behaved stockmarkets, particularly in Europe, that had not fallen prey to wild speculation, *schadenfreude* reigned. Held back by weak economies, the average price of shares on European markets had hardly risen since the end of the war. Thus in 1929 the European stock index was just 20 per cent higher than in

1919, one of the very few exceptions being France, where the Bourse de Paris had risen *formidablement*, as a French historian wrote.

Remoteness from the United States also lent a measure of protection. For example, far-off exchanges in Japan, South Africa, Australia and New Zealand had very different characteristics from Wall Street and they practically ignored the Crash. Indeed, the fledgling New Zealand stockmarket, southernmost in the world, remained relatively buoyant because prices had grown steadily on the back of a robust programme of public works. Conversely, proximity to New York proved fatal. The markets in Montreal and Toronto crashed in tandem. Having copied the worst features of the American markets, for instance by issuing avalanches of new stock on margin, prices had gone sky-high. Some leading industrial shares had sold at forty times annual earnings.

And so the chickens came home to roost. Entertainer Eddie Cantor lost a fortune but kept his sense of humour. As he told radio listeners on the very day of the rout, 'Well, folks, they got me in the market just as they got everybody else. In fact they're not calling it the stockmarket any longer. It's called the stuck market. Everyone is stuck. Well, except my uncle. He got a good break. He died in September. Poor fellow had diabetes at forty-five. That's nothing. I had Chrysler at a hundred and ten.' Not generally the most astute category of investors, many other entertainers came unstuck. Beetle-browed Groucho Marx, who had already made a fortune as a comic actor and live performer – he had just starred in the movie *Animal Crackers* – claimed to have lost $800,000. Boxer Jack Dempsey, the first multi-millionaire athlete, was $3 million poorer.

The chief apologist of the boom, Irving Fisher, was wiped out. He lost investments estimated variously at between $7 million and $30 million, and his house; he had to move in with his daughter. For all his rational calculations, the professor had learned that poverty could be democratised just as easily as wealth.

As for Jack Morgan, still waiting to board the *Olympic*, he did not feel any sense of guilt over the events leading up to the Crash. 'I do not believe there is any lack of a sense of responsibility on the part of men of wealth,' he would later say. 'I know that the best of these did what they could to discourage speculative excesses in the forepart of the year and to limit the panic ... and protect the community as far as possible from the natural consequences of the excesses of its more speculative members.' But Jack's faith in 'men of wealth' would soon be shaken by the evidence that emerged in searing post-mortems.

The immediate task, though, was what to do about the collapse in the markets, if anything. Should the authorities intervene, or should they do nothing?

3

Liquidate Everything

Joseph Schumpeter was a visiting economics professor at Harvard. An Austrian aristocrat by upbringing, he was the adopted son of a general and probably the only important economist who was also an excellent horseman. Although still in his forties, Schumpeter had arrived at the university after a dramatic early career. He had practised law in Egypt, returned to Austria to take over a professorship in economics at the age of twenty-six, written three much-quoted books by his mid-thirties, served – albeit briefly – as finance minister, been president of a private bank whose collapse left him bankrupt, and finally gone back to teaching at university. He was regarded as a heavyweight in economic matters, a product of the learned European school, and in this crisis he was about to become famous – or infamous, depending on the viewpoint – for his theories of 'creative destruction'.

Schumpeter was an authority on business cycles, and was convinced that capitalism could not proceed on a smooth path. Instead it was prone to storms and tempests, and could even destroy itself. 'Economic progress, in a capitalist society, means turmoil,' he wrote. The economist's upbringing during a period of upheaval in war-torn Austria may have further convinced him of this doctrine, but there was no doubt that he regarded the slump in the United States as a normal manifestation of the business cycle. He belonged to the school loosely known as liquidationists. Highly influential, they tended to regard the

events of October 1929 as positively healthy. As far as they were concerned, the Crash and its immediate aftermath had lanced the boil
disfiguring the economic face of the United States, and the poison
would now drain away.

Paid-up members of this school included President Hoover's treasurer Andrew Mellon as well as most of America's influential
economists. Revelling in the post-Crash wreckage – banks were
already failing at an average rate of seventy-five a month – Mellon saw
the collapse almost as a visitation from on high for the speculative
excesses of the multitudes. 'It will purge the rottenness out of the
system,' he preached to Hoover. 'High costs of living will come down.
People will work harder, live a moral life. Values will be adjusted, and
enterprising people will pick up the wrecks from less competent
people.'

Although Mellon was well into his seventies and might be forgiven
for his views, he still held the most important financial post in the government and should surely have known there was no evidence that
Americans in general had become lazy or decadent in the roaring
twenties, nor that struggling factories and unprofitable farms were the
result of incompetence or lack of enterprise. Nor could depositors be
held responsible for the collapse of those banks to which they had
entrusted their life savings. Nevertheless, Mellon quickly arrived at his
own solution for the disaster about to unfold. Put simply, it was to do
nothing. 'I see nothing in the present situation that is either menacing or warrants pessimism,' he declared in early 1930, a few months
after the Crash.

His economic strategy, if it could be called that, demonstrated the
gulf between the very rich and everybody else that had become a feature of what had once been the world's most egalitarian society. As the
material well-being of people began to deteriorate in the United States
and beyond, the bitter medicine of liquidationism would polarise
economists and politicians on both sides of the Atlantic as well as in
the wider world.

However, whether you were a liquidationist or not, in the months
following the Crash few expected it to contaminate the economy at
large. The boom had lasted so long that the sense of prosperity and
endless economic growth preached by people of influence had

invaded the national psyche. Also, many Americans saw the stock-markets as a thing apart, an entertaining sideshow that was almost irrelevant to the rest of the commercial world, and therefore the Crash was unlikely to affect the wider economy. Like Mellon, most people did not see anything untoward that at that stage justified pessimism and were confident the good times would return. 'I thought it was temporary,' recalled Al Gordon, then a twenty-eight-year-old working at a New York investment bank. 'Most people thought it was temporary.'

But as the situation steadily worsened, confirming a link between the state of the stockmarkets and the material well-being of individuals, violently opposed schools of thought developed within the halls of universities and the corridors of government. Essentially, American liquidationists were classical economists who believed in a predominantly laissez-faire style of economic management, basing their case on the painful but short recession of 1921 just before the twenties began to roar. At that time the economy bounced back quickly. History was on the side of this view. Over the previous half century, the United States had suffered a series of banking and financial upsets but had quickly worked through them to attain rising levels of material well-being. There had been the 'crisis of 1873, the panic of 1884, the stringency of 1890, the crisis of 1893, and the crisis of 1907', pointed out economic historians Michael Bordo and Barry Eichengreen, authorities on the gold standard. Liquidationists therefore believed the Crash was only a prelude to the next boom, just as long as things were left alone and the poisons within the economy were allowed to drain away.

The classical economists held sway on both sides of the Atlantic. In Britain, they included Viennese-born Friedrich Hayek, still in his early thirties and another product of the authoritarian Austrian school of economics; the outspoken Lionel Robbins, who had just become the youngest economics professor in Britain and was a devotee of Hayek (he read him in the original German); and Dennis Robertson, who was doing brilliant spadework within the Treasury. The versatile Robertson, who was also an actor and poet, was progressively falling out with his former tutor, John Maynard Keynes, over their respective responses to the mounting crisis: Robertson favoured the more classical solution of a savings-based recovery while Keynes leaned towards the daring theories of a liquidity-based one.

Sitting unhappily in the White House, Hoover was somewhere in the middle of these schools of thought. He could see all too clearly that he might yet inherit the very disaster he had so much feared and which Coolidge had so cheerfully helped foment. The president had had an earlier brush with a similar situation while chairman of an emergency conference under President Warren Harding during the post-war slump of 1921, and he knew what it might mean. 'There is no economic failure so terrible in its import as that of a country possessing a surplus of every necessity of life in which numbers [are] willing and anxious to work [but] are deprived of dire necessities,' he declared in a speech at the time. 'It simply cannot be if our moral and economic system is to survive.'

Americans were certainly being deprived of motor cars, dire necessities to many. Already the automobile industry was in trouble, partly because banks were rapidly reining in the credit that had financed much of the boom in sales. Within months of the Crash, sales were heading towards a 40 per cent decline and auto workers were being laid off in droves. Van Alen, Walter Chrysler's architect, had already become an indirect victim of this decline. The automobile magnate never paid his final fee, nearly ruining van Alen as a result. Although he had designed one of the world's most admired buildings, van Alen never again accepted a similarly prestigious commission.

Hoover did not, however, believe in doing nothing. Within two months of the Crash, he had organised at the White House an emergency symposium of industrialists, unions, farm leaders and bankers. Heartened by the president's determination to bully the economy back into life, this group displayed a rare sense of unity. Big business promised not to cut wages; indeed, Henry Ford increased those of his remaining assembly-line workers from $6 to $7 a day, even though sales of his Model A were in a state of collapse (they would eventually decline from their peak of 1.5 million in 1929 to 232,000 in 1932). In a quid pro quo that demonstrated their goodwill, labour immediately withdrew outstanding wage claims. Power and railroad companies committed themselves to spend $1.8 billion on new projects, repairs and maintenance. Greatly encouraged, Hoover promptly set up a task force of four hundred businesspeople charged with the responsibility of enforcing the voluntary wage restraint and overseeing the capital spending programmes he had just secured.

Next, the new president tackled the second front of a heavy public works programme. He appealed to the governors of all forty-eight states to commission dams, roads, hospitals, schools, harbours, public buildings and anything else that could conceivably serve the public interest and employ people. Over the objections of Mellon, who feared for his precious balanced budget, Congress was quick to approve Hoover's proposal for $160 million in tax cuts.

The president's rapid-fire measures brought equally rapid results. In April 1930, the sharemarket rallied and the Standard and Poor 500 composite index nudged 26 points, 4.5 points above the 1929 close. This was still well down on the highs of the boom but it was nevertheless taken as a promising sign. 'No one in his place could have done more,' approved the *New York Times*. 'Very few of his predecessors could have done as much.' The organ of the establishment was convinced that Hoover had done enough. And so was the president. In mid-February, three and a half months after the Crash, he was confident enough to inform a worried deputation of bishops and bankers that the government had the situation well under control and his measures would soon restore the economy to full health. 'Gentlemen, you have come six weeks too late,' Hoover told them. Many others believed the same, among them the British economist Keynes, who believed the recovery had started before Christmas 1929. In short, the liquidationists were being proved right. All it had taken to limit the losses from the Crash was patience, some judicious intervention, an optimistic outlook and a steady nerve. The toxins had oozed from the system and the patient was making a rapid return to full health.

—————

Reed Smoot was a deeply conservative senator from Utah who had in a long career distinguished himself with his jingoism. He was, for instance, an implacable opponent of the League of Nations and little interested in the non-American world. Posted to Britain in his youth as a Mormon missionary, he so disliked the experience that he served only ten months of the usual two years and returned to Utah where he steadily rose up the Church ladder, eventually becoming an apostle of The Church of Jesus Christ of Latter-day Saints. A banker by profession, Smoot had served as a senator for most of the century and now held the powerful position of chairman of the finance committee where he had made a name for himself by scrutinising everything that smacked of free trade. His three major beliefs, biographer F. Ross Peterson noted, were 'Mormonism, Americanism, and protectionism'. Smoot believed that 'every American product, agriculture or manufacturing, deserved protection'. Now sixty-eight, he was about to set his stamp on world history in the unlikely area of tariffs – trade barriers erected against foreign-made products.

The issue of protection had a history in America. It had long been a winner in American politics, and particularly in the 1920s. Stooping to conquer, Hoover had pretty much pledged protection to farmers during his presidential campaign. Agriculture was the only major sector of the economy that had not boomed during the roaring twenties – farm incomes had actually steadily declined – and Hoover won votes by undertaking to launch a thorough examination of the tariff issue. Its purpose would be to combat, as the Republican platform put it, 'foreign producers [who] because of lower foreign wages and a lower cost of living abroad' undercut America's own men of the land, particularly in states such as Reed Smoot's Utah. But it was not just farmers who favoured protection. Manufacturers had also prospered behind the towering invisible barriers the federal government had erected around America's ports.

Hoover had hardly got his feet under the desk in the Oval Office when he convened a special session of Congress for the express purpose of raising tariffs on farm products. This was exactly what local Congressmen had been waiting for, and they approved the bill with unseemly haste, largely through the good offices of a self-made farm boy named Willis Hawley from Monroe, Oregon, who took charge of its passage. Congressman Hawley had become a professor of history and economics but without, it seems, learning much, because the bill, as approved, turned out to be a deal more comprehensive and menacing than Hoover had envisaged. It threatened to raise tariffs on a multiplicity of over twenty thousand dutiable items. Not only that, these tariffs were to be raised by record percentages from already high levels. Now Hoover's fear was that America's trading partners would immediately retaliate in kind, which could have the effect of stifling world trade.

The bill went to the Senate where it stalled, despite the ardent support of Reed Smoot, whose economic convictions were based entirely on an iron-clad concept of American self-reliance. He had little or no world view. Despite Smoot's evangelism, the majority of senators were frightened by the bill's extremeness. But before it could go any further, the stockmarket collapsed and Congress did not reconvene until the spring. When it did, the evidence of the mounting economic damage, especially in rural areas, was sufficiently persuasive for the bill to harvest the votes necessary to see it through the Senate. Most of the Democrats voted against, but a few were very much in favour. 'Democrats voting for final passage [of the bill] were from Louisiana or Florida and represented citrus or sugar interests that received significant new protection under the bill,' American historian Anthony O'Brien pointed out. The thinking seemed to run along the lines that if the previous, high-tariff regime known as Fordney-McCumber had applied through the boom, higher tariffs again should work even better.

On 17 June 1930, Hoover reluctantly signed the Smoot-Hawley bill into law over the protests of no fewer than one thousand economists, who put their names to a petition arguing that the law would damage world as well as American trade. It had now become clear that the fitful stockmarket recovery of early 1930 was a deception, a false rally preceding the death throes, and that the economy was sinking into a trough. Many of these petitioners were anti-liquidationists, a bolder breed who refused to accept that doing nothing was the answer. However, even liquidationists argued that it was wrong to put up the shutters against global trade – perhaps the single most powerful force in Europe's hard-won and still incomplete recovery from the 1914–18 war.

One of the bolder breed was Seymour Harris, who was about to become an important figure in the forthcoming debate. Author of a study of the finance of the French Revolution called *The Assignats*, the New York-born Harris favoured the heretical solution of higher government spending – total anathema to Mellon – in order to get

America out of the impasse. Like Schumpeter's fellow (but dissenting) economist at Harvard John Kenneth Galbraith, who would write the classic study of the Crash, Harris believed in the beneficent effect of a well-disposed, big-spending government.

These views put Harris on a collision course with older colleagues at Harvard such as Schumpeter. Probably the most quoted of the classical economists, the Austrian argued that interfering with the natural course of economic cycles, for instance by trying to throw more money into the system, was 'particularly apt to produce additional trouble for the future'. In summary, ill-advised meddling in economic downturns only made things worse. Highly erudite, the professor could muster impressive theories to support his case. In truth, it was time for stock-market values to adjust, and it was true, as Mellon predicted, that wiser heads who had refrained from rampant speculation would profit from the carnage. Nor was Schumpeter a cold-blooded economist. He believed, for instance, that victims of the recession were fully entitled to support from public funds because it was irrational they should bear the brunt of recession through having been unlucky enough to work in the worst-affected industries. As an authority on the economic debate of the period would write sixty years later, 'The advocates of the "liquidationist" point of view during the Great Depression were mistaken, but not crazy.'

In the meantime, several other younger American economists continued vehemently to disagree with their elders, lining up behind John Maynard Keynes, of whose work they were well aware. Like the Englishman, they were convinced that it was 'replete with folly' to sit by and allow deflation and unemployment to spread. At prestige universities all over America, the debate grew more and more heated. Junior lecturers at Harvard such as Harry Dexter White, who would become one of America's most practical and influential economists, challenged the orthodoxy of their superiors by writing papers that attacked the leading liquidationist torch-bearers. In what was nothing less than a full-scale rebellion, the school was damned for its sterile and 'nihilist' theories. The young lions took no prisoners, savaging famous and respected classical economists, authors of books that were almost bibles in academe.

On the other side of the Atlantic, *The Economist* tended to back the liquidationists, hoping there were good grounds for expecting some global good from 'the deflation of the exaggerated balloon of American stock values'. Hayek, one of the most respected of the liquidationists, was similarly convinced that economic shocks of this kind were simply manifestations of underlying ills that had to be allowed to work their way through the system. Less forgiving than Schumpeter, he believed that attempts to alleviate unemployment only had the effect of 'holding up those redistributions of labour between industries made necessary by changed circumstances'.

The new boys were unimpressed. They propagated a radically new and warmer-hearted theory at whose core was the provision of financial liquidity. Essentially, the rebels wanted action to stimulate the economy in the form of judicious doses of public funds. They believed a government could spend its way out of recession; it was not a time to hoard money.

The debate raged ever more fiercely, creating lifelong enemies. Keynes, the most prolific essayist of the rebels, labelled those pulling the economic strings as 'madmen in authority', plucking half-understood theory from the air and turning it into public policy. As for the liquidationists themselves, they were 'austere and puritanical'. The basic argument of Keynes and his fellow heretics was that there was no immutable economic law that insisted a creative burst of productivity like that of the roaring twenties must necessarily be followed by a purgative bust. In one bitter sentence he wrote that liquidationists desired 'a victory for the mammon of unrighteousness if so much prosperity was not subsequently balanced by universal bankruptcy'.

But there were many economic puritans on Keynes's side of the Atlantic too. Lionel Robbins, a passionate economist who had been dispatched to the western front in the 1914–18 war at the age of nineteen and returned with a hunger to study the subject, would write, 'In the present depression we eschew the sharp purge. We prefer the lingering disease.' In fact, Robbins' metaphor did a disservice to the medical profession which prided itself on treating symptoms; it did not see itself as being faced with a stark choice between brutal intervention and prolonged suffering.

Another puritan was Sir Otto Niemeyer, soon to earn notoriety in Australia for his proposals for its own economic salvation. Niemeyer had spent his entire working life at the Treasury, joining straight after achieving an outstanding degree at Oxford University, and later at the Bank of England. Son of a German merchant who emigrated to England, Niemeyer stood four-square for sound money and the gold standard. Six years earlier he had been influential in persuading Churchill to put Britain back on gold, a decision the latter now greatly regretted, principally blaming Niemeyer and his boss at the Bank of England, Sir Montagu Norman. In one of the more entertaining sideshows of the Great Depression, Niemeyer would soon be dispatched around the world on a mission to instruct the Empire's financial ministers – and especially those in Australia, a species he held in low regard – in strict adherence to the orthodox writ of the Bank of England.

In America, however, the nub of the problem – and it was already plain for all to see – was that almost all Americans were now affected by the reverberations from the Crash, not just those who had plunged wildly into the sharemarket. With his enormous wealth safely in the bank (which he owned), Mellon could afford to be philosophical, indeed almost joyful, about the financial and human destruction. But not so Hoover. His policies were now diametrically opposed to those of his treasury secretary. As he would later unhappily remember in his memoirs, 'The "leave-it-alone" liquidationists headed by Secretary of the Treasury Mellon felt that government must keep its hands off and let the slump liquidate itself. Mr. Mellon had only one formula: "Liquidate labour, liquidate stocks, liquidate the farmers, liquidate real estate."'

And Mellon was still determined to balance the budget by raising taxes, because Washington's tax take had fallen so low in the wake of the falling profits and rising unemployment that the government could not make ends meet. 'We are in the midst of a grave emergency,' Mellon told a worried Congress. 'It is essential to raise additional revenue, not just to cover current expenditures but to maintain unimpaired the credit of the United States government.' Though a great treasury secretary in his own way, Mellon had utterly misread the situation and had no answer to the depression enveloping America. By contrast, Hoover believed higher taxes would only worsen the situation by prolonging the slump (and requiring ever higher taxes to balance the budget). Money needed to be left in the system, not with-drawn from it.

So Mellon was dispatched across the Atlantic to serve as ambassa-dor to the Court of St James, where he lasted an unhappy year before returning to America. Despite massively generous philanthropy in his final years, he would die in the middle of the Depression, unforgiven as the arch-liquidationist and regarded as one of the architects of the people's misfortunes.

While the debate continued to rage, the Federal Reserve adopted Mellon-like liquidationist policies. Between 1930 and 1931, the Fed would allow the money supply to shrink by a third, to the frustration of Hoover, who had little control over it. Money, the fuel on which all economies run, was simply being allowed to drain out of the tank.

4

A Visitor from the Bank of England

A broad column of striking coal miners, swinging along to the skirl of the Kurri Kurri pipe band, marched on the pit as an early-morning light broke over the hills in Rothbury, northern New South Wales. The grey dawn revealed a barricade of heavily armed police, some of them mounted, standing between the miners and the entrance. The coal miners, who had been on strike for nine months and were marching to protest against the use of scab (or 'free') labour at the mine, were startled by such a show of force. All of them staunch members of the local miners lodge, many had spent the previous night at a picnic with their families, singing songs and telling yarns about their union experiences as they prepared for the coming confrontation.

Some of the marchers had stones in their pockets while others concealed 'waddies' – heavy wooden clubs; at least one had a shanghai, or catapult. As well as revolvers, all the police carried batons. It must have become quickly apparent to the miners that in a firefight they would be hopelessly outgunned. The police, most of whom were drawn from outside the area, were under instructions from the state government to keep the rebel miners out of the pit at all costs. In short, the work of the mine was not to be disturbed. Heavily influenced by the colliery owners who presided over the most combative industry in Australia, the government feared growing unrest among the unions but particularly in the mines. It was determined to stamp out trouble, and today – 16 December 1929 – presented a good opportunity. One of the longest strikes in Australian history was coming to a head.

Most Australian union bosses believed their members had not shared equally in the growth of the late 1920s, and they were certainly right. Although the standard of living was relatively high in Australia, certainly compared with industrial workers in Britain, wages had hardly budged. On average they had crept upwards by about half a per cent a year – a meagre increment in the circumstances. The unions had grown numerically stronger during the industrial boom, with membership up to around 900,000 – an increase of nearly 30 per cent over the decade. Nearly 60 per cent of male workers and over 40 per cent of female were trade unionists – an unusually high ratio compared with most other Empire countries.

Australia was a highly authoritarian nation, the powers-that-be almost routinely intolerant of dissent. Employers broke the law with impunity; sweat shops were rife, especially in the rag trade. Yet most governments had long looked askance at growing union power, adopting in general a hard line against large-scale stoppages even when they had legitimate origins. For instance, when Australian seamen walked off their ships in sympathy with British sailors in the legendary strike of 1925, the government did its best to have the ringleaders deported – not the British ringleaders but the Australian ones! This was on the grounds that, as well as reputedly being communists, they were immigrants and therefore not true-blue Aussies. It required the intervention of the High Court to declare the expulsion unconstitutional, to the fury of the federal government. In this dispute, the government had the support of the fast-rising Sydney fascist Eric Campbell, who had helped recruit a clandestine five-hundred-strong force of armed men to try to repress the strike.

The unions had scored a few successes during the 1920s, but not enough to assuage their sense of injustice. Battles in a ten-year war for a shorter working week throughout industry, from forty-eight to forty-four hours, had been repeatedly won in arbitration courts and Parliament, only to be lost through changes of government, reversals of rulings and other flip-flops by the various arbitrations. Indeed, one labour judge resigned in protest at government interference in the court's decisions. And the authorities did not hesitate to use force to break up even legitimate strikes. In 1928, police opened fire on a demonstration by Melbourne waterside workers over the use of free labour; unsurprisingly, the 'wharfies' lost that battle too. A year later, a strike across four states by timber workers collapsed when non-union mills reopened with non-union labour. And a month after that, New South Wales mine-owners led by the notoriously hard-headed John Brown gave the men just fourteen days to accept a 20 per cent wage cut. Although the employers cited a loss of profits in a declining economy, this tactic stood in total contradiction of an award that both parties had agreed and signed. Although unions were regularly prosecuted for illegal strikes – the timber workers had in fact just been hauled before the courts – the federal government took no action against 'Baron' Brown and other mine-owners for this blatant breach of labour law. The result was a catastrophic nine-month strike by ten thousand men.

This was the tense situation inherited by the new government of Jim Scullin, the first Irish immigrant to become the prime minister of Australia. Amid growing unrest among employees, especially those in industry, the miners' stoppage had become a campaign issue. On the way to victory, Scullin had promised to force the mine-owners to honour their agreement and to 'secure a reopening of the locked-out collieries on the pre-lockout basis' – in other words, on the terms agreed by both parties under the law. As good as its word, the new government took the issue up, winning two straight decisions in the Commonwealth Arbitration Court; but with reckless disregard for social cohesion, not to mention the judiciary, 'Baron' Brown took the fight to the High Court. To the government's and the miners' dismay, the judges reversed both rulings.

Next, adding insult to injury, the mine-owners induced the stationary engine-drivers to return to work, a tactic that opened up the mines for the hire of free labour. Not only were the miners incensed at this cavalier treatment of their legal rights, so were their wives. Many of them members of the highly partisan and long-established Miners' Women's Auxiliary, the women took up the cudgels on their men's behalf by marching on to the rails and stopping trains carrying free labour to the pit head. Having done so, they subjected the passengers to a cacophony of 'tin-kettling' – the banging of pots and pans designed to fray the strike-breakers' nerves.

Thus, on 16 December, after a string of setbacks, the miners were spoiling for a fight.

As police, heavily outnumbered, took cover, the miners suddenly broke into a run and charged the colliery gates to the tune of 'The Campbells are Coming'. The Battle of Rothbury, as it would go down in union history – the first serious violence of the Depression within the British Empire – was launched in a fusillade of bullets, stone-throwing, vicious beatings and fistfights. Almost immediately men on both sides started going down, bruised and battered and shot, a bloody confrontation of Australians against Australians watched by horrified bystanders including wives and daughters and sisters from ringside seats on the verandas of nearby houses. Although none of the partici-pants suspected it at the time, the day would become 'legendary in mining communities and indeed throughout the labour movement in Australia', as Dr Robin Gollan later wrote in *The Coalminers of New South Wales*.

Newspaper accounts of what happened at Rothbury are contradic-tory and biased. 'Police Fire on Mob' headlined the *Newcastle Sun*; 'During the affray, three shots were fired by the miners,' reported Sydney's *Daily Telegraph Pictorial*. Some facts are, however, indis-putable. All the police were armed (several miners suffered bullet wounds) and the miners were not (the police were treated mainly for cuts and bruises, not gunshot wounds). Fifty years later, miner Alf Purcell was still adamant: 'There were no guns on our side – no one expected shooting to happen.' George Booth, a former miner and Member of Parliament, told the legislative assembly, 'Let me tell the House and the country ... that the miners never fired a shot at all. I was there from start to finish.' Despite the evidence, the police chief continued to insist that 'three shots were fired by the miners, who indulged in a fusillade of stones'. It is equally certain that the police were hopelessly outnumbered and must surely have felt threatened and overwhelmed by such a huge column of men, variously described as numbering between four and nine thousand.

The true casualty count – the next day one paper had it at '45 wounded', another at 'many' – was never established, for good rea-sons. During the fighting, which continued for several hours punctuated by long lulls, the miners made sure to drag away their injured 'in case their wounds were used in evidence against them', noted Gollan. It is certain, though, that the strikers suffered the most serious injuries by a wide margin.

There were two deaths: one miner collapsed in the fray, probably from a heart attack, while another, twenty-nine-year-old Norman Brown, died from a gunshot wound to the stomach, apparently fired at point-blank range. The young miner immediately became a martyr to the cause. On the day of his funeral, attended by thousands from all over the district, local shops and businesses closed 'as a tribute to the memory of the deceased', recorded the *Cessnock Eagle*. A miner with a flair for words produced a song for the occasion:

> *There was music at the graveside and in grief the mourners stood,*
> *Still the wind a hymn was humming with the trees upon the hill,*
> *The sun was shining brightly on sad friends from every town,*
> *And the minister started praying for our dead pal Norman Brown.*

The official version of the Rothbury riots was a whitewash. The coroner's report cleared the police of all wrongdoing, and the government backed the police action to the hilt. Indeed, the police chief was commended for his actions. The official organ of the forces of law and order, the *NSW Police News*, expressed outrage at the 'despicable tactics' employed by the 'Reds' at Rothbury and concluded by congratulating the force on how capably it had helped avert the threat of civil war. Nowhere was there an expression of sympathy for the men who, after all, only wanted to get back to work under the terms of their agreement with the colliery-owners so that they could hew out of the ground the raw material that provided the nation's warmth and power.

In the wake of the Battle of Rothbury, the state government practically gave carte blanche to the police to behave as they wished. Locals found themselves under constant surveillance by a virtual army posted to the area with firm instructions to break up any 'unlawful assemblies'. Even if they were merely having a smoke and a yarn, groups of miners were kicked and bashed and some severely injured. One recalled a later police commissioner coming across a group and ordering his men, 'Into the bastards.' According to Robin Gollan's fair-minded account, the police 'seem to have conducted themselves with an arrogance and brutality that went far beyond the requirements of maintaining order'.

The strike did not end for another three months, at which point the miners, many of them now poverty-stricken, returned to work on lower pay rates and conditions than those provided for in the original agreement. Baron Brown and the mine-owners had won the Battle of Rothbury while leaving behind a simmering resentment among their employees and unions in general that would break out over the next two years in protests, disruptions and riots in nearly all of Australia's major cities.

The Australian economy was in trouble before the Crash, although it was not the stock exchange that was the problem. Australia's markets had bounded along on a bull market for the best part of fifty-five years, mainly because listed companies had a long history of paying generous dividends which proved attractive to investors and helped them overlook any vagaries in share prices.

In 1929, Australia's predicament was essentially the same as the one it had faced repeatedly since its founding as a penal colony at Port Jackson, Sydney Harbour, 142 years earlier, namely, an inadequate supply of capital to match the ambition of a young and impatient nation that happened to be spread over a vast and largely hostile continent, which posed enormous difficulties for infrastructure. The City of London had long provided the necessary funds for development just as long as Australia paid its way through its imports and exports, buying and selling from the mother country. However, the provision of that sorely needed capital had often been erratic and, because of that, destabilising. 'The psychology of the British investor ... is incalculable and generally irrational', economist Lyndhurst Giblin observed at the time.

Australia's dependence on Britain was indisputable: in 1929, 45 per cent of all her exports went to Britain and 41 per cent of imports came from Britain. But now, as the overstretched economy fell into decline, Australia could neither meet interest payments on its overseas loans nor raise new ones. Earnings from its major exports, especially wool and wheat, were in a state of collapse. Prices for butter and all metals except copper were on a downward spiral. Result: the nation suffered 'from a gross deficiency of income'.

It was the construction boom of the 1920s that had impoverished the public finances and alarmed the City. The towering Sydney Harbour Bridge was the most visible symbol of a breakneck growth in public infrastructure that in short order had produced Sydney's underground railway system, a network of highways and rural railways, electricity supply for the outback, and the first excavations for the massive Murrumbidgee irrigation project. It had all been done on borrowed money, and borrowed foreign money at that. Jack Morgan's arm in the City, Grenfell, Morgan, had been instrumental in organising a $75 million thirty-year loan at 5 per cent for the Commonwealth of Australia. The projects that the London office had helped fund were of national importance, giant stepping stones towards nationhood, but they had been expensive and it would be many years before they paid for themselves, if at all.

For much of the 1920s, Australians had enjoyed this burst of much-overdue spending after the penurious war years. 'Very striking is the new consumption – in motor cars, movies and talkies, wireless, gramophones, tobacco for women, and the increased expenditure in confectionery, and dress, dancing and travelling,' observed Giblin at the start of the Depression. But as the first tremors of the Crash reverberated across the Pacific, exacerbating Australia's precarious position, her national wealth began a decline that would eventually reach 30 per cent. Just as worryingly, the collapse in gross domestic product would be almost exactly matched by the rise in the unemployment rate, from already serious levels. Even before the Crash, 10 per cent of the male population was unemployed, far higher than elsewhere in the Empire. On top of that, a fast-growing population was putting extra pressure on employment. Boosted by a wave of not entirely welcome subsidised immigrants from Britain, the population was approaching eight million. The resentment towards the new arrivals came from longer-established immigrants who feared these 'blow-ins were stealing Aussie jobs'.

Scullin's government had swept to power on a promise to maintain living conditions in spite of these looming economic difficulties. The prime minister's working-class background – one of nine children, he was the son of a platelayer on the railways – made him naturally sympathetic to an electorate with an unusually high proportion of wage-earners compared to land-owners and other employers. But the timing was disastrous for Scullin. Two days after the government was sworn in, the Crash in Wall Street threw plans into disarray.

In the fast-tightening conditions, London bankers looked hard at their loan books and refused to roll over even sovereign loans – generally blue-chip business – to long-standing customers such as the Commonwealth of Australia, except on increasingly tough terms. Thus Scullin soon found himself presiding over a nation approaching insolvency. As the old sovereign loans ran out, the public works programmes that had sparked the economy during the 1920s slowed to a stop, throwing more and more out of work. For instance, the construction of Canberra, the proud new federal capital, ground to a halt and workers were laid off. The Federal Capital Commission, the authority responsible for developing the emerging city of some seven thousand, was abolished in mid-stride.

Desperate men abandoned the cities for the Bush, remote country towns where they hoped to find work as farmhands, drain-diggers or wood-choppers, anything that paid a few quid. They generally found that others had got there before them. It was nothing new for men to walk huge distances to find work in a country where wealth had historically been slow to reach the interior. 'Depression!' remembered a bush worker at the time. 'There's always been a depression in Australia as far back as I can remember. I was walking the country looking for work from the end of the First World War until the start of the Second, till 1939!' With men on walkabout all over the country, relief work had been hastily organised as early as December 1929, long before this became the practice in other countries, but it was no more than a drop in an enormous bucket. Australia faced 'the menace of catastrophic unemployment', with all its implications for civil unrest in an employer-dominated society.

In this declining economic environment, Scullin's Labour government soon found itself ambushed by its own campaign promises. As more and more Australians lost their jobs, national revenue declined rapidly. Yet federal and state governments still had to pay the interest on their increasingly burdensome overseas loans. Long before the United States and Europe slid into the Depression, Australia was already in an 'exceptionally grave' situation, as Giblin described it. It had the unenviable distinction of being easily the most indebted of all Empire nations. Indeed, some City bankers were convinced Australia was on the verge of default – a calamity for a sovereign state. And so it was decided that the nation needed an emissary to remedy its improvident ways.

Although it had become home for many of their former subjects, British governments had never quite comprehended Australia, and not just in economic matters. It was far away, very different, and even eccentric, a place where people spoke with a nasal twang and used odd home-grown expressions. Because of its origins as a place populated mainly by convicts, its relative youth and its institutions, which were modelled on those of the mother country but considered inferior versions, Australia was not really regarded as British at all. It was a member of the Empire and played excellent cricket, but the nation was beyond the mother country's ken. Most heinous of all in the eyes of the Treasury and the Bank of England (which generally thought alike), it was considered recalcitrant in matters of public finance.

Even academics did not understand Australia. As one consternated British reviewer complained about *An Economic History of Australia*, published at the very start of the Depression and written by Tasmanian-born Edward Shann, 'Professor Shann's Australian is Greek to foreigners. I read ten of his expressions to an American professor of economic history; only one was correctly translated. How can English students be expected to know all that lies behind "sundowner", "swag man", "wowser" and "cockatoo farmer"? And how can a reader in the land of speak-easies be expected to know what "after hours" means?' In fact, the professor who had offended his reviewer by omitting to include a glossary of Australian expressions was a particularly astute pioneering economist and historian. Basing his theories on an analysis of earlier slumps (which he had experienced), Shann had predicted years before that wild public spending would create the very conditions that were now enveloping Australia.

It is most unlikely that Sir Otto Niemeyer knew the meaning of sundowner, let alone cockatoo farmer, when he arrived in Australia on 14 July 1930 for a four-month visit. He did, however, come fully armed with the Bank of England's sense of superiority in matters of public finance. 'The British always took it for granted that finance was too important a matter to be left to mere colonials, even white ones,' one economic historian remarked. For better or worse, the emissary from the Old Lady of Threadneedle Street had arrived.

Sir Otto – or 'Sir Rotto' as a hostile politician would soon describe him – was the Bank of England's globe-trotting ambassador for the gold standard. Accompanied by Professor Theodore Gregory, an authority on the gold standard, he went to Australia at the invitation of Prime Minister Scullin but at the prompting of Australia's senior banker, the stiff-necked Scots-born Sir Robert Gibson. Niemeyer's purpose in Australia was to appraise its economic state and, in his mind anyway, to pass on the benefit of his wisdom. He was an ortho-dox, highly respected Bank of England economist who had been hand-picked for the job by Sir Montagu Norman. A City man to his fingertips, Niemeyer undoubtedly saw himself as a headmaster disci-plining wayward schoolboys (he once referred to his Australian counterparts as 'colonial savages'). If Britain was the mother country, the Bank of England regarded itself as the mother bank. One of its directors, Sir Josiah Stamp, would soon write in what can safely be seen as the founding document of the 'sterling area', 'The Dominions on a sterling exchange standard are critically interested in the fortunes of sterling and must join with Britain as custodians of the validity of sterling.'

'Validity of sterling' – it was a fascinating expression that bore much more than merely monetary implications; in the mix too were connotations of Empire, patriotism and, of course, sound finance. And it certainly flew the banner of the gold standard in which, nat-urally, the Bank of England should take the lead. According to Sir Josiah, the Bank of England could safely assume 'a right to leadership' in the management of sterling through efforts to 'influence financiers in the Dominions to its own way of thinking'. Although Stamp was a brilliant and largely self-made economist who had, unlike most of his peers, not arrived in the corridors of economic power via Oxford or Cambridge, he was undoubtedly expressing a form of financial imperialism.

He was also expressing the unbending view of Sir Montagu, the Bank of England's long-serving governor. Here was another true son of the City, Britain's financial powerhouse that the writer J. B. Priestley would sarcastically describe as regarding itself 'as if it were the very beating red heart of England'. Certainly the City had an inordinately high opinion of itself, placing its activities without a hint of apology as the central pillar of the entire British economy. This was a view shared by many commentators, such as A. S. Wade, who rhapsodised about the City in his *Modern Finance and Industry* as 'a perfect machine which liquefies credit and irrigates trade from day to day'. Thus the City saw itself as the global hub of commerce. It loaned to sovereign governments – several Latin American administrations drew all their funds from the City – to wealthy individuals, to certain industries (especially those headed by like-minded people), to diamond magnates in South Africa, to railway-builders in a dozen countries, to coffee and tea growers in the Empire. And, of course, in Australia it loaned to governments and graziers alike.

Sir Montagu was imbued with a passion for the dominating role of the City in Britain's economic life, and he saw his mission as protecting that role by maintaining the integrity of the British pound. A critical part of that crusade was a long-term plan to erect a ring of central banks in the Empire along the lines of the Bank of England model, albeit subservient to it. It would be the business – duty, in fact – of this network to unite behind sterling. As it happened, it was also a dream of the Australian Labour party to have a proper central bank – 'a Bank of Australia to be in Australia what the Bank of England is in England', as its main flag-bearer King O'Malley had put it years earlier. Thus in 1930, the Bank of England 'was eager to train the colonial savages in the niceties of financial management'.

To be fair, the sense of superiority exemplified by Niemeyer dated back many years, and with good reason. The Australian banking system had proved to be a ramshackle edifice too often in the past to justify any other view. The Treasury had long managed the Empire nations' foreign exchange strategies for them, and effectively still did.

Representatives from London routinely stepped in with advice if it was thought Empire countries, in particular the 'white' Dominions such as Australia, Canada and New Zealand, were spending too much public money. On these occasions invariably the advice was to deflate, to slow spending down even at the risk of causing pain to the general population.

Niemeyer arrived in the middle of a full-blown economic crisis, not a banking one. The federal government relied for much of its income on customs duties, which were diminishing rapidly because of the fall in imports, and on taxes, which were dwindling with the rise in unemployment. At the Commonwealth Bank, actually a private institution with specific public responsibilities, Robert Gibson sat at the head of a cabal of bankers that was in many ways more fiscally powerful than the government. Incredibly, it was the Commonwealth Bank that controlled the issue of notes – the right to print money – from its handsome pillared headquarters in Sydney's Martin Place. As a result, Gibson clearly saw himself as the gatekeeper of the Australian pound, proof of which is that at times he had refused to produce more notes and coins than he considered prudent, in direct defiance of the federal finance minister. This thrifty Scot believed in saving, not spending. Indeed he flooded the nation with money boxes – miniature reproductions of his bank's headquarters – to encourage household thrift.

Now approaching seventy, this self-appointed conscience of the nation's money supply had made good since emigrating from Falkirk forty years earlier with little more than a few coins in his pocket. Already wealthy from building up a series of businesses, Gibson had been a member of the Commonwealth Bank's board since 1924. He was not, however, an economist, and had the counting-house attitude towards money that might be expected of a self-made Scot. With his narrow, ascetic face and goatee beard, he bore a passing resemblance to Sir Montagu Norman with whose views he broadly agreed. By 1930 he had been chairman of the Commonwealth Bank for four years, and he ruled it with a rod of iron. Gibson believed in the gold standard, an Australian pound that was worth a British pound, balanced budgets, and all the rest of sound finance. He had little truck with economists, and in fact was known to indulge in tirades against them. For Gibson, money was tangible and concrete, something that could only be spent if it had first been saved. As such, he did not believe in the creation of credit. Nor did he trust government with money. Thus, in the absence of a steady supply of domestic credit, governments were forced to borrow abroad. The huge burden of Australia's loans was a direct consequence of bankers', in particular Gibson's, control of the monetary supply. It was a ridiculous situation that tied the hands of the federal treasurer and severely limited his options in good times and bad.

Whereas various schools of economic thought in the United States, Britain and Europe were engaged in an often vituperative contest for the high ground, taking sides in one camp or the other, it was very different in Australia where the debates were conducted in a spirit of collegiality. Less constrained by their backgrounds, the nation's economists felt freer to work together towards often original solutions that reflected the unique circumstances of their native country. Additionally, most of these Antipodean economists had much more interesting and varied backgrounds than their European and British counterparts, an accident of birth having allowed them wider perspectives. For instance, New Zealand-born Douglas Copland, one of the pioneers of economic studies in Australasia, was the son of a wheat farmer who came to economics via stints as a statistician, maths teacher and lecturer at the Workers Education Association. As it happened, Copland stood more in the Niemeyer camp in the early years of the Depression than did his colleagues, though he later changed his views and would become much sought after around the world for his advice.

As for Professor Edward Shann, one of Australia's most important economic historians, he was unclassifiable. He had come through the depression of the 1890s and put himself through university with the financial help of his family. Something of a Renaissance scholar, he had taught constitutional history and philosophy, acted as political secretary to a radical liberal politician, studied at the London School of Economics (where he made the acquaintance of George Bernard Shaw and the Fabians among other intellectual leading lights, such as historian G. M. Trevelyan), and made a study of French syndicalism for his doctorate, a thesis that made sweeping excursions into political theory, sociology and economics. Throughout all these experiences, Shann remained quintessentially Australian, a scholar who never forgot that his scholarship served a humane purpose. As one of his biographers wrote, '[His books'] common theme – the individual's struggle against restriction – is an imaginative fusion of Australia's underlying economic problem with the general condition of mankind.'

But of them all, Lyndhurst Giblin had certainly the most adventurous background. In his late fifties at the time of the Depression, he had been a distinguished scholar at King's College, Cambridge, and represented England at rugby. Instead of taking the easy option into the civil service after graduation, he took ship for the wilds of British Columbia where he prospected (unsuccessfully) for gold, helping make ends meet as a lumberman and teamster. He then ended up back in London, teaching ju-jitsu among other things, before embarking for the Solomon Islands. Next, he established an orchard in his native Tasmania, all the while teaching mathematics and, in his spare time, climbing peaks and accurately measuring their height. The 1914–18 war saw him fighting on all the horror fronts – Ypres, Passchendaele and the Somme – and being wounded three times. Although he was not even a trained economist, Giblin united his other disciplines to produce unusually penetrating analyses of Australia's economic situation. Above all, he was highly suspicious of economic theory that had not been substantiated in practice.

All of them were prepared to give Niemeyer a fair hearing, and Sir Otto's visit immediately sparked much debate about how best to extricate Australia from its difficulties. The longer he stayed, the warmer the debate became, largely because of the emissary's lordly attitude. According to one commentator, he thoroughly enjoyed himself on a 'junket of port drinking and golfing' while projecting an air of pompous certainty. If Niemeyer's own, later pronouncements are anything to go by, he must have trod on many toes. He gave hardly any credit to the views and contributions of his Australian colleagues. 'I thought Giblin pretty disappointing . . .' he wrote about the man who had been a star student at Cambridge. As for Copland, he preached 'dangerous nonsense'. (Later, Copland would be invited by Cambridge University under the auspices of Keynes, who did not get on with Niemeyer, to deliver the inaugural Alfred Marshall lecture on Australia's emergence from the Depression.)

Very soon, there was hardly an Australian economist who was not incensed by Niemeyer's airy cure-alls for their nation's travails. Some of these nostrums were met with disbelief, such as his view that Australia was over-populated (its population would more than double over the next half century). Carrying on in similar vein, he ridiculed suggestions that Australia should come off the gold standard, and he was absolutely adamant that agriculture would always employ more people than manufacturing (it was already the other way around). It is hardly surprising, therefore, that, in the years since, Niemeyer has become a poster boy for the deeply resented British sense of intellectual superiority, as well as a much-cited example of the havoc sometimes wrought by the 'visiting expert' bearing ready-made solutions.

In August 1930, Australia's premiers arrived for a conference in Melbourne where Niemeyer was the star, if not particularly welcome, speaker. The occasion would become one of the earliest political showdowns of the Depression. The premiers arrived hoping to soften the effect of the fast-spreading slump through more generous welfare budgets. After all, this was exactly what Scullin had promised. But hanging over the conference like a black cloud was the price of Australian bonds – effectively, government loans. Their value was slumping and the quality of the nation's credit deteriorating alarmingly. London's bankers, also under pressure from the deteriorating capital flows around the world, had made it perfectly clear they were prepared to turn off the tap.

Niemeyer, the City's delegate, was in vintage form. Standing up before the nation's elected leaders, he delivered a two-hour broadside that treated them like undergraduates. 'I assume everyone in this room is in agreement that costs must come down,' he said, laying down the gauntlet. 'Australia is off its Budget equilibrium, off its exchange equilibrium, and is faced with considerable internal and external unfounded and maturing debts,' thundered the man from the Bank of England. 'The credit of the country is at a lower ebb than that of any of the other dominions, not excepting India.'

In any economic debate, especially with a Bank of England ambassador, Scullin and most of the other premiers were at a considerable disadvantage. The prime minister had left school at fourteen and variously worked behind a grocery counter and as a wood-chopper, a miner and a farmer, all the time educating himself at night school like so many other Labour leaders. At best, he had a rudimentary grasp of economics. And so Niemeyer's highly orthodox views prevailed. Having been warned that Australia's living standards were too high, the premiers submitted with remarkable meekness and adopted the classic economic strategy of most other governments around the world. Like the liquidationist medicine, it treated the economic body as if it were suffering from a poison that needed to be purged. Balanced budgets, no more overseas borrowing until all external debts were settled, cuts in government expenditure including social services, cuts in wages – in fact, cuts all round. It became known as the Melbourne Agreement.

Backing the Melbourne Agreement, the Commonwealth Bank's Robert Gibson had a large consignment of gold shipped to London to buttress the trading banks' London-based funds – an action which further impoverished Australia. The Melbourne Agreement for which Niemeyer had argued so strongly would soon prove ineffective in the face of a fast-collapsing economy, mounting misery and spreading unrest.

Having won the day for the Bank of England in Australia, Niemeyer sailed on to New Zealand. On his return to Britain he would say about Australia, 'This is an odd country, full of odd people and even odder ideas.' If anything, he was even less impressed by the politicians and bankers in New Zealand, where the situation was deteriorating nearly as rapidly as that of its neighbour. The smallest of the Empire nations with the exception of tiny Newfoundland, its two million people were culturally and economically linked to Britain. Its pound was pegged to sterling, nearly all its exports of wool, butter and meat went to Britain, and much of its spare cash was held in Britain in the so-called London balances – stockpiles of sterling earned by New Zealand's exports but permanently and lucratively lodged in the City. If the London balances were healthy, the City was inclined to turn on the money tap, and vice versa. In the absence of a central bank, New Zealand's public loans were arranged for fat fees by the City's banks. As a result, New Zealand governments lived in constant fear of losing favour with London's bankers.

The prime minister at the time of the Crash was seventy-four-year-old Sir Joseph Ward. Seriously ill with diabetes, he was out of his depth. His speeches, a biographer wrote, were 'rambles down memory lane'. Like most of his country's prime ministers to that date, Ward had little formal education. He had grown up in the bleak and windswept fishing village of Bluff on the southernmost tip of the South Island and left school at the age of thirteen. Although he was finance minister as well as prime minister, Ward was completely bewildered by the sudden turnaround in the fortunes of his country's economy, although he claimed he had a solution ready at hand. He quickly became a figure of fun, much lampooned by cartoonists. Eventually, in May 1930, under pressure from his own ministers, he resigned. He died soon afterwards.

The economy, however, which was highly vulnerable to shocks from beyond its ocean-washed borders, continued to 'go to the dogs', in the local vernacular. This was a nation that lived off the sheep's back as well as the cows' udders. Entire country towns depended for their prosperity on profits from big grazing estates and dairy farms. As overseas earnings declined in the general blockade of trade, men were being laid off meat-slaughtering lines in giant meat freezing works. Woollen mills slowed to half-pace. Ships started to leave the ports half-empty. State-owned railways freighted less and less cargo. Dairy factories processed less milk. Sales at the nationwide farmers' co-operatives – retailers supplying everything from grass seed and weed-killers to bush shirts and gumboots – rapidly collapsed. Country pubs dispensed less beer and city brewers laid off staff.

Reinforced by Niemeyer's visit, the influence of the City and the Bank of England set New Zealand's course for the rest of the Depression. New prime minister George Forbes, a representative rugby player in his youth known as 'Honest George' for his straight-speaking style, and finance minister W. Downie Stewart, who in 1931 took over the reins of the public purse from Forbes, adopted classic deflationary tactics *à la* Niemeyer. Downie Stewart, a capable minister who had become quite a favourite of London's bankers during visits for imperial conferences, also enthusiastically adopted Niemeyer's proposals for a central bank modelled along the lines of the Bank of England.

However, Niemeyer and Professor Gregory had hardly left New Zealand on the next leg of the mission to South America before the situation began to unravel . . .

⬤━━━◗

Rather like New Zealand's Sir Joseph Ward, Canadian prime minister Mackenzie King remained largely unconcerned about the first tremors after the Crash, outwardly at least. Known as Rex to his friends, he had led the Liberals through prosperous, big-spending years boosted by a raging cross-border trade with the United States. King was an economist who had studied at both Chicago and Harvard universities, where he had been lectured by liquidationists, and he was confident the sudden post-Crash downturn in his own economy was merely a brief interruption to years of robust growth. Companies had banked fat profits for nearly a decade in what was the fastest-growing economy in the world, and the general quality of life had risen steadily. Additionally, the prime minister's education at the hands of classical economists had left him with a strong bias towards frugality in the management of public finances. King valued a balanced budget as dearly as did most of his contemporaries. So even though he was facing a general election, he saw no need for special measures, and certainly not for provisions for special assistance in this brief hiatus in the grand plan. In one of the most unfortunate observations of the Depression, he told parliament he would not grant 'a five-cent piece' for unemployment relief.

However, to King's disbelief, the United States exported its problems across the border almost overnight, largely because of Canada's commercial and financial integration with it. Soon gross domestic product began a precipitate decline. In fact, the tightness of Canada's link with its neighbour's economy was probably unique at the time. It bought roughly two thirds of imports from United States producers and much of Canada's financial business was executed in New York, which also happened to be (in the absence of a central bank) the repository for much of its gold. As a result, King should have known that a contraction in the money markets over the border would hurt Canada, as it soon did. Within months of the Crash, the supply of money –

essentially, the sum of currency held by public and total deposits –
began to dwindle and would eventually contract by one third. As for
the sharemarkets, they were already heading for a fall of 80 per cent.

The Smoot-Hawley tariff laws did not help King's cause. He had
repeatedly lowered tariffs during the 1920s, but now he had to raise
them to match the new higher ones imposed by the United States. 'For
the present we raise the duties on these selected commodities to the
level applied against Canadian exports of the same commodities by
other countries,' he said in a conciliatory way, 'but at the same time we
tell our neighbour we are ready in the future to consider trade on a
reciprocal basis.'

King's opponent in the 1930 elections, millionaire businessman
Richard Bennett, who led the Conservatives, was far less tolerant of
Smoot-Hawley. 'How many thousands of American workmen are
living on Canadian money today?' Bennett roared on the election
stump. 'They've got the jobs and we've got the soup kitchens? I will
not beg of any country to buy our goods. I will make [tariffs] fight for
you. I will use them to blast a way into markets that have been closed.'
Not only was Bennett prepared to fight back over tariffs, he was also in
favour of unemployment relief as well as pump-priming economic
programmes. Increasingly dismayed by the turn of events, the electorate went for it. Mocked as 'five-cent King', the prime minister lost
office to the Conservatives in a landslide.

In the meantime, the mother country had troubles of her own.

5

Iron Chancellor

When the order for the ship arrived in the offices of John Brown & Co, it was seen as a blessing for Scotland's beleaguered Clydebank. A few short years earlier, it had been one of the most productive ship-building localities in the world as well as one of the least likely because of its distance from the sea. But the yards along the Clyde river had struggled for work during much of the 1920s. The resurgent ship-builders of Germany and France had won prestige orders for Blue Riband transatlantic liners, as attested by the 51,000-ton SS *Bremen* now plying the lucrative route from Europe to New York. Launched in July 1929, about the same time that John Brown & Co got the new commission, the streamlined *Bremen* had immediately snatched the transatlantic speed record from the British-built *Mauretania*.

The commission, from the Cunard Line, would put Clydebank back in the business of building transatlantic liners. More importantly for one of Britain's most impoverished workforces, her construction would employ about three thousand Clydesiders from riveters to upholsterers on the banks of that legendary twenty-mile stretch of river that W. H. Auden, the poet of industry, once described as 'a glade of cranes'. Almost immediately, John Brown & Co began to order materials for the vessel – designated simply as Hull No. 534 – that would revive the Clyde.

If there was any place in Britain that needed work, it was the Clyde. Although it had long been the hub of British ship-building supremacy, little of the profits made there had rubbed off on the ship-builders themselves. The slums to the south of the river, particularly in the suburbs of Gorbals and Hutchesonton, were probably the most notorious in Britain and certainly among the most depressing in Europe. In 1930, nearly eighty-five thousand people were squeezed into those two suburbs, living cheek by jowl in thousands of mid-Victorian, soot-blackened tenements in which half a dozen families might share a single outside privy. 'Sanitation is virtually non-existent,' a contemporary observer recorded. Most of the dwellings were within sight and sound of the belching smoke stacks, and the crashing and clanking of heavy industry. Overcrowding was several times higher than anywhere else south of the border in England.

In general, however, the state of housing in the poorest areas of Glasgow at the onset of the Depression only reflected what had long been a blot on the conscience of the (mainly church-going) industrial elite and the middle class who occupied the city's more congenial suburbs such as Kelvingrove and Pollokshields with their spacious Victorian terrace houses and villas. While amassing enormous profits right up to the end of the 1914–18 war, and in some cases well beyond, few big employers had felt any need to redistribute any more of these gains in the form of wages than was absolutely necessary. Nor did they see it as their role to provide housing or much else in terms of facilities for their workforce. The public authorities were not indifferent to the misery of the Gorbals and Hutchesonton and had encouraged new housing, but they lacked the funds to make a decisive difference to the quality of life there.

Only hardened stoics could survive in and around those tenements. The streets were dirty, and so were the youngsters. Photos of tough and grimy faces, filthy knees and boots (if they had footwear at all) became emblems of the Gorbals of the period. Everything had to be made to last. Cardboard was inserted inside shoes when the soles wore out; clothes were handed down almost like artefacts, or were made out of other items of clothing such as Dad's worn heavy jackets. Books were luxury items. In the absence of hot, running water, baths were usually taken in a tin tub in the kitchen, the one big room in the house. Three or four children often shared a bed; six in a bed was not uncommon. Rats bred freely, scurrying around on dirt floors. When the man of the house was out of work, which was common during the 1920s, his wife went hungry almost as a matter of routine so that the children might have something to eat. Even so, the diet was severely deficient, even in reasonably good times. Many 'Bankie' kids grew to adulthood without ever seeing a piece of fruit. As a result, diseases of malnutrition were rife in the Gorbals. 'Rickets was common,' wrote Ralph Glasser, son of a Lithuanian Jew, who grew up there. 'Many children had bone and joint deformities, bow legs, knock knees, limbs of unequal length. Some clanked along with a leg enclosed in iron struts from ankle to knee, or thumped the ground with an iron frame attached to the sole of a boot – a device to make a short or bowed leg function as though it were of equal length with the other. These were everyday sights.'

Overcrowding had worsened in the 1920s, mainly because employers continued to pursue a strategy of importing cheap labour from across the Irish Sea or from eastern Europe to keep down wages – a tactic that served only to provoke the constantly simmering militancy of the Clydesiders. Inevitably, the newcomers settled into the cheapest available accommodation, which was of course also the least desirable; and in the absence of welfare, everybody wanted work. When there was any prospect of employment, men would gather outside the gates of the yards and wait for news. They might cool their heels for hours, days, even weeks, hoping for a call for extra hands. As Glasser remembered in his moving memoirs, 'Outside the twenty-foot-high gates [of blast furnace Dixon's Blazes] were clustered a couple of dozen men in cloth caps, fustian jackets and mufflers, heavy black trousers tied with string below the knees. Lantern-jawed, saturnine, faces glazed with cold, collars turned up under their ears and heads bowed, they stood huddled in upon themselves, sheltering within their own bodies, as sheep do on a storm-swept hillside.' And whether they were in or out of work, cheap booze was the working man's opiate, as the vomit-strewn streets revealed. It was almost expected of Clydesider men to drink half the week's wages and give the rest to the wife.

Overcrowded and dirty, freezing in winter, vermin-infested, roamed at night by knife-bearing street gangs and drunken bully-boys, the suburbs inevitably became the breeding ground of the discontented. Baffled and angry at their plight, Clydesiders had long been united by their general misery against the rest of the world. As more and more immigrants were foisted on them, they drew tighter together in a sometimes vicious intolerance of newcomers, especially Jews and those of competing religions. But above all they hated the 'capitalist classes', an all-encompassing expression that covered landlords, employers of most descriptions, and of course Tories.

When threatened, Clydeside women could be just as implacable. If landlords sent in agents to evict tenants for non-payment of rents, the women were known to drive off the hated intruders by pulling their trousers down. Many an agent fled holding his pants up with one hand and fending off foul-mouthed *besoms*, in the vernacular, with the other.

It was almost a miracle when somebody escaped these slums for a better life. Ralph Glasser was one who did so, albeit against impossible odds. Having left school at the age of fourteen to work as a soap-boy and then as a presser in a garment factory, he studied at night school for years before eventually winning a scholarship to Oxford. He sent his entire library of three books ahead by post, and cycled the four hundred miles south.

Revolutionary movements had inevitably incubated in the Gorbals as the luckless thousands sought a way out of their wretched lives by trying to force the bosses to give them a fair share of the cake. To a growing number of these most downtrodden of employees, Karl Marx seemed to offer a solution, and they sent their children to Glasgow's Proletarian Sunday Schools established by the Marxist Social Democratic Federation. There the children learned to sing from the Proletarian Song Book ('Ours is the world despite all'), published by the highly productive Proletarian Bookstall, and to sit at the feet of teachers who spread the gospel of Marx and revolutionary socialism in preference to the Bible. Indeed, in some of these schools Jesus was presented as a revolutionary who deliberately undermined the established order in the name of justice for all. Throughout the 1920s, all kinds of unlikely clubs and activities were organised with a revolutionary or at least proletarian flavour, such as the Workers Music Association that 'provided a counterbalance to the perceived wisdom of industrial capitalism'. Even the Clarion Cycle Club was used as an opportunity to discuss ways and means of improving the members' lot. All these organisations were of course entirely outside the orbit of the state system and were therefore regarded with suspicion by the commercial establishment, few of whom seemed to be aware that they were sitting on a powder keg.

The general sense of hopelessness perforce produced its fair share of mutinous individuals plotting the overthrow of the established order. One of these was engineer David Kirkwood who had worked at John Brown & Co's shipyard, something of a production line for revolutionaries. At the onset of the Depression, Kirkwood was one of the ringleaders of Red Clydeside, the hotbed of Glasgow's insurgency movement. He was already a local hero for having been expelled from Glasgow by the authorities after stirring up opposition to the 1914–18 war (he was banished virtually around the corner to Edinburgh). Returning to Glasgow after a spell cooling his heels, he was beaten up and arrested during the 1919 'Battle of George Square' that flared up over a strike for a forty-hour week; Kirkwood was fortunate to be acquitted of incitement to riot. Now, in 1930, he had converted his militancy into a parliamentary career by getting himself elected Labour Member of Parliament for Dumbarton Burghs, a constituency that happened to include his old workplace at Clydebank. Kirkwood, who would call his biography *My Life of Revolt*, saw Hull No. 534 as a blessing for his birthplace and was determined to make the most of it.

His fellow Red Clydesiders were nearly all tradesmen hailing from the rougher suburbs of Glasgow. Willie Gallacher was a brass fitter who, as a founding member of the Communist party in Britain, was about to become a thorn in the Labour government's side. Engineer Harry McShane, another early communist, was a staunch supporter of Soviet Russia, at least until he went there in the early 1930s. Like many other communists, McShane would throw his weight behind Britain's most benighted workers by playing a leading role in the National Unemployed Workers Movement that would terrify successive Depression governments.

The Red Clydesiders' intellectual conscience was represented by the intense, dark-eyed Labour MP James Maxton. He was a local schoolteacher who turned to socialism, he said later, after witnessing the wretchedness and poverty of so many of the children he taught (he also managed to convert his siblings to the cause). Even then Maxton, a powerful orator who earned the admiration of Winston Churchill, was urging fellow Scot and Labour prime minister Ramsay MacDonald to adopt more effective measures to solve unemployment. Not one to mince his words on matters affecting his chosen constituency of the downtrodden, Maxton was once suspended from Parliament for calling a Tory MP a 'murderer' over the withdrawal of free milk from schools.

Another notorious Red Clydesider was Manny Shinwell, son of Polish-Jewish immigrants who cut his socialist teeth as a machinist in a rag-trade sweat shop. Shinwell shared with Kirkwood a charge for incitement to riot, but unlike Kirkwood he had been convicted and had served five months in jail. Having also been elected an MP, he was now secretary for mines in the new Labour government where he had to deal every day with the very colliery-owners who had helped put him behind bars.

The commission for the transatlantic liner was one of the few bits of good news in Glasgow in late 1929. The Depression was spreading quickly and visibly in a city that relied on heavy industry. The three North British Locomotive yards, which had built steam-powered engines for railways all over the Empire, were almost idle. The order book of Glasgow Corporation's tram-manufacturing works had emptied fast. Most of the coal mines around the city's outskirts were in the process of closing down. And it was the same story in other corners of Britain long reliant on the established 'staple' industries, the old warhorses of the economy that were now transparently under long-term threat.

The human evidence of the steady decline of the staples was known as the 'intractable million' – referring to the people who had been unable to find permanent employment throughout the 1920s. The expression had been coined by Arthur Cecil Pigou, an eminent economist at Cambridge University. When the Labour government took office in 1929, chronic unemployment was a nine-year-old problem without any obvious prospect of a solution. Nearly all of the 'intractables' had been occupied in the hoary export-based industries such as coal, textiles, ship-building, steel production and other heavy engineering in which Britain had once gloried. It was through these industries that Britain had achieved domination of global markets. But the 1914–18 war had smashed them apart and they had never been properly repaired, at least not to Britain's satisfaction. As a result, the decline in the global power of Britain's major export earners varied between merely significant and ultimately disastrous, depending on which sector was concerned. Coal was one of the worst-affected industries with exports down by over a third during the 1920s; cotton was definitely the worst hit, with exports down by a half. These sectors were big employers: the average cotton-weaving firm employed between a hundred and three hundred workers, and they were shedding in droves. According to government studies, there was a surplus of two hundred thousand men in the coal industry alone.

In the absence of alternative prospects, the intractables were lost in a cul-de-sac. They possessed increasingly dated manual skills, and many of them lacked the temperament or desire to learn new ones, let alone to move to areas where they might find more permanent work. The intractables lived mostly in the north of England, in the Celtic fringe of north Wales and in the flatter lands of Scotland north of the Borders. Governments had tried to shift the unemployed – or at least some of them – out of hopeless one-industry towns to more promising locations where they could work on special projects such as a new fish dock at Grimsby, port extensions, reservoirs and sewerage schemes. Known as the Industrial Transference Scheme, it was 'an attempt to take the workers to the jobs'. The strategy was not, however, particularly successful. For whatever reasons, many of the transferees were unable to hold down their new jobs and drifted back home.

Thus, successive post-war governments had not had much luck in dealing with the problem, but nor had they shown much determination. Practically every attempt to develop a full-scale public works programme – similar to that in Australia, for instance – had foundered for lack of political and commercial support. 'Had the great schemes which were outlined three or four years ago been started, they would today be in operation,' regretted Sir Alfred Mond, a former chairman of the Cabinet Unemployment Committee. Mond had particularly in mind a scheme for the creation of a canal from the Forth river on the east coast all the way to the Clyde on the opposite coast. Like many similar projects intended to get men working again, it had been rejected on the grounds that it was superfluous, a mere stop-gap that was in any event unnecessary. Unemployment, the detractors said, was only temporary and would soon disappear without the aid of such schemes. 'That was three years ago,' Sir Alfred added. 'That scheme would almost be completed today. It would have employed a hundred thousand men.'

This foot-dragging had gone on for most of the 1920s. 'For eight years, more than a million British workers, able and eager to work, have been denied the opportunity,' pointed out a 1929 report written by a Liberal committee headed by former prime minister David Lloyd George, an eloquent advocate for public works programmes. Fulminating against this 'tragedy of human suffering, waste of fine resources and bankruptcy of statesmanship', the report proposed to use central planning – anathema to the business community, as well as to the City – to stoke the fires of the 'great machine of industry'. Britain's long-neglected road system was considered a sensible place to start, with a comprehensive investment programme fuelled by loans. As one MP remarked at the time, the Roman government was the last one in Britain to take an interest in roads, and that was 1800 years ago. The Liberals estimated that a hundred thousand men – a tenth of the intractable million – would be gainfully occupied in such a nationwide programme, to their own and Britain's mutual advantage.

Labour's Chancellor of the Exchequer Philip Snowden was the main roadblock, seemingly almost taking pleasure in rejecting one scheme after another. According to the *Manchester Guardian*, he applied himself to his job 'with a puritanical rigour'. Although Snowden's own government had identified road works as an economically justifiable and practical way of putting Britons to work, the Chancellor would have none of it, repeatedly stone-walling transport minister Herbert Morrison when he came looking for money. Backed by a parsimonious Treasury with whom he was a great favourite, Snowden clung to the view that any government funds invested in public works should deliver a measurable profit – and preferably in the shortest possible period. For Snowden, the litmus test of the worth of a public project was that it must produce a benefit 'to productive industry in the near future'. Anyway, the Yorkshireman was quite convinced that 'Britain's roads were already the best in the world'. For Morrison, self-educated son of a policeman who was at the time writing a book called *Socialisation and Transport*, the economic benefit of a road works programme was obvious. It would arrive later rather than sooner, however, especially for the main trunk roads. 'Must not the argument rest on the enormous growth of traffic, including commercial and industrial traffic, which uses roads and which will continue to increase?' he presciently asked. Morrison was far ahead of his time.

There was a public works scheme of sorts – mainly for fixing roads, bridges, railways and the nation's drains – but it amounted to little more than a wish list. It was also ill planned, especially compared with the Liberals' programme. In the event, Britain's road improvement programme was implemented in a desultory and reluctant way – the Roman legionaries did far better – and much of the toil of digging and breaking rocks was done by men in work camps for a pittance.

In view of his opposition to something with such obviously practical uses, it is hardly surprising that Snowden killed another grand plan to settle hundreds of families on small farming plots, particularly in Scotland. This was too much for some of the Chancellor's Cabinet colleagues who became increasingly angry at Snowden's unsympathetic style of economic management, in particular the Glaswegians, all of whom had endured tougher adversities than the Yorkshireman. They wanted public money spent for the good of those Britons most vulnerable to the slump. Snowden was, however, very much in thrall to the prevailing economic wisdom, which held that a nation's books had to be balanced otherwise the devil must be paid at a later and not too distant date. Indeed the Chancellor was an arch-exponent of that wisdom; he even resented the cost of job-creating schemes. 'There is one item of national expenditure which is distressing me almost beyond measure, and that is the cost of unemployment,' he would observe in a speech. Like so many other holders of the public purse strings who would soon be grievously disappointed by the coming economic onslaught, Snowden was confident that world trade would recover by the end of the year and carry Britain with it.

The deteriorating state of the warhorse industries was the result of a clash of powerful, irreversible and random forces. In Russia, the Bolshevik revolution had decimated the economy, wiping out the ravaged nation as an export market for coal. In Germany, which was desperately trying to rebuild its war-shattered economy, a coal cartel had been formed to undercut Britain. Thus France, Italy and Belgium, all long-standing customers of Welsh and Scottish mines, now bought much of their coal from Germany under the war reparations arrangements.

The war had also changed everything for cotton. Unable to obtain supplies during the conflict, long-standing overseas customers had sought alternative sources of raw material, or started producing cotton themselves, India in particular. To cotton manufacturers' shock, even Japan had emerged as a major producer of high-quality cotton. Almost from a standing start, by 1929 Japanese mills, which had installed automatic looms that ran rings around Britain's much slower hand looms, had cornered 19 per cent of the world cotton trade. And as Britain's cotton producers constantly reminded the unions, wages in the Japanese mills were one fifth of those prevailing in Britain and the only way to compete was to cut costs to the bone.

However, yearning for the bumper export profits of yesteryear, textile manufacturers such as Sir Charles Macara, the self-made Scot who was then British cotton's senior figure, were still convinced (against all the evidence) that Britain could once again occupy 'our former supreme and prosperous position in the cotton trade of the world'. As it turned out, he was hopelessly wrong. But Macara, son of a minister of the Free Church, was an enlightened employer who 'believed that industrial harmony could only come from social harmony between capital and labour'. Unfortunately, because he might have exercised a considerable influence on government policy in the hard times just around the corner, Macara died in 1929. The industry lost an important figure at a critical period.

In Whitehall, committees were meeting almost weekly to try to devise ways and means of restoring three of the biggest industries – cotton, iron and steel – to their former global glory. Or, as the brief put it, 'to make recommendations as to any action which may appear desirable and practicable in order to improve the position of this industry in the markets of the world'. But when the report on the iron and steel industry was ready, its conclusions were so grim and 'too damaging', according to a senior civil servant who saw the details, that it was quietly buried. Any hope that the staples might rescue the intractables from their miserable plight was thus dashed.

For this passive state of affairs, the owners had to shoulder much of the blame. Their industries had been in flux for decades, especially in terms of technology and competition, yet they still presided over nineteenth-century methods of management and organisation. They failed to invest in modern machinery and, jealous of their industrial fiefdoms, wasted one opportunity after another to amalgamate and achieve the economies of scale that might have made their products internationally competitive. As far as they were concerned, the world had stood still and it only needed another round of economies for Britain to regain its old supremacy.

The owners did, however, have a common plan, and it was called cutting costs to the bone. And when employers talked about cutting costs, they invariably meant wages. 'If other competing countries have increased their production and captured our markets,' Sir Adam Nimmo, vice-president of the Mining Association, observed, 'it is because British coal has been too dear.' For Nimmo, the solution was lower wages. But how much lower? If wages were reduced to those prevailing in competing countries such as the almost starvation rates being paid in Germany, they would have to be halved or even quartered.

This would become a theme song of the employers in all wage negotiations during the Depression, as it had been for much of the 1920s. Bit by bit, this one-eyed strategy would lead – indeed, it already had – to a mounting sense of resentment and confusion among workers, stoking the conviction that they were the victims of forces beyond their control. Coal miners had already swallowed a wage cut, plus a longer working day, after an ignominious defeat in the General Strike of 1926. 'Every day miners are driven into taking risks which they should not take in order to produce enough coal to enable them to draw at least the minimum wage,' Wal Hannington, a leading light of the National Unemployed Workers Movement, would write in *The Problem of the Distressed Areas*, still probably the best and fairest account of the misery of Britain's Depression unemployed.

Hannington, son of a bricklayer who had already seen the inside of several jails for his role in organising strikes and protests during the 1920s, knew hundreds of miners and had seen how the odds were stacked against them. It did not pay to complain when you were in a position of weakness, as most pitmen were: '... they know from bitter experience that if they go to the colliery office and complain that their money has not been made up to the minimum the management will soon find reasons for discharging them. The fear of victimisation amongst the men drives them to keep their mouths shut when they should be able to expose widely the grave violations of the minimum wage act practised by colliery companies.'

With notable exceptions such as the Fitzwilliams in Wentworth, Cambridgeshire, who fed and entertained their own miners during the General Strike, colliery-owners were generally regarded as the most callous employers in all of Britain, with the possible exception of the jute barons of Dundee. Obdurate, unimaginative and short-sighted, the coal industry had no serious ideas for improving productivity, as the new Labour government was quickly learning. For instance, in discussions about the future of the coal export trade, Miners Federation negotiators bluntly informed ministers that a restoration of the seven-hour working day (which miners had lost in the 1926 General Strike) would add another two shillings to the cost of each ton of coal and subtract 20 per cent in wages. Thus a seven-hour working day was totally *outré*. Costs had to be cut to the bone.

As for Manny Shinwell, who was thoroughly enjoying political respectability as minister of mines, he thought the colliery-owners were burying their heads in the sand. He argued that Polish and German pits were producing 'better and cheaper coal than Britain'. (He was certainly correct: most colliery-owners had failed to invest their profits, and their mines were woefully unproductive.) When he urged the owners to go to Europe and 'study the problem on the spot', they refused, so he went himself and corroborated his own opinion.

While colliery-owners remained convinced the recovery of their industry must be predicated on lower costs, their product was fast losing its value. Coal was no longer the staple fuel it had long been. The world's merchant fleet, including British-built ships such as the *Mauretania*, was already feeding alternative fuel into its giant engines.

By the late 1920s it was oil rather than coal that propelled 30 per cent of vessels plying the world's oceans, up from a mere 2.6 per cent in 1914.

Despite overwhelming evidence, Prime Minister Ramsay MacDonald retained a stubborn faith in the staple industries, insisting they would show Britain the way out of the 'economic blizzard', as he put it. On its way to election victory in 1929, Labour had presented itself as a party of compassion that would right the wrongs committed by the Conservatives, a party that had 'thrown thousands of workless men and women onto the Poor Law', as its general election manifesto accused. Not only that, 'vast areas of the country are derelict' and 'a million of our fellow countrymen are needing food and clothing'. To right these wrongs, Labour would launch public works schemes on 'new roads and bridge improvements'. The central theme of the manifesto was to 'restore prosperity to the depressed industries' through all kinds of support for exports. As a result, ship-building and shipping would prosper on the back of an increase in foreign trade. And if none of this worked, it would even assist Britons to emigrate, but only after being equipped with 'training and assistance . . . for those who wish to try their fortunes in new lands'. In general, 'new lands' meant Empire nations such as Canada, Australia and New Zealand where there was already rampant unemployment.

The majority of voters saw MacDonald as an apostle of socialism, their saviour. Illegitimate son of a poor Scottish seamstress, he was one of the three founding fathers of the Labour party who genuinely believed socialism was the panacea for most of Britain's ills. On his way to Number 10, he had written a string of idealistic books such as *Socialism and Society*. A tweedy and comfortable figure with a silver tongue which could charm trade union audiences, he even won the backing of the Clydesiders, albeit with reservations about the depth of his commitment to the cause. As for the establishment, and particularly City grandees such as Edward Grenfell, they had been nervous about Labour but willing to help.

For years, the Bank of England had done what little it could to try to revive increasingly derelict companies in the staple industries, particularly cotton and steel, through a process of merger and rationalisation. Sir Montagu Norman's main concern was not so much for the

unemployed, but for the integrity of the provincial banks whichun-
derpinned the strength of the British pound but which had loaned
heavily to the factories. He lived in constant fear of bank failures, and
the fortunes of many of the regional institutions were so closely inter-
twined with local industry that they risked going down with it.

The Crash made the job of rescuing the staples more urgent. In
early February 1930, a month after Labour took office, the aristocracy
of the City met in the Westminster office of Jimmy Thomas, a former
leader of the railwaymen's union. Also present were Sir Montagu,
Edward Grenfell, Lionel Rothschild, Charles Hambro and senior
people from other merchant banks, all of whom had been invited to
discuss the situation following a passionate speech Thomas had made
in Manchester, the heart of the cotton industry. In this peroration,
Thomas, who tended to let his mouth run away with him, had
declared that Britain's important industries 'must be fundamentally
reorganised and modernised in order to be able to compete at prices
which will enable them to compete with the world'. His remarks made
it sound as though the City was ready and waiting to pump money into
the rebirth of the threatened staples. As he put it, 'Industries which
propose schemes that, in the opinion of those advising the City, con-
form to this requirement will receive the most sympathetic
consideration and the co-operation of the City in working out plans
and finding the necessary finance.' In fact this was far from the case.
Apart from Grenfell and one or two others, the City grandees were
decidedly lukewarm about dirtying their hands with industry. They
were lenders, not investors. Anyway, the merchant bankers could see
little return in the business. For his part, Grenfell regarded it as a
public duty 'to help in the general situation'.

It was because of its history that Morgan, Grenfell was more
inclined to don its overalls, so to speak, than most of its competitors.
Though known as an American bank, the House of Morgan had actually started in London, putting down its roots nearly a century earlier
when an expatriate American named George Peabody established a
counting house in the City. Later he hired another expatriate, Jack
Morgan's grandfather, and made him a partner. Soon the house was
doing a thriving business, channelling profitable loans into the United
States in competition with longer-established City merchant banks

such as Baring Brothers, Brown, Shipley and others. And if there was money in it, the bank got involved with industry such as America's McCormick Harvesting Machines. 'Morgans soon found itself registering McCormick's patents in Britain, New Zealand and Australia, and even arranging displays of their farm equipment at agricultural fairs,' noted Kathleen Burk, biographer of Morgan, Grenfell. This willingness to work with industry and to take on massive assignments sharply distinguished the bank from others in the City. It was, for instance, J. S. Morgan & Co that had helped Thomas Edison develop his Edison Electric Light Company in Britain. And it was Junius, Jack's father, who had tried to corner the shipping trade through International Mercantile Marine. Similarly, in America, J. P. Morgan & Co preferred to play formative roles in entire industries rather than merely loan money to them. In this way it had paved the way for the amalgamation of companies, even those that had once been competitors, into powerful, semi-monopolistic entities that could sway the markets. It was the House of Morgan that bought out Scots-born tycoon Andrew Carnegie and launched mighty US Steel. In time, this readiness to immerse itself in the restructuring of huge enterprises would come to hurt the bank, provoking wild accusations that it controlled vast webs of United States industry. But in the 1920s, this kind of activism was regarded as good for America.

And so, in the long and honourable tradition of the bank, Edward Grenfell took on the chairmanship of the Bankers Industrial Development Company. To put it plainly, its brief was to identify tottering businesses that could be saved and then do what it could to revive them. But this was far from the City's forte, and the Bankers Industrial Development Company would quickly prove a disappointment. Indeed, the joke would be that its initials stood for 'Brought In Dead'. And so the City went back to its role of a largely passive lender.

'Thump, thump, thump, thump – at 3.30 p.m. the sound of the crippled chancellor's rubber-tipped canes was heard, at 3.46 the great budget speech was on,' wrote *Time* magazine memorably in April 1930.

This particular Budget came at a critical time in Britain, several months into the Depression. Labour had now been in power for nearly a year and the entire nation, from wage-earners to industrialists, was anxious to hear what lay in store for them in terms of taxes and welfare. Nobody outside the government knew quite what to expect from Philip Snowden, who was probably more loved and hated, depending on your camp, than any Chancellor in years.

A lifelong Methodist and teetotaller, constantly in pain from spinal damage as a result of a fall from a bicycle in his youth, he was known to espouse an austere economic philosophy which, like so many others holding the public purse strings, he liked to call 'sound finance'. In this determination, Ramsay MacDonald was right behind his Chancellor. Essentially, sound money meant that responsible governments did not spend more than they made in any single year, if at all possible. Ominously, as Chancellor in an earlier Labour government, Snowden had produced a purely housekeeping document at a time of high unemployment, one that sought to reduce the national debt. At the time he expressed a bank manager's view of the job: 'The function of the Chancellor of the Exchequer is, as I understand it, to resist all demands for expenditure made by his colleagues and, when he can no longer resist, to limit the concession to the barest point of acceptance.' Debt was abhorrent to this son of a Yorkshire weaver and former tax official who had scrimped and saved through his early life. Somehow this background had induced him to identify expenditure on public works schemes as wasteful. Indeed he once described Sir Alfred Mond, the champion of such schemes, as a 'charwoman economist' who imagined that 'Englishmen could live by taking in each other's washing'. As far as Snowden was concerned, money spent on relief works was 'from the economic view almost wholly wasted'. He was extremely jealous of his portfolio. A later Chancellor, Roy Jenkins, would describe him as 'a powerful, famous, cantankerous and rigidly orthodox head of the Treasury'.

Watching from the crowded galleries as Snowden stumped into the House was his wife Ethel, a striking-looking teacher, socialist, feminist and temperance campaigner who was highly ambitious for her husband. Also present were as many of the industrial elite as could find a seat; the world's greatest shipping magnate, Lord Kylsant, chairman of Royal Mail and White Star lines, and Sir Montagu Norman were among them. The latter worked closely with the Chancellor, who seemed to revere the Bank of England governor. 'He might have stepped out of the frame of a portrait of a handsome courtier of the Middle Ages,' Snowden would later rhapsodise. 'It took but a short acquaintance with Mr. Norman [as he then was] to know that his external appearance was the bodily expression of one of the kindliest natures and most sympathetic hearts it has been my privilege to know.'

Sipping water where his predecessor Churchill, who now sat opposite, had drunk whisky and soda, the Chancellor did not take long to summarise the damage already caused by the fall-out from the Crash. Although it had happened barely six months ago, he described an economy that was already in difficulties. The public finances had slumped into a significant deficit, and Snowden made it clear he intended to make up the shortfall, every last penny. 'As long as I hold this office, the country shall pay its way by honest methods,' he rasped. Having nailed his colours to the mast, he raised taxes on middle incomes by $2^1/_2$ per cent before taking revenge on the 'idle rich', as he often described them: henceforth the government would extract in death duties exactly half of the estate of every deceased person of wealth, regardless of whether the money had been inherited or self-made. 'Take the lot!' yelled the Tory benches, many of whose MPs were directly affected.

Snowden was battening down the hatches. If he could possibly help it, there would be no public works schemes on his watch. Even though Labour had been elected on the back of posters plastered on walls all over Britain that declared 'The works are closed! But the ballot box is open. Vote Labour in your own interests', Snowden could not have read them.

6

Rise of the Fascists

By the early summer of 1931, the Macmillan Report was nearly complete. After nearly eighteen months of heated debate among its members, the committee was putting the final touches to what amounted to a gloomy summary of the state of the public finances. And committee chairman Hugh Macmillan, the Glasgow-born judge who had made something of a career out of running major inquiries of this kind, knew the report could prove highly controversial.

Chancellor Snowden had asked him to establish how best to harness public and private finance – banking and credit – for the greater good of the economy in the wake of the Crash. Apart from professional economists such as the ubiquitous Keynes, who was writing most of the report, the committee included banker Robert Brand from Lazards (a Keynes ally), former Chancellor of the Exchequer Reginald McKenna (who was also in growing sympathy with Keynes's anti-liquidationist arguments), three industrialists, Labour MP Ernie Bevin, several former Treasury people, and J. Walton Newbold, the first declared communist to be elected to Parliament. In the last few years the versatile Macmillan had chaired inquiries into lunacy, coal-mining disputes and ship-building, among other subjects. This, however, was the one for which he would be remembered.

The committee had been deliberating since late 1929 after the first tremors from Wall Street had demonstrated Britain's vulnerability to an abrupt disruption in global money flows. The situation had deteriorated markedly since Snowden's Budget a few months later, unemployment growing rapidly and unrest mounting in the hardest-hit areas. In the light of events it had also become clear that Snowden's Budget was inadequate for the worsening conditions. The public finances were unravelling, and so were those of the City. The liabilities of the 'perfect machine' now stood at four or five times the Bank of England's gold reserves – a dangerous situation for a nation that saw itself as the guardian of the gold standard underpinning the value of most of the world's currencies. Just as seriously, indeed probably more so, the City's income from abroad was falling rapidly. Foreign dividends, invisible earnings, fees and other cash flows, all of which buttressed the gold standard, were in an unstoppable decline.

Sir Montagu Norman was one of the most worried men in London. A particular concern for him was the parlous state of Germany. This was because he had encouraged many City banks, including Morgan, Grenfell, to loan heavily to the old foe in a coordinated effort to shore up its finances. Some City institutions had loaned so much to Germany that they relied on the repayments to meet their own obligations. And those payments were now in jeopardy.

Germany's Chancellor (roughly the equivalent of a prime minister) was a forty-four-year-old bachelor named Heinrich Bruning, leader of the Catholic Centre party. The much-decorated lieutenant of a machine gun company in the 1914–18 war, the bespectacled and intense Bruning had assumed power in 1930 with the approval of the generals who exercised a pervasive control over the nation's politics. Bruning had inherited a deeply troubling situation as a direct result of the Crash. Although the City was a big lender to Germany, the United States had been an even bigger one, and it had turned off the tap. Indeed, after the Crash some Wall Street banks, worried about the state of their own reserves, had given Germany just ninety days to repay her loans. Those American businessmen who had 'flocked into the country to spot profitable investment opportunities' in the mid-1920s were now much more preoccupied with trying to save their own businesses.

The nation had made, at best, a partial recovery from the war it had inflicted on Europe. The great German economist Gustav Stresemann had warned an American banker that the country was living on short-term credits – in effect through day-to-day borrowing – to meet its domestic and external obligations. 'Germany is in fact dancing on a volcano,' he said. But the precipitate withdrawal of American funds had served to deepen Bruning's problems. By 1930, the German mark was in such bad odour with foreign bankers that it could hardly raise the money abroad for such mundane purposes as the payment of civil servants' wages.

Bruning was very much under the thumb of the eighty-four-year-old president Paul von Hindenburg. The magnificently moustached Hindenburg was a Prussian general of the old school who loved to dress up in uniform complete with spiked helmet. Knowing little of economics, and verging on senility, the old general approved a dose of austerity as the prelude to a return to economic stability. Although Hindenburg did not take the threat too seriously, he hoped this would happen soon enough to stop the political progress of the Nazis under the theatrical leadership of a mere corporal, Austrian-born to boot. This despised individual was Adolf Hitler. Undisputed champion of the fascists, as most English-language publications described his party, Hitler was regarded as more threatening than dangerous, but the old general did not want the Nazis gaining more power than they already had. Hindenburg was probably more concerned with the rise of the communists than the mounting popularity of Hitler's faction. The corporal had at least served in the German army.

Only too happy to oblige the president, Bruning launched a hair-shirt programme of tax increases and spending cuts, not unlike that of Snowden. An economist by training, Bruning's main goal was to maintain the power of the mark, thus enabling Germany to pay off its international debts as rapidly as possible. Most of these debts were the result of post-war reconstruction, but they also included the reparations imposed on Germany as the fiscal punishment for having started the 1914–18 war. A sound mark was fundamental to the Bruning strategy because the higher its value, the more debt it would repay.

However, a divided parliament refused to approve the Chancellor's medicine, forcing him to fight a general election in September 1930. The result shocked every government in Europe. Although Bruning regained power, it was only in a technical sense because of the complicated nature of the new government. The Nazis emerged with over 18 per cent of the votes – nine times higher than two years earlier – while the communists improved their support by a third. For the first time the parties of rebellion had shot into contention as genuine political entities instead of mere rabble-rousers that had hitherto been dismissed as creatures of the night. And Bruning was forced into the impossible position of negotiating with them over his economic policy.

Bruning did all he could to block the progress of the Nazis. In a forty-six-page decree he took a blanket series of anti-fascist measures such as three-month prison terms for 'anyone defaming public officials' (something Hitler did at every opportunity as part of a concerted plan to undermine the authorities), the banning of all political meetings until 2 January 1932, plus further prohibitions on the wearing of political uniforms outside one's front door, and curbs on the sale of firearms, blackjacks, clubs and other blunt instruments, all of them weapons of choice for the Nazis. But Hitler's party had an aura of invincibility about it. Its success at the polls followed an astute campaign that exploited to the hilt the growing contamination of the Depression. Among other disaffected voters, Nazis won the support of the rural poor, who were among the worst-hit victims of the slump, and many in the middle class. As for the communists, they made gains among resentful employees of big industry such as coal and steel with their derisory wages. Between them the Nazis and the communists now occupied nearly a third of the seats in parliament.

As the Nazis, with Hitler in the lead, filed up the steps of the massive Reichstag building with its magnificent cupola of steel and glass to take their seats after the election, they represented probably the most visible evidence to date of how deeply the Depression had affected everyday life. Before the Crash there were 1.25 million unemployed in Germany; a year later, after the flight of American dollars, there were four million; now, in 1931, unemployment was heading towards a catastrophic 8.5 million. There could hardly have been more fertile ground for the rise of a radical alternative party such as Hitler's.

In less straitened circumstances, Hitler would very likely have come to nothing. Once seen as a poor man's Mussolini, he would have served his year in prison in 1923 for the farcical proclamation of the 'national socialist revolution' in a botched demonstration in Munich's biggest beer garden, and would in all likelihood have subsequently been released into obscurity. 'So perhaps it would have been, but for the Depression,' surmised *Time*. But as unemployment rose and the prospects for individual Germans, especially the youth, deteriorated markedly, he was seen as something of an economic prophet rather than the head of the 'Joke Party' – a sobriquet the Nazis had once attracted. After all, this was a man who had predicted the economic disaster that had now all too obviously descended on the nation. 'Adolf Hitler gave thousands of young Germans a chance to escape from reality,' wrote *Time*'s correspondent from Germany. 'Hitlerites had uniforms, brass bands, roaring mass meetings, plenty of free beer.' Thus the Nazis had become the party of hope, far more appealing than Bruning's austere and humourless Catholic Centre party. 'There cannot be any doubt that the Nazis were the party of the Depression,' explained economic historians Barry Eichengreen and Peter Temin. 'They were a fringe group in the 1920s and grew to electoral prominence only in 1930 when economic conditions deteriorated.'

The swastika cross, which party members wore proudly on their brown shirts, was about to become the best-known symbol in Europe.

Fascists everywhere were riding two waves: the misery of the Depression and fear of the communists. Benito Mussolini, the fascist dictator of Italy, had been inspiring imitators far beyond Germany who saw him as a strong man who could not only revive a tattered economy but who was also able to stand up to the Bolsheviks. Fascism had the added attraction of appealing to people who liked to dress up in uniforms, a human trait the Italian leader had exploited to great advantage. Jackboots and jodhpurs offered drama, hope and a sense of solidarity to those men who had been to war and, hankering for the discipline and comradeship that once bonded them together, were fiercely intolerant of dissenters who might threaten the fabric of a society for which they had spilt blood. Hitler had learned a lot from Mussolini.

A propagandist and opportunist who made his name as the editor of the socialist newspaper *Avanti* ('Forward'), Mussolini was by turns socialist, syndicalist, anti-capitalist, anarchist, anti-Bolshevik, anti-monarchist and, in his winning format, champion of industry. Having become prime minister seven years before the Crash, he also quickly discovered a fierce patriotism and a talent for totalitarianism. 'Everything with the state, nothing against the state, nothing outside the state,' he used to rant. The role of the masses was reduced to the level of automatons; they were to 'believe, obey and fight'.

Somehow it all worked, after a fashion. By 1929, the strutting fascist had organised the economy into a semblance of a recovery under what was known as the corporate state based on a close partnership with industry. It was employers' support that kept him in power, and Mussolini was duly grateful. The state protected industry from foreign competition and even bought most of its products, although they were generally higher-priced than competing foreign goods.

Even now, it is difficult to distinguish what it was about fascism as a movement that inspired so many copycats around the world. As a force it certainly did not provide a remedy for the Depression – the majority of Italians benefited little from it. And it was violently intolerant: Mussolini's Black Shirts routinely beat up dissenters. Yet, as Italians said, fascism 'made the trains run on time'.

Just as the Italian fascists forged a partnership with industry that promised to lift the nation out of the post-war economic trough, the Nazis nailed their colours to an economic programme that would save Germany from what they liked to call the 'Wall Street Depression'. Under the slogan *Brot und Freiheit* (Bread and Freedom), the programme amounted to nothing less than a revolution. Hitler intended to smash the existing economic order and replace it with one managed by an iron-fisted state. No mention was made at that time of the iron fist, but the elements of the programme presupposed exactly that. The new economic order would be created and managed by the state. And, the Nazis promised, it would create stability out of chaos.

Hitler knew hardly anything about economics, but more than anything else he knew what the voters wanted, and it was a return to prosperity. On his side he had capable advisers such as Hjalmar Schacht, Germany's senior central banker and a friend of Sir Montagu Norman. Indeed it was the pair's collaboration that had helped Germany borrow about £130 million from Britain. The Nazis' programme for recovery was based on borrowing and spending. With a bold disregard for the threadbare state of Germany's public finances, they would pour money into highly visible assets – bridges, railroads, canals, public buildings and autobahns – that would inspire pride in the nation. The Nazis were certainly not liquidationists, airily supporting painful economic solutions while the people suffered. They would spend Germany out of trouble through exactly the series of publicly financed projects that Chancellor Snowden considered a waste of money.

Hitler also had a remarkable gift for plausibility. Even highly experienced and practical economists such as Sir Josiah Stamp would be highly impressed by his grasp of the subject when he met him later in the 1930s. And, of all people, so was Henry Ford. A committed anti-Semitic, the automobile magnate had published a best-selling four-volume tome in the early twenties called *The International Jew* in which he accused the race of a concerted campaign to control the world by monopolising money flows. In an almost perfect echo of the Nazi party's own cant, Ford prophesied that they would achieve this nefarious goal 'not by territorial acquisition, not by military aggression, not by governmental subjugation, but by control of the machinery of commerce and exchange'. Naturally, the Nazis practically adopted the publication, so much so that they printed nearly thirty editions complete with a preface praising Ford for the 'great service' he had performed for their noble cause. As a taste of things to come, the Nazis had hardly taken their seats in the Reichstag when they proposed a law to seize the 'war winnings' of the Jews.

With Hitler's basilisk stare boring into his back, Bruning's task became much more difficult after the election. Steeped in classical economic doctrine, he had a horror of debt and remained convinced that Germany needed a dose of hard times. If nothing else, it was in his view the only way to regain the credibility of the foreign lenders who were absolutely crucial to the nation's recovery.

Despite the difficulties, Bruning did remarkably well at first, paying off large chunks of Germany's obligations and negotiating standstill arrangements with foreign creditors that effectively froze repayments. Unfortunately for most Germans, the price of maintaining a high mark was a collapse in their own material well-being because the only way Bruning could prop up the currency was by forcing massive economies through the system. Wages collapsed, unemployment soared, the economy shrank, and resentment mounted.

The capital markets also took fright at the sudden emergence of the fascists in the polls, adding greatly to Bruning's tribulations. In fewer than two months, between 15 September and 10 November 1930, a torrent of foreign deposits poured out of Berlin's banks. This was ominous for a nation that depended on foreign capital for its economic survival. Unable to produce sufficient income of its own, foreign money was 'essential for the functioning of the private sector of the economy as it was for the liquidity of the state'. As we have seen, although the Crash had reduced the supply of foreign investment, the German economy had been revived through foreign loans, overwhelmingly British, and its immediate future depended on continuing to attract whatever funds it could. As a risk market, foreign lenders had long charged higher rates of interest for loans to industry, city and regional authorities in Germany. But now they demanded stratospheric rates measured by normal international standards. Within a month of the Nazis' success at the polls, the basic rate on the German money markets shot up from 4.7 per cent to 7.1 per cent, double that prevailing in New York.

And it was not just foreign funds that were fleeing Germany. Fearful of these uniformed new radicals in the corridors of power, wealthy residents were dispatching huge sums into safekeeping beyond Germany's border.

Fighting like an eagle in a sack, Bruning kept tightening the noose further during the summer of 1931. He cut public servants' salaries not once but several times, starving the cities and towns of funds, and forcing down wages as well as prices. All of this was grist to the Nazis' mill. Ridiculing the Chancellor's efforts, they continued to promise *Brot und Freiheit*.

Housed in an immense pillared building, Credit-Anstalt was no ordinary bank. It was *the* bank in Austria, the holding company for the

Rothschilds in that part of Europe, the main lender to the nation's industry, an emblem of its banking industry, the presumed possessor of enormous reserves and impregnable security, and the parent of half a dozen branches elsewhere in Europe. Indeed, Credit-Anstalt was so imposing a symbol of Austrian capitalism that it had become an object of hate for the nation's socialists who attacked it for having 'its capitalist foot on the neck' of the nation's manufacturing industries through its monopoly on 'the money control of the Austrian state'.

The House of Morgan had a direct interest in the impregnability of Credit-Anstalt. Without it, the huge loans Jack Morgan had raised for Austria would be at risk. In a collaboration with the Bank of England and the Federal Reserve Bank of New York, the London and New York branches of the bank had floated the reconstruction loan that helped war-torn Austria out of the rubble after the war. Morgan, Grenfell had led a syndicate in London while J. P. Morgan & Co did the same in New York. Between them they assembled the capital that restored the economy – no small feat at the time. Probably only the House of Morgan could have achieved this; so important was the imprimatur of the two banking houses that both loans were heavily oversubscribed within minutes.

But now the situation was very different. Credit-Anstalt had loaned heavily to an industrial sector caught in the grip of the widening economic crisis, and its debtors were having trouble meeting their payments. The bank was also being dragged down by a loss-making mortgage-lender called Vienna Bodenkreditanstalt that the city authorities had forced it to take under its wing, greatly weakening its capital structure. As the repayments on which the solvency of Credit-Anstalt depended began to dwindle, its management was keeping the bank afloat only through short-term borrowings from London, including some funds from the Bank of England and some from New York. Scenting trouble, nervous foreign depositors began to withdraw their money from the early summer. Some of these depositors had already been burned by the failure of France's Banque Oustric the previous year and did not want to get caught twice.

Worried by the turn of events, the Rothschilds appealed to the Austrian government for help. The administration responded by seeking extra funds from the capital markets in Paris, which had for decades been the nation's main source of credit. However, alert to the subtleties of the politics of capital markets, the French government immediately got involved and offered a lifeboat on the unacceptable condition that Austria drop its plan to form a customs union with Germany.

A scheme inspired by the rapid decline in world trade in the wake of the Smoot-Hawley tariff law, the customs union was intended to provide a guaranteed market for the two countries' manufacturers. Wary of what a German recovery might mean, it was also a scheme France greatly feared. Having been mauled by Germany in two wars in the last sixty years, it much preferred an economically weak Germany. The government of the opportunistic Pierre Laval, later a collaborator with the Nazis, was already alarmed that Bruning had managed to persuade President Hoover to agree a freeze on reparations payments. In any event, France had sailed through the immediate aftermath of the Crash and Laval did not see any particular threat to its economy from the failure of an Austrian bank, even one as big as Credit-Anstalt. Factories in his country were still at full stretch and there was little unemployment. So France, sitting on ample gold reserves, failed to come to the rescue.

In London, Sir Montagu did what he could for Credit-Anstalt by arranging an emergency loan from the Bank of England. In fact the governor had his own problems. He had just discreetly coordinated the rescue of Lazards, one of the big names of the City, after the discovery of a major fraud in its Brussels office that left the institution with outstanding liabilities of £7.15 million – five and a half times total assets. The imminent collapse of Lazards could not have happened at a worse time, right in the middle of the Austrian banking crisis and mounting nervousness over the British pound. For Sir Montagu, who feared some institutions in the City might go the same way as the Austrian banks as a consequence of a failure by Lazards, and totally undermine his credibility, his main preoccupation was sterling and the gold standard. The latter had to be 'defended à l'outrance [to the bitter end] for the sake of honour', he wrote in the time-honoured tradition of the Old Lady of Threadneedle Street. Therefore a large loan, including a substantial contribution from the Inland Revenue, was quietly slipped to Lazards over a fraught weekend, saving the bank from the same fate as Credit-Anstalt. It was beautifully done. The outside world, even the City, knew nothing about the rescue; the only known record of the emergency was an internal note in the Bank of England that lay undiscovered in the archives for years. Sir Montagu never told the truth about it; indeed, he lied. When asked about rumours of Lazards' near collapse, he insisted they were 'devoid of any foundation whatsoever' in a central banker's fib designed to maintain faith in the British pound.

The Banque de France, which now shared most of the world's gold with the United States, regarded Britain as an economic power in permanent decline and any hint of bank failures in the City would have weakened the governor's position in the constant negotiations forced by the increasingly rickety structure of the gold standard. 'Britain finds herself in a bad situation,' a French politician confided to a German ambassador in early 1931. 'The Empire is falling more and more apart, and in England itself the belief in her own ability to recover is disappearing. The British people also lack courage and the resolve to work.'

The rescue of Lazards was also a matter of pride for Sir Montagu. Bank failures were rapidly turning into a national indictment – shameful events reflecting badly on the nation – and Norman knew that the French banking system was standing up well to the Depression. It was standing up so well that France was showing the United States how to run a nationwide banking network. As economic historian Pierre Villa pointed out, 'the banking system as a whole was always very liquid'. Unlike their American counterparts, France's bank managers had invested most of their clients' deposits with an impeccable sense of responsibility, not in shares and corporate bonds but in long-term government paper such as treasury bonds, as well as in gold. Thus the value of those investments had not collapsed in tandem with the sharemarket.

But not even the Bank of England's intervention was enough to save Credit-Anstalt. If France had helped, combining with other central banks to arrange a loan to prop up Austria's banking system, Credit-Anstalt might have been saved and serious consequences averted. With a population of some ten million, Austria was not so large a country that its deposits and reserves could not have been assured with some judicious and coordinated intervention. For one, the Berlin correspondent of *The Economist* could not understand why international institutions did not come to the rescue in view of the catastrophic implications. 'It was clear from the beginning ... that such an institution could not collapse without the most serious consequences, but the fire might have been localized if the fire brigade had arrived quickly enough on the scene,' he wrote. 'It was the delay of several weeks in rendering effective international assistance to the Credit-Anstalt which allowed the fire to spread so quickly.'

On 11 May 1931, Austria's mightiest financial institution declared itself insolvent and closed its doors. When the details emerged, the revelations of the bank's position were appalling. More than half the share capital was gone along with all of its reserves. Clearly the bank was ruined beyond repair, and the reaction was immediate. Fearing a run on funds, Austrian banks hurriedly cashed up their accounts abroad and brought the money home. Similarly, their counterpart banks were forced to pull back funds to protect themselves. All over Europe, banks rushed to safeguard their assets. If they could, foreign depositors withdrew funds from Austrian and European institutions, albeit too late in many cases. In a bid to shore up the public finances, a panicking Austrian government blocked all but essential gold and foreign exchange transactions, locking £300 million of foreign deposits inside its borders.

Just as had already occurred in the United States, Europe was starting to hoard capital. The fire was spreading.

About the same time, an eagle-eyed German banker named Carl Doerner was working his way through the accounts of one of his nation's biggest companies. A director of Danat-Bank, Doerner was alarmed to discover that his institution's biggest customer, the Bremen-based textile manufacturer Nordwolle, had been systematically falsifying its books. This was a considerable shock because the firm was one of the world's biggest textile companies. Although Nordwolle was notorious for employing immigrants on pitifully low wages, it was assumed to be highly profitable. Digging deeper, Doerner found that the owners of the company, the famously high-living Lahusen family, had steadily withdrawn large sums of money while concealing enormous losses incurred largely as a result of the collapse in world trade. The more Doerner analysed the books, the more worried he became. It seemed to him that the financial position was so serious the entire concern hovered on the brink of a collapse. And he well knew that the implications for Danat-Bank, the fourth largest of the nation's banks and considered a gold-plated institution, were almost too fearful to contemplate.

Packing up the books, he hurried back to Berlin. Doerner was about to inadvertently put in train a series of events that would bring down Bruning's government and pave the way for Hitler's ascent to power.

As it happened, Danat-Bank chairman Jakob Goldschmidt was entertaining Nordwolle owner Carl Lahusen when Doerner arrived at his Berlin villa. Finding an excuse to take his chairman aside for a few minutes, the worried director explained the situation. Goldschmidt was stunned: 'Nordwolle is gone, Danat-Bank is gone, I'm gone.' Having spent thirty years in banking, he knew the institution could not survive the collapse of its biggest debtor. In fact, Goldschmidt was the author of his own troubles. Under his chairmanship Danat had transgressed most of the golden rules of banking. The bank was over-exposed to a single borrower; it was also paying excessively generous dividends out of its reserves and offering interest rates it could not afford.

Now Goldschmidt descended to trickery. He tried to spark a rally in the bank's shares by buying them himself in a reckless splurge of three million Reichsmarks. But he was not a popular figure in the banking sector, having aroused resentment for aggressively competitive tactics and a publicity-seeking style. Even worse in highly status-conscious Berlin, he was a self-made, lower-middle-class parvenu. Out of pride and resentment, Goldschmidt maintained the deception by refusing to divulge the bank's true position for weeks on end, and when the news finally leaked out, other senior bankers were reluctant to lend their support. In the single month of May, Danat lost about 40 per cent of its deposits. On 10 July, it closed its doors. Inevitably the collapse provided fuel for the Nazi campaign against a race allegedly responsible for Germany's plight.

This latest failure of a major European bank was another blow for

Sir Montagu, Chancellor Snowden and the entire British economy. Trapped in the vaults of Danat-Bank was £60 million of the Bank of England's precious reserves.

Next day, another pillar of the German financial community, Dresdner Bank, revealed it was also in trouble, precipitating a rush by increasingly panicked investors to withdraw funds. Almost immediately there was a run on Germany's gold reserves as nations and individuals, fearful of their bullion, withdrew it to presumably safer havens. Everybody with money in Germany – and foreign funds accounted for nearly half of all bank deposits – wanted to get out. The collapse of American faith in the value of German bills was disastrous: New York banks alone held around $500 million of them. 'Out of the crisis of a single bank there was a much bigger one shaking Germany's biggest institutions to their foundations,' wrote one authority.

A total default by Germany was imminent.

Jack Morgan was furious at the revelations emerging from Berlin. Having used all his prestige to help get Germany back on its feet, he felt the House of Morgan had been roundly deceived. After all, he had acted as President Hoover's emissary in the matter of German reparations, intervening in the discussions on Bruning's behalf. What particularly sparked his anger was the way wealthy Germans were removing their money from Germany at the same time as Reichsbank president Hans Luther was in London, begging for emergency loans to save the fatherland. It was high time the Germans 'understand here and now that they are not going to be babied any longer', Morgan cabled from New York.

Many US banks with loans out to Germany felt the same way and flatly refused to bail out the government. As Kathleen Burk pointed out, American banks held 40 per cent of Germany's long-term external debt; they were propping the nation up at a time when US banks were failing by the thousands in their own country. As long as rich Germans emigrated their capital, Germany was tarnishing the House of Morgan's reputation with its peers. However, it was not possible to abandon Germany in its hour of need. If the nation effectively ran out of money and reneged on its obligations, the business of the City's big acceptance houses would be put under threat. And so was the British pound under threat: its stability was based on a steady stream of foreign currencies flowing into London.

Facing a collapse of the monetary system – a spectre that had haunted all Germans ever since the runaway inflation of the early 1920s – Bruning had no option but to order the closure of all banks under an emergency decree. Thus, on 14 and 15 July 1931 not a single bank was open throughout the country. Next, his back to the wall, he rammed through a swathe of measures designed to stop money fleeing abroad. Access to foreign exchange was strictly limited, even for the purchase of vital raw materials and food. Foreign deposits in German banks were frozen. The discount rate – the base rate for short-term borrowing – was more than doubled from 7 per cent to 15 per cent in a bid to tempt foreigners to keep their money in Germany. (Of course this made the cost of borrowing for Germans prohibitively high.) The banks were unceremoniously bundled into a regime of strict surveillance that required them to report regularly on the state of their liquidity, their capital reserves, gross debt and other measures of solvency. On average, their reserves of capital had sunk to frighteningly low levels of around 3 per cent, several times below what was considered prudent, and they had to be replenished through a reluctant and massive infusion of government funds that Bruning could not afford. Finally, Bruning took his revenge by kicking out half the directors of the recalcitrant institutions and forcing a marriage between the fatally weakened Danat and other banks.

Adolf Hitler watched and waited, knowing that his moment drew closer every day.

In an unfortunate coincidence of timing that nevertheless says much about the rapidity with which events were unfolding in Europe, the Macmillan Report was released on 13 July in the middle of the German crisis. It revealed large cracks in the position of Britain's public finances and inadequate gold reserves. Two days later, gold started to drain from the vault of the Bank of England.

7

Sir Montagu's Nightmare

The cable to Sir Montagu Norman from George Harrison, the governor of the United States Federal Reserve, was terse. 'We are concerned and surprised at sudden drop in sterling exchange today,' Harrison stated, dispensing with the usual niceties. 'Can you throw any light on this?'

As it happened, the Bank of England supremo could not. 'It was sudden and unexpected,' he wired back.

But not entirely unexpected. The governor knew better than anybody that Britain's reserves were sitting at a precariously low level. In addition, the London money market was showing worrying signs of drying up. Large sterling sums were frozen in Germany, Austria and central Europe following the bank collapses there, and nervous foreigners, both banks and individuals, were pulling out funds to shore up their own defences. Following the Bank of England line, the British press generally described these as 'panic' withdrawals, although they were nothing of the sort; rather, they were a rational response to widespread concerns about the state of the British pound. The Macmillan Report had revealed a gaping net short-term deficit of £254 million in the public finances, a statistic instantly noted in the world's fragile capital markets. The document 'revealed Britain's position, for the first time, as an international short-term debtor, and suggested that the Bank of England's reserves were inadequate relative to London's external short-term liabilities'. Simply put, the foreign debt of the City and Britain was not adequately covered at home.

The guardian of the gold standard was flouting its own rules.

In an unusually wet summer, half the British Cabinet were away on holidays, including Prime Minister Ramsay MacDonald who had repaired to his Scottish base in the fishing village of Lossiemouth. Philip Snowden stayed conscientiously at his desk but was ill, as indeed he always was. As he prepared the Budget in a fast-deteriorating economy, the Chancellor was under extreme pressure. The overwhelming weight of opinion in the City and the commercial world was that he should produce another 'sound finance' document that demonstrated Britain to be a virtuous economy guided by steady hands. In short, a Budget of responsibility that held firm to the classical principles of fiscal management espoused by the liquidationists, industrialists (insofar as they understood those principles), by most politicians except 'socialists' (as the quality papers usually described them with palpable condescension) and, it was assumed, by other right-thinking members of the community.

The letters pages of *The Times*, which was edited by Old Etonian Geoffrey Dawson, regularly carried diatribes against unbalanced budgets and high company taxes, which contributors repeatedly claimed were 'the heaviest in the world', as indeed they probably were. A typical complainant was one Sir Robert Horne. Airing his classical education as well as his hobby-horse, Sir Robert charged that 'industry is burdened with charges which disastrously reduce its power to turn out goods at competitive costs', adding that these same charges were underwriting 'political programmes designed to pile the Pelion [a mountain in Greece] of waste upon the Ossa [Roman goddess of gossip] of extravagance',[I] whatever that might mean.

In fact the issue of company taxes was a theme song of *The Times'* readers. Walter Runciman, an MP, sometime president of the Board of Trade and a member of the family that owned the Newcastle-based Moor shipping line, co-signed a letter to the editor in early 1931 urging the government to cut taxes, not on wage-earners – a measure that would have made their lives easier – but on company profits. 'Present taxation is starving industry of the capital necessary for its expansion and development,' he warned. His solution was the slashing of 'wasteful expenditure and swollen staffs' that allegedly could be found in government departments. In no time at all, he predicted, this strategy would lead to 'an immediate stimulus to industry' and 'restore a large measure of hope and confidence to the manufacturing and trading community, and at the same time enable our industries to absorb into their normal occupations an increasing number of those who are [at] present unemployed.'

As it happened, Runciman was probably right. Heavy taxes were an obstacle to the growth of commerce, but so were heavy taxes on individuals an obstacle to the growth of the economy, because they cut spending power. However, the MP and shipping magnate was hardly the most balanced of observers. His father, the biggest shipping owner on the Tyne river, was an unabashed admirer of Mussolini, in common with many others, and would soon argue that strikes should be handled 'in the Mussolini way'. That is, any miscreants daring to protest against low wages by removing their labour should be given the heavy-handed treatment.

The Times was obviously under the influence of its proprietor, the American-born Old Etonian John Jacob Astor, most of whose friends formed the top brass in the army or the elite in the City. Indeed, Astor was a director of Hambro's Bank. In their enthusiasm for sound finances, the editor and the proprietor clearly saw eye to eye. Dawson's leader writers, who grew increasingly to resent his interference, were obliged to weigh in with editorials to order. 'An unbalanced Budget would be not only a national discredit but an acute national danger,' one leader typically argued in early 1931.

What mainly exercised Astor and his friends was the cost of unemployment insurance, which had more than tripled in three years. At most levels of government it was regarded as out of control, a serious threat to the stability of the public finances – in short, frightening, in the fiscal scheme of things. Nearly all unemployment insurance was funded out of debt rather than unemployment contributions extracted from those in work, and the arrangements were proving woefully inadequate in the circumstances.

Furthermore, there was a suspicion among the middle classes, the gentry and nobility, the letter-writers to *The Times* and certainly in the mind of editor Dawson that the dole was being blatantly abused. And it was true that men and women were dropping in and out of unemployment benefit according to their circumstances, while the system of payments seemed incoherent. For instance, as an appalled government actuary pointed out, a coal trimmer might have two or three days' work a week, toiling for long hours for £5 to £7 a day, and drawing the benefit for those days when there was no work. However, a professional footballer, who might earn over £6 a week for a couple of hours' work, would collect the dole on the other four days. Similarly, the sandwichmen who walked up and down the high street bearing advertising hoardings might get one day's honest pay plus another four days' pay on what was known as 'the fund'. Then there were the 'girls and women' who worked gainfully as shop assistants during busy weekends but who claimed the dole during the rest of the week rather than take lower-paid domestic work. As far as the government actuary was concerned, the fund was sending the country to the cleaners, and *The Times* agreed with him. 'By far the most serious indictment which can be brought against the financial policy of the government is its abject inability to deal with the question of unemployment insurance,' it thundered.[2] Never mind that the dole saved hundreds of thousands of men, not counting their families, from near-starvation, it was 'a growing menace' to the public finances as far as *The Times* was concerned. And of course these same public finances had to be balanced.

Pretty much sidelined in this debate by Snowden, who had no time for mere theorists, Maynard Keynes fumed at the incompetence he believed he saw around him while the Depression deepened. He saw Britain as an essentially still wealthy country, just one undergoing temporary difficulties that could be fixed with a little flair and imagination. The world's economies were 'as capable as before of affording for everyone a high standard of life' he had already written in 1930. 'But today we have involved ourselves in a colossal muddle, having blundered in the control of a delicate machine, the working of which we do not understand.' In the absence of enlightened policies that would spin the wheels of commerce, he was now predicting a global calamity that 'might last for years with untold damage to the material wealth and to the social stability of every country alike'. *The Times* occasionally ran Keynes's views in its pages – indeed, it could hardly ignore the opinions of such an eminent economist – but generally buried them in obscure corners as they contradicted the essential principles of sound finance and balanced budgets.

Snowden had form in the matter of Tory-pleasing balanced budgets, despite his working-class origins. No fewer than twenty-one left-leaning Labour MPs had threatened to leave the party in February after he foreshadowed cuts to the dole while abjuring taxes on industry. 'I say with all the seriousness I can command that the national position is so grave that drastic and disagreeable measures will have to be taken,' he warned a House hanging on his every word, as it usually did when the Chancellor was up. Spiralling costs of unemployment insurance threatened the golden rule of balanced budgets, according to the 'wizened, gnomish little Yorkshireman', as America's refreshingly irreverent *Time* described him.

Unimpressed at Snowden's claim that his only purpose in forty years in politics was 'to improve the lot of the toiling masses', the disaffected MPs informed the Chancellor in no uncertain words that he was a traitor to his own party. On that particular occasion, one of them, William John Brown, roared at Snowden, 'This socialist government has neither the guts nor the grace to get out ... The Labour party has accepted the capitalist ideas they were sent to the House of Commons to expose.' He sat down to deafening applause from like-minded members. Dangerously for Labour, the militant wing of the party, and the Red Clydesiders in particular, was becoming increasingly alienated from its own government, which they believed was aligning itself with the interests of hard-hearted employers such as Lancashire's cotton-manufacturers who had just locked out thousands of workers over wage claims. But other major industries were getting tougher with unions.

Now, five months after Snowden's pessimistic speech, the national position was even more grave. The Chancellor knew the world was watching what actions he took, and as both the Treasury and Sir Montagu constantly reminded him, any suggestion that the government had abandoned the golden rules of prudent finance would only put the British pound deeper in jeopardy. Norman never let Snowden too far out of his sight. The governor had once crafted the perfect description of his role. The job of a central bank, he wrote, 'should be like a good wife. It should manage its household competently and quietly; it should stand ready to assist and advise; it can properly persuade and cajole and on occasions even nag; but in the end it should recognise that the government is the boss.' In these strained times he was probably cajoling and nagging more than assisting and advising, but the governor knew the kind of Budget he wanted and it was a bankers' one, a Budget for the City that would improve the deteriorating position of the 'perfect machine'.

Jack Morgan wanted a Budget like that too. On 26 July he turned up in London for a meeting with Sir Montagu to discuss an emergency loan to defend sterling from the drain on gold. The Treasury wanted £25 million. Like all the figures quoted in this book, it seems a trifling amount from today's perspective, but it is not the absolute sum that matters so much as its proportion in terms of total public finances. And right then, £25 million was life or death for a British economy tottering on the edge of an abyss. Jack told Sir Montagu he could only raise such a loan in the United States if Britain were to produce 'at least some plan of restoration of financial stability'. In practice, that meant a Budget of austerity, a document that would satisfy the City while inevitably enraging the growing army of unemployed. Assured that this was indeed the plan, the American immediately went to the capital markets seeking two stop-gap loans, both for £25 million: one was with the Federal Reserve of New York and the other with Banque de France, which was now much more cooperative because of the repercussions from the collapse of Credit-Anstalt.

It was now that Snowden lost one of his key allies. For months he had been in constant touch with Sir Montagu about the level of gold reserves that fundamentally affected the terms of the Budget, but suddenly the governor was no longer available. Stretched beyond breaking point, on 29 July he collapsed from exhaustion and took to his bed in the middle of the biggest crisis of his twenty-year stewardship of the British pound. Presumably for appearances' sake, the governor's ill health was kept quiet for over two weeks before the Bank of England finally issued a statement acknowledging that Sir Montagu 'has been indisposed as the result of the exceptional strain to which he has been subjected during recent months', and that 'acting on medical advice, he has had to abandon all work for the present and has gone abroad for rest and change'. What had been prescribed was a period of total isolation from Bank of England affairs. In fact the governor had already set sail for Canada aboard the *Duchess of York*. 'I have not been feeling as well as I should like and I feel that I should like a little rest,' he told reporters as he stepped aboard the vessel. 'I have been kept hard at it lately.'

Always a highly strung individual, Sir Montagu had in his youth consulted Carl Jung, the Swiss psychologist. The doctor filled the young man with doom by diagnosing him as a victim of a general paralysis of the insane that would kill him within two years. So much for pioneering psychology: Norman went on to perform a valuable central banker's role for Britain for many years. He first became a Bank of England director in 1907 when sterling was the world's dominant currency, he helped arrange the loans that provided the finance for eventual victory in the 1914–18 conflict, he had gone on to nurse the pound through one post-war crisis after another, and in 1925, of course, he was one of those who cajoled and nagged a reluctant Churchill into restoring Britain to the gold standard. It is no exaggeration to say that Sir Montagu had dedicated his working life to the system. But now, as 'confidence in London was steadily ebbing' and his precious gold standard was under threat, the grand panjandrum of the gold standard had folded under the pressure.

Into the breach stepped deputy governor Sir Ernest Harvey, facing the very real prospect of the dissolution of the gold standard. From all over the world, demands were pouring into the Bank of England seeking to buy gold at official prices. Buyers simply did not believe sterling was worth the official rate of $4.8665 and they wanted to acquire gold while that inflated rate lasted. The fundamental principle of the gold standard, to which most currencies adhered, was that the metal was worth a fixed amount of money. That meant the Bank of England was obliged to provide the gold if the buyer had the currency.

Although Sir Ernest was a stalwart of the Old Lady of Threadneedle

Street, he had hitherto been out of the spotlight. Son of a vicar, he had risen through the ranks at the Bank of England, which was most unusual at the time. Indeed he was only the second employee of the bank to have been appointed to the court of directors; all the other directors were politicians, private bankers or aristocrats with financial expertise, real or otherwise. Harvey had long played a skilled second fiddle to Sir Montagu, taking over much of the donkey work of running the bank during the governor's frequent and lengthy absences. He was an old-school Bank of England man, steeped in the doctrine of the gold standard and balanced budgets. But then he would never have become deputy governor had he not been.

As soon as he could, at the close of the foreign markets that night, Sir Ernest sat down with officials to go over the books. They revealed an appalling picture. Reserves including gold and foreign exchange had collapsed in the last two months. There was practically nothing left in the vaults. And worse, much worse, was to come. Another report – the May committee's investigation into national expenditure – was released on the last day of July. Unfortunately, it more than confirmed the pessimism of the Macmillan Report, calculating the deficit for next year at about £120 million. As *The Times'* parliamentary correspondent wrote, the document 'bears out the forecasts of those who have declared that Sir George May and his colleagues would make no attempt to disguise the serious financial position with which the country is confronted'.[3]

Sir George was the son of a grocer and wine merchant who had started his working life as a clerk with Prudential Assurance at the age of sixteen. In 1931 he was still with the firm, albeit as secretary, and had been appointed by the Chancellor to identify where the government could save money. The official remit of May's committee was 'to make representation to Mr. Chancellor of the Exchequer for effecting forthwith all practical and legitimate reductions in the national expenditure consistent with the efficiency of the services'. As such, the assignment suited May perfectly. Although able and industrious, he had a counting-house mentality rather like the Chancellor's.

The report conscientiously reflected its remit by recommending wage cuts for police, teachers and pre-1925 entrants to the armed forces, not to mention wholesale economies in public works schemes and social services. These last were predicated on the basis that, in the light of previous experience, public works schemes and social services 'cannot be essential'. The road fund, cherished by the champions of public works programmes, was singled out as 'a liability on the national finances' for the 'grandiose schemes' it had espoused. Thus a host of apparently grandiose schemes were recommended for the axe, especially in London such as that for a new bridge at Charing Cross, road works at Elephant and Castle, and a plan to improve traffic in London which, the report said, 'we cannot afford to deal with at this rate of expenditure'.

Most disturbingly for the Labour party – and encouragingly for *The Times* and its letter-writers, who continued to demand all-round 'retrenchment' – the proposed cuts in social services were to fall most heavily on unemployment insurance. In summary, two thirds of total savings were to come from the unemployed while the City was to get off scot-free. The Labour members of the May committee disagreed so strongly with Sir George's recommendations that they wrote their own report, which totally rejected the notion that labour, and particularly those out of work, should bear the brunt of the sacrifices. In its place they urged an emergency taxation of the rich. For this effrontery the dissenters earned the demonisation of *The Times*: 'The minority, in effect, echo the familiar Socialist contention that taxation of the rich can be indefinitely increased and the familiar Socialist fallacy that the rich – by which they mean the *thrifty* [author's italics] – can be segregated and taxed without harm to anyone except the rich themselves.' In short, the minority report was 'an absurdity'.[4] In the same month, the paper reported a record total of Britons out of work.

Predictably, Chancellor Snowden quickly identified with the May Report and set up an 'economy committee' to take the hard decisions. The committee would include himself, Prime Minister MacDonald, Foreign Secretary (and revered Clydesider) Arthur Henderson, and Jimmy Thomas, former railway union secretary, Lord Privy Seal, enthusiastic drinker and rash speech-maker. The first meeting was set for 25 August, when MacDonald returned from holiday, but the money markets did not observe the proposed timetable: as soon as the May Report revealed the unhappy position, gold began to pour out all over again. Within less than a fortnight, more than a quarter of the emergency £50 million raised by Sir Montagu and Jack Morgan would flee the country. In these circumstances it was just about impossible to raise further loans. The entire British economy was hanging on a lifeline.

Jack Morgan was now the only person the government could turn to. After all, J. P. Morgan & Co had found the money that rescued the post-war economies of Italy, Germany and Austria. Now it was Britain's turn to join the list of supplicants and only hope the banker could produce the same result.

Fortunately, for the next ten days or so the torrent of withdrawals reduced to a trickle and the Chancellor dared to hope for salvation from the terrible fate of presiding over the collapse of the gold standard. In the meantime the parties – Morgan, Snowden and other senior government figures, the Treasury and the Bank of England – conferred constantly about the details of another loan while the Cabinet argued bitterly over the intended surgery – in effect the amputation of the dole.

Suddenly the withdrawals recommenced, this time in even bigger amounts. This latest run was probably triggered by adverse publicity. 'London Banks Could Suspend Payment' warned headlines in the Geneva newspapers, among a wave of similar stories. The media's general assumption was that the closure of Germany's banks put Britain at risk, as indeed it did, because of the huge sums frozen in foreign vaults. Right on cue, bankers in Belgium, Switzerland, Netherlands and Sweden among other countries hurriedly disengaged from London, extracting their deposits in a headlong flight to liquidity. Scenting profits, speculators now launched a beggar-thy-neighbour attack on the pound. They lined up at the window of the Old Lady of Threadneedle Street, presenting sterling and demanding gold.

On Tuesday 11 August, Prime Minister MacDonald reluctantly abandoned his holiday in Lossiemouth and jumped on the train back to London while other ministers rushed back from all over Britain. Like everybody else involved, MacDonald was facing the greatest test of his career. Quite simply, the money was running out. Indeed, the financially able Scottish peer Lord Lothian confided to a colleague that the pound could go any time.

In this crisis, the first essential was to shore up the fiscal defences. It was not a time for long-term economic reform which, if it was going to come at all, should have come much earlier. With the prime minister's approval, the Bank of England urgently requested an emergency loan from the Fed on 13 August. Governor George Harrison's reply was immediate and favourable, assuring deputy governor Harvey that £50 million could be raised in the United States and probably the same amount in Paris, but only 'provided the programme of economy was adequate and received the approval of Parliament'. Working through the correct channels, the Treasury promptly made a formal approach to J. P. Morgan & Co, its official New York agents.

Like Harrison, who was technically superior to him in United States banking circles, Jack Morgan was convinced there was no hope of raising a loan unless Snowden's Budget slashed government expenses to the bone. In this, he was only being realistic; right or wrong, it was what lenders would demand. Not even J. P. Morgan & Co could conjure up such a vast sum on behalf of Her Majesty's government if lenders feared the loan might depart the Bank of England's vaults almost as soon as it arrived – and by now the entire banking world, a highly risk-averse industry, knew that Britain was haemorrhaging its reserves. What was needed was a statement of confidence that would convince the money markets that sterling was sound, and that statement would have to come in the shape of a 'sound finance' budget. In short, tax increases and ruthless cuts in government expenditure needed to be made. There was no time for a more enlightened solution.

It was against this frightening background that the Labour government's inner circle, fortified by copious cups of tea, met on the Sunday evening to discuss what could be done. MacDonald and Snowden had already briefed the opposition parties, both of which demanded even heavier cuts to public expenditure than Snowden had foreshadowed. The obvious difficulty was getting the economies past their working-class colleagues. Arthur Henderson, the highly influential foreign secretary, was the Glaswegian-born son of a cotton spinner; Manny Shinwell was a machinist; others had been everything from truck-drivers to shop assistants. And all of them knew that MPs outside

Cabinet, like Red Clydesiders James Maxton and David Kirkwood, were waiting in the corridors to prick their consciences. They also knew that the leading trade union body, the Trades Union Congress, was certain to turn down flat further cuts, especially if they applied to unemployment insurance. In fact, the TUC was already demanding that people in work must make the sacrifices rather than those out of work. Yet it was unemployment insurance – the dole – where Snowden and the prime minister were convinced the most brutal surgery had to be done.

With time fast running out, Edward Grenfell dispatched a cable to J. P. Morgan & Co in New York where, in the absence of the boss, veteran partner Thomas Lamont was holding centre stage at the partners' daily conferences. It was a discreet cable sounding out the position across the Atlantic:

> Have intimated to authorities here that there is no likelihood of bankers being able to place British loan [over] five or ten years in New York unless government makes satisfactory announcements as regards balancing Budget. If such a statement were to be made which appeared to you to paint a satisfactory picture would you think it possible to make such an operation for say $250,000,000. This is purely a private message for you in order that I may give an opinion if asked by authorities.

The New York banks had heard on the grapevine that the earlier stop-gap loans were disappearing rapidly. If they had known the true picture, it is most unlikely they would have countenanced any kind of a loan, let alone one for $250 million. No fewer than 60 per cent of the emergency loans had already evaporated, within a month. The Bank of England now had just enough gold in its vaults to last four days of normal business, and without further contributions of gold from South Africa and Australia even that might prove optimistic.

The pressure on everybody – the prime minister and his government, the Bank of England and the House of Morgan – was immense. The Cabinet was now meeting daily, scrapping with increasing bitterness over the proposed cuts. Every time MacDonald and Snowden were able to wrest a saving – a million here, a million there – the prime minister passed the information to New York through Grenfell, although not always letting his ministers know he was doing so. As easily the most financially literate of the Cabinet, Snowden dominated discussions and brooked no opposition; 'Snowden was not a man to change his mind,' remembered Manny Shinwell in his memoirs. Eventually the Chancellor hewed and harried his way to savings of nearly £70 million – enough to convince the opposition parties that this might indeed be a Budget sound enough to restore confidence. From the sidelines *The Times* cheered them on: 'Every one hoped that Mr. MacDonald and Mr. Snowden would win their gallant fight for what they know to be the necessary and indeed the only way to end the present emergency.'[5] At least the paper was consistent in its one-eyed stance.

The details now went to the US Federal Reserve. Harrison, a lawyer by training, had no ideas about how to repair his own fast-failing economy, beyond sitting tight and waiting for things to improve, but the Fed chief was disappointed and wanted even deeper cuts. J. P. Morgan & Co's New York partners happened to agree, doubting that enough had been done, and they immediately dispatched a cable back to Grenfell. While not wanting to give 'undue discouragement', they proceeded to scold Britain for fiscal mismanagement over an extended period. They pointed out that 'the banks and banking houses have for a long time looked with great apprehension upon the continued neglect of the present government to establish sound fiscal policies and it is going to take a great deal more than simply the joint declaration of the three party leaders to convince the investment and banking public here that real amendment has been undertaken and that the government is in a position to command heavy foreign credit favours'.

This was rich, to say the least. Here was the United States sinking rapidly into an economic mire, one largely precipitated by the failings of its own banking industry, yet J. P. Morgan & Co's partners felt perfectly justified in ticking Britain off for its inability to 'establish sound fiscal policies'. What kind of cuts did they envisage? No dole payments at all? Here they were straying deeply into a sovereign nation's territory, its right to manage its own affairs. Yet J. P. Morgan & Co was the only organisation of any kind that could find the money in these circumstances, and as the piper it was entitled to call the tune.

The partners assembled on a Sunday in a private home on Long

Island to await a formal request to raise the loan. Other cables from Grenfell had already made it clear that if it were not bailed out, the Labour government would fall. The fate of the British government now hung on the contacts and reputation of a Wall Street bank.

With MacDonald waiting by the phone, his political fate in the balance, J. P. Morgan's partners discussed what could be done. Of all the loans they had orchestrated, this was probably the most difficult. As bankers, they much preferred certainty to risk, especially so in the case of a sovereign loan involving numerous other parties with whom they had a long relationship based on trust and goodwill, the two commodities that were everything in their circles. Yet the partners had not seen the austerity Budget; indeed it had not even got through the Labour party, let alone through Parliament. All the partners could rely on was the opinion of the City and the assurances of the Bank of England that it was indeed a 'sound finance' kind of document.

While J. P. Morgan's partners deliberated, the Labour government began to fall apart, a victim of internal tensions. Foreign Secretary Henderson could not stomach a Budget that stabbed his own constituency in the back. A cotton spinner, iron-moulder, locomotive apprentice, foundry worker and dedicated and unpaid trade unionist, 'Uncle Arthur' had spent his entire political life – nearly thirty years – working for the betterment of poorer people. At the age of sixty-eight he could not tolerate a 10 per cent cut in the dole, not when many of his constituents were living in hovels and struggling to feed their families. He could turn a blind eye to £56 million in other economies, but not to cuts in unemployment insurance. So Henderson rebelled, warning his colleagues that he could not support a government that deepened his people's destitution. For the prime minister, this was a terrible defection. Henderson had long been his most loyal supporter.

In the middle of the government's argumentative disintegration, a carefully phrased, highly diplomatic note arrived from Edward Grenfell, the well-connected intermediary. Although he could be stiff-backed in manner, Grenfell was the very model of discretion and, after more than thirty years with the bank, well used to dealing with British governments. The son of Henry Riversdale Grenfell MP and a director of the Bank of England, Edward was himself an MP and a director of the Bank of England. Indeed he had been a director for more than a quarter of a century, but never had he performed a more delicate task. Passing on the views of the partners, the cable confirmed that New York could probably raise 'a short-term credit of $100m to $150m', with a view to finding the rest later.

To MacDonald's relief, it looked as though the money could be found and the twin edifices of sterling and the gold standard might yet be saved. That was certainly what *The Times* wanted. 'The universal reputation of the pound sterling and the fact that it is the principal financial medium for financing international trade invests it with world-wide interest,' it argued in a highly patriotic editorial that included a warning that the government had only a few hours in which to save the currency. 'Every country in the world desires its stability, and is vitally interested in maintaining it, because London has been for generations the depository of foreign funds ...' *The Times'* overriding concern was 'British credit', and it routinely ran scare-mongering stories about housewives having overnight to pay a shilling for six pence worth of groceries should the pound go off gold.

However, a public loan with all the formal covenants and other fine print would have to wait until Parliament followed through on the Budget cuts by passing the appropriate legislation. In a passage that illustrated the world's fears about sterling, Jack Morgan had asked, 'Are we right in assuming that the programme under consideration will have the sincere support of the Bank of England and the City generally and thus go a long way towards restoring internal confidence in Great Britain?' Like a good banker, he was asking in effect if the lenders would get their money back. It would be disastrous for J. P. Morgan & Co, not to mention his own reputation, if the pound were to collapse and put the repayments at risk. But the 'programme under consideration' – cuts in expenditure that would take food out of the mouths of the swelling army of unemployed – certainly did not have the support of all the Labour government. Although the Cabinet agreed by a slim majority to reduce unemployment benefit by 10 per cent, the decision had split the government down the middle. The Red Clydesiders absolutely refused to put their names to it.

Having made one last attempt to talk his ministers around, an exhausted Ramsay MacDonald admitted defeat. Late at night, he went to Buckingham Palace where King George V, alerted to the situation, was waiting. The king had ordered up a special train to bring him down from his Scottish seat at Balmoral castle to lend his gravitas and support to his ministers. Met at Euston station by Sir Josiah Stamp, the faithful Bank of England man, the king had been provided with a few minutes' briefing on the situation before being driven to Buckingham Palace. Close to despair, the prime minister had no option but to offer his administration's resignation. More measured than MacDonald, the king advised his prime minister to sleep on it, and proceeded to consult the other parties' leaders.

Late next day, 24 August, MacDonald resigned as prime minister and formed a National government of all three parties. That did the trick. With the Clydesiders and other fiercely working-class warriors out of the way (to the relief of *The Times*, which scorned their 'ignorant prejudice'), the J. P. Morgan partners were able to assure the new government that they could raise $150 million in a short-term loan secured by Treasury bills issued by the Bank of England. Effectively, it was a bridging loan that the new all-party government hoped would tide Britain over the run on gold. 'Thanks to the National government,' MacDonald told Parliament on 25 August, 'this House meets with the pound worth twenty shillings.'

The Times immediately wallowed in a nautical metaphor: 'Meanwhile all those who understand how near British credit and the well-being of the British people have been to shipwreck will rejoice that, though the sea must be rough, a sound crew has been picked to launch the lifeboat.' It was a perfect reflection of the City's view. Still, the loan that would refloat the boat was expensive. America's bankers were not prepared to get involved in these parlous circumstances unless the rate justified the risk, and $4\frac{1}{2}$ per cent was their price. The New York partners made the position clear in a cable that must have made the prime minister and his Chancellor wince. There was 'not a single institution in our whole banking community which actually desires the British Treasury notes on any terms either as to commission or interest,' it humiliatingly explained. In fact the American banking community were only pitching in out of a sense of obligation 'to co-operate in the support of sterling'.

The loan still had to be cleared with President Hoover, who was caught in a cleft stick. While not wanting to stand by and witness the

'Everybody ought to be rich': Punching out thousands of quotations a day, the Western Union self-winding stock ticker was the essential tool for investors.

'Liquidate everything', urged hard-hearted Treasury secretary Andrew Mellon after the Crash hit Wall Street. The arch-liquidationist is aboard the transatlantic liner *Berengaria* at Southampton in 1926.

A genius of the automobile industry, Walter Chrysler ran rings around Ford and General Motors during the Depression and owned what was briefly the world's tallest skyscraper.

Automobile magnate Henry Ford and son Edsel in their heyday, at the 1928 Ford Industrial Exposition in New York's Madison Square Garden. A year later, sales of Ford automobiles began to slide in the wake of the stockmarket crash and the great industrialist became steadily more delusional.

America's 'most luxurious motor car', the colossal Stearns-Knight, and similar high-end automobiles became the symbols of the roaring twenties preceding the big bust.

Labour prime minister Ramsay MacDonald (*left*) relied on American loans to save Britain, while skinflint Chancellor of the Exchequer Phillip Snowden (*right*) begrudged spending money on the dole. They are outside 10 Downing Street before a cabinet meeting in 1929.

The overcrowded, soot-blackened and often dangerous Gorbals slums of Glasgow, where the quality of life was among the lowest in Britain and Europe. It became a hotbed of communism.

An ailing Sir Montagu Norman, governor of the Bank of England, leaves Britain aboard the Canada-bound *Duchess of New York* in the middle of the crisis over the gold standard, in 1931.

Son of a plate-layer on the railways, Australian prime minister Jim Scullin came to power in 1929 promising relief from the Depression.

An emissary of the Bank of England, Sir Otto Niemeyer earned the dislike of practically everybody in Australia except bankers.

Dinky-di prime minister: 'Honest Joe' Lyons, wife Enid and the barefoot kids arrive to take up residence in Canberra at a critical time in the Depression, in 1932, when Australia was on the brink of revolution.

destruction of sterling, which would also damage the dollar, he was also mindful of the political risk. Here were American institutions finding $150 million for Britain at a time when banks in his own country were falling like ninepins. The first significant run on America's banks had begun in Nashville, Tennessee, the year before (in November 1930), and then rolled through much of the South. In 1931, no fewer than 2294 banking institutions of various kinds would put up their shutters. Newspapers were running pictures of confused people congregating outside closed banks, wondering if they would ever get their money back. A photograph in a New York paper on 20 March 1931 showed a burly policeman in peaked hat and buttoned-up tunic standing guard outside the city's grandly named World Exchange Bank while three well-dressed men tried to peer inside through a window. When the president told Morgan partner Thomas Lamont the media would come down heavily on him for 'permitting domestic banks to fail with heavy losses to depositors in order to utilise available assets in helping out the British banking and government situation', he was only being realistic. Nevertheless, he gave his approval – an action for which Britain was duly grateful – and the loan went ahead. It had been a close-run thing.

As it happened, J. P. Morgan & Co did better than its word. By exploiting every available contact, including 'our newspaper friends', the partners were able to promise $200 million. Thus on 28 August, Jack Morgan signed documentation in London committing the New York house to raising the money. And when it was all done, the New Yorkers reported back to Grenfell that they had never met such a negative reaction to a loan-raising. Even the funding of Mussolini's fascist regime had proceeded more smoothly.

———

The labour movement's unalloyed hostility towards banks now had a field day. The *Daily Herald*, part-owned by the Trades Union Congress, ran a story accusing New York bankers of dictating the swingeing terms of Snowden's Budget. In a movement highly prone to conspiracy theory, the story gained immediate credence and was adopted by the left wing and cherished for years afterwards as evidence of the callous influence of the richest man in the world and his equally ill-disposed partners. The incident became known as the 'bankers' ramp'.

As far as it went, all this was perfectly true. J. P. Morgan & Co could never have assembled the lifeline if the partners had not been able to convince contributing parties that Britain was determined to cut its cloth to size. It was not a matter of economics because few of the lenders understood economics; they only wanted to be sure their money was safe. However, the left wing of the party never understood this because they never really fathomed how the world's money markets worked. Yet the story survives.

Snowden certainly pursued the wrong strategy for fighting the Depression. But it may also be true that the Red Clydesiders and other relatively untutored dissenters from orthodox economics had only managed to stumble intuitively on a better solution. Simply stated, their answer was based on getting people back to work, whether through public works schemes or any other means, so that their pay packets would serve to stimulate the economy. Certainly the oratorical left-winger James Maxton saw the fixation on a balanced budget as 'a trivial thing', given Britain's underlying wealth. Talking from his Scottish home in Barrhead, the former schoolteacher raised the human factor – the fate of the poorest and most helpless – that was tellingly absent in the debates in the pages of *The Times*. 'The only big crisis I see is whether the rich or the poor are to pay,' he said. 'My attitude is that I shall fight strenuously any combination of parties, however imposing the personalities, in any attempt to take one penny out of the pockets of underpaid workers, unemployed men and women, old-age pensioners, and widows and orphans, or to reduce in any way the educational and health opportunities of our children. I do not believe that there is any need for any human being to be deprived of a loaf of bread.'

In time that viewpoint – namely, that a short-term mortgage could be taken out on Britain's basic wealth – would prevail. Theoretically speaking, it was a viewpoint remarkably close to that of Maynard Keynes. For the moment at least, though, it had been crushed. It would take years for the realisation to sink in that there were genuine alternatives to existing notions of 'sound finance'.

But there could be no doubt that the immediate trigger of this crisis was the rigidity of the gold standard with its fixed rates for currencies.

The gold standard was a system designed for stability in a different, pre-war era when sovereign and private investors alike had faith in the values attached to currencies. Now, with vast deposits of sterling trapped in Europe, amid revelations of Britain's economic vulnerability, stockmarkets in rapid decline, iconic banks failing and trade suffering a global collapse, the true value of currencies such as sterling was turning into a guessing game. Yet the entire gold standard depended on these highly suspect values. In this perturbed atmosphere, every bank failure or even rumour of one was sparking a scramble for gold. Whole nations were in competition with one another for the yellow metal. So, instead of serving as a source of strength and constancy, the gold standard had turned into a conductor that transmitted nervousness throughout the distribution channels of the world's money markets. Far from promoting stability, as Sir Montagu believed, the system was now propagating the very opposite.

Still, Britain had its loan, and J. P. Morgan & Co could take some of the credit. 'Let me call attention to the magnificent helpfulness and goodwill shown us by New York and other American bankers from the beginning to the end,' Prime Minister MacDonald told a packed emergency session of Parliament. 'If this loan had not been made, the pound sterling would have stumbled. It would have been twenty shillings one day and ten shillings the next. It would have tumbled without control. I am not scaring you. I am giving you history.'

On 10 September, Philip Snowden – 'his deep-lined face white as a handkerchief', *Time* reported – unveiled his long-awaited Budget to a hushed House. Leaning on his canes, he said, 'I am about to discharge one of the most disagreeable tasks that has ever fallen to my lot.'

Taxes went up all round: income tax by six pence to five shillings in the pound, surtax on the highest incomes by 10 per cent, a penny a pint on beer, two pence on a gallon of petrol, a penny on a packet of cigarettes, and entertainment taxes by over 16 per cent. The social welfare cuts proposed by the May Report were duly implemented. To the horror of Labour militants, who jeered and interrupted throughout much of the speech, even children's allowances were lowered.

A highly taxed country beforehand, Britons emerged from the Budget under an even more immense burden of imposts. The left-wingers were particularly incensed by the tax on the lowest paid. A married man with two children earning a bottom wage of £823 now had to pay nearly 20 per cent of that in tax compared with not a dollar in the United States, as *Time* pointed out. Even somebody earning a subsistence income of £309 was taxed. In fact, the economy was pretty much taxed dry. The Bishop of London, the Right Reverend Arthur Ingram, told reporters that taxes took more than two thirds of his official income of £11,000 – and that was *before* the Budget.

Snowden did not feel the need to apologise for implementing his disagreeable task. 'You'd better hurry up for you haven't got much time,' he retorted when the rebel MPs booed the extra penny on a pint. 'This increase on beer goes into effect tomorrow.' (The rebels, in common with the rest of Britain's beer-drinkers, could not have taken his advice because the government's tax take from a pint immediately began to drop despite the higher rate, thus proving that taxes can be pushed so high that governments actually receive less from them than when they are set at affordable levels.)

Having battled through the speech, visibly draining in strength, the Chancellor gathered himself for a dramatic conclusion. Stunning the House, he launched into a paean for his native land by quoting 'England, an Ode' by Algernon Charles Swinburne, dead now for over twenty years:

> All our past proclaims our future;
> Shakespeare's voice and Nelson's hand,
> Milton's faith, and Wordsworth's trust in this
> Our chosen and chainless land.
> Bear us witness; come the world against her,
> England yet shall stand.

The rebel MPs, most of whom were Scots, sat down in disgust during this startling recitation while the opposition benches – the Conservatives and Liberals who had been privy to the Budget all along – leapt to their feet and launched into a volley of cheers. Little wonder the working classes felt abandoned by their Labour government.

By and large, big business approved the measures, being by far the least hurt. Its main complaint was that they did not go far enough. 'The Federation of British Industry has for many years past urged upon successive governments the need for a drastic curtailment of public expenditure,' that worthy body editorialised. 'This is now a vital and urgent economic necessity ... A change of policy and of outlook is now requisite. We must curb our desire to find a short cut to Utopia and rest content with the standard of life which we can afford.'

The City practically adopted the Chancellor as one of their own, especially when he justified the document a couple of days later in a radio broadcast. Explaining that London was the world's hub for trade capital because the British pound was regarded as being as good as gold, he went on, 'Anything which shakes foreign confidence in the stability of our money naturally leads foreigners to withdraw their money from London.' Snowden and like-minded MPs were in the middle of what looked very much like a concerted campaign to evoke the horrors of the collapse of the German mark during the early 1920s, even though this had occurred in a very different, anarchic situation. 'Had we gone off the gold standard, wages, pensions and all incomes would have followed that course, and it is impossible to say at what point it would have been arrested.' Warming to his task, Snowden painted a picture of a doomed Britain embroiled in industrial chaos, with rampant unemployment and a practically worthless pound – in short, an economic Armageddon.

The Times weighed in along similar lines, commending the Chancellor for 'an heroic achievement' while pointing out incomprehensibly that 'an infinitesimal share of direct taxation is born by members of the Labour Party'. Apart from the increase in direct taxes, 'the new burdens are limited to beer, entertainments, tobacco – the trimmings, not the necessities of life'. (In that month, the paper reported that unemployment was up by nearly seven hundred thousand in the last year.)

The Times was far from alone in its wholehearted support for the Budget. Many Britons approved of this skinflint document. Inspired by the king, who told the nation he would forfeit £50,000 of his annual income from the Civil List, and also by the Prince of Wales, who donated £10,000 to the public finances – to the admiration of *The*

Times, which hoped this sacrifice would be 'effected at the least possible cost to the necessary dignity of State functions and to the livelihood of the servants of the Household' – queues actually formed outside the offices of Inland Revenue to pay taxes in advance. A certain Mr Philip Jackson, a confectionery manufacturer from Doncaster, sent a cheque for £1000 to Snowden 'towards the reduction of the National Debt'. Gratefully received, the cheque was duly banked and the Chancellor wrote back, 'Please allow me to express my thanks and warm appreciation of the patriotic spirit which prompted you to make this gift.' And a woman from Bristol, seventy-year-old Mrs Walter Hoddinott, returned her pension book to the Chancellor because she wanted, she told reporters, 'to do her bit'. A Conservative MP gave up his salary 'during the present crisis'.[6]

But the left wing remained incandescent with rage at a prime minister they regarded as traitorous and would never accept his justifications. MacDonald later wrote an explanation to his fellow Scot Manny Shinwell: 'We were on the verge of a financial crisis which if not dealt with within the space of days would have meant not cuts of ten per cent, or anything of the kind, in unemployment pay, but would have disorganised the whole of our financial system, with the most dire results to the mass of the working classes.' The prime minister would always maintain that the formation of the all-party National government had avoided 'a crushing calamity'.

In fact, the calamity was about to occur.

⸺

When the Budget was delivered, the Royal Navy's Atlantic fleet was anchored in the natural harbour of Cromarty Firth near Invergordon in Scotland, ready to set sail for routine battle practice. There were some twelve thousand sailors in the fleet and they were resigned to a pay cut. But they did not expect what they got. Incomprehensibly, Snowden had merely told the Admiralty the size of the economies he wanted and left it to the navy brass to sort out how they would be distributed. The admirals compounded this blunder by cutting a few pence off the pay of serving officers such as midshipmen while slashing by a quarter the already meagre pay of the ordinary seamen and lower ratings. Hardest-hit was the backbone of the navy, the long-serving veterans who had fought through the 1914–18 war, whose pay fell to three shillings a day. Ordinary seamen, who lost nine pence, ended up with just over two shillings a day. As one of them said, 'The cuts cannot hit us aboard ship, but our wives, after the rent is paid, have only a pound left.'

The Admiral of the Fleet, who was on £8 a day, took his pay cut on the chin as 'a sacrifice for King and currency', but the lower ranks were fuming. After the port watch went ashore on normal leave, some Irish sailors reportedly from the *Rodney* gathered in the canteen and launched into 'The Red Flag', to the consternation of the officers. When it was the turn of the starboard watch to go ashore next day, there were mass meetings in the canteen, irate gatherings in the pubs of Invergordon and other impromptu assemblies, and a few broken windows.

A worried commander-in-chief, Rear Admiral Wilfred Tomkinson, immediately ordered the battleship *Valiant* to hoist anchor and lead the fleet into the Atlantic, hoping thereby to nip any further reaction in the bud. But, incredibly, the *Valiant*'s seamen refused to come on deck to get the vessel under way. When officers went forward to do it in their place, they found a guard of burly sailors in their path. 'Beg pardon, sir, but it's no go,' the protesters' spokesman reportedly told his superiors. 'If you get one anchor up, we'll drop the other.' Discretion being the better part of valour in these historically rare circumstances, the officers retreated. Seeing the *Valiant* stay on her anchors, the bay rang with cheers from the lowest-paid seamen in the Royal Navy, and they burst into song:

> *The more we are together, together, together,*
> *The more we are together*
> *The merrier we will be;*
> *For your friends are my friends*
> *And my friends are your friends ...*

The immediate result was that the Atlantic manoeuvres were cancelled and the ships were ordered to return to their home ports, but the unrest continued to ripple through other branches of the navy. Further down the coast, at Rosyth on the Firth of Forth, seamen presented a list of grievances. The mood got ugly enough for some officers to wear Webley service revolvers as sidearms.

The press promptly dubbed the protest the 'Invergordon Mutiny', even though the *Daily Herald*, the working-class paper, carried a pledge of loyalty by the seamen to their king. Highly exaggerated reports flew around the world, further alarming those who still had investments in Britain. Britain's armed forces were in open revolt! Although they were nothing of the sort, the 'mutiny' sufficed to destroy the last vestiges of confidence in the British pound by suggesting that the fabric of the nation's society was being rent apart. To Snowden's horror, there was another wave of withdrawals of gold. The beleaguered Chancellor must have felt that whatever he did, there was always a currency crisis. Within the next three days, a further £33 million in reserves emptied from the vaults of the Bank of England. Because of the 'mutiny', the very pay cuts on which J. P. Morgan & Co's partners and their lenders had insisted were having exactly the opposite of the intended effect. They were inadvertently helping to destroy sterling.

It was on 21 September, acting on the prime minister's instructions, that the Bank of England refused to pay out gold to private individuals even if they had the money. That meant Britain was no longer selling the yellow metal to all comers at the fixed price of $4.8665 an ounce, the official but clearly optimistic value attached by the Bank of England. Thus Britain was officially off the gold standard, albeit 'for the time being'. For the first time in six years, the pound was a floating currency; instead of having a fixed value pegged to gold, its worth would be determined by the market at large. And after Britain went off gold, other nations began to follow suit. Soon, thirty-five countries had abandoned gold in another direct legacy of the Crash.

Eyes staring out of heavy pouches set in a haggard face, the Chancellor thumped his way back into the House to explain this latest in a catalogue of disasters. Nothing had gone right for Snowden during his stewardship of the public finances. In a stoic speech, he told a packed House, 'The consequences are bound to be disagreeable. In some ways they may be serious. But they will not be disastrous or catastrophic. The pound will not go the same way as the mark or the franc.' This was of course in complete contradiction to the dire consequences he had predicted before Britain went off gold. Like a poodle at the Chancellor's heel, *The Times* performed an adroit somersault and was now in complete agreement. 'A suspension of gold payments by a Socialist government would have been one thing,' it editorialised. 'But suspension by a National government committed to retrenchment and reform is another.' So seemingly it was not the gold standard that mattered after all; it was the quality of the people who repudiated it.

Some saw the abandonment of the gold standard as a cause for rejoicing. Canadian-born Lord Beaverbrook, proprietor of the *Daily Express*, was delighted: 'The fact remains that we are rid of the gold standard, rid of it for good and all, and the end of the gold standard is the beginning of real recovery in trade.' Cornered by reporters, the normally publicity-shy Jack Morgan also saw trade as the cornerstone of a recovery. 'This step seems to me to be the second necessary stage in the work of the National government, the first being the balancing of the budget. The completion of the government's work will be the restoration of trade in this country.'

As he spoke, the pound was falling. It plunged as low as $3.75 at one stage in New York before bouncing back to $4.30, in part because Wall Street refused to attack it out of sympathy for an ally, and probably out of fear of repercussions from the House of Morgan. The important point was that the government's fears of a headlong sell-off were briefly allayed; the pound did not go the way of the mark or the franc, as MacDonald too had so grimly warned before Britain went off gold. In the meantime, that stalwart of the Bank of England Sir Josiah Stamp hoped for a return to gold, clearly reflecting the official view. 'If you keep sterling in the belief that Britain will restore the gold standard later, then everything will be all right,' he said reassuringly. 'But if you get panicky and decide to sell your pound, then naturally the result will be that the pound will depreciate.' The National government had done its best to frighten Britons to death about the consequences of going off gold. Now, apparently, all would be well.

In this ferocious debate there was, however, one point of unanimity, and it was the importance of a recovery in trade. The newspaper magnate Beaverbrook, the banker Morgan, the tight-fisted Chancellor Snowden, the easy-going prime minister MacDonald, even the embittered Clydesiders – all agreed that the revival of the economy depended on more British goods being sold abroad.

Unfortunately, the opposite was happening.

8

Sinking Ships

When the siren sounded at the end of the day, the 3800 men working on Hull No. 534, the hope of the Clyde, downed their tools and went home as usual. This time, however, they would not come back. Nearly twelve months after it had started, the construction of the mighty vessel ceased at the John Brown & Co yard on Clydebank. Cunard's managing director, Sir Thomas Bell, a distinguished-looking Scot, had reluctantly pulled the plug on the entire project for the inarguable reason that the Depression had ruined its viability. No. 534 had been designed for a thriving transatlantic passenger trade that was now in rapid decline. Cunard had ordered a ship capable of carrying four thousand passengers, but even the smaller liners plying the run were losing money as their former passengers stayed ashore and bookings dwindled. Not only were businesspeople, film stars, aristocracy and royalty not travelling as much, or as lavishly, as they did before the Crash, the low-fare immigrants who booked the cheaper cabins were no longer welcome in the United States where unemployment was rising at a frightening rate. One of Cunard's other John Brown & Co-built ships, the handsome *Aquitania*, known as the 'ship beautiful' by her regulars, had been crossing the Atlantic with much less than her normal complement of passengers. Similarly, the Anglo-American Red Star line had tied up most of its fleet, including the liner *Belgenland*, in Antwerp in response to an unimaginable slump in passenger numbers – down to one thirtieth of pre-Depression levels.

The stopping of work on No. 534 was not entirely down to the Depression; other political and financial factors were certainly involved. French, Italian and German ships were winning more of the business on the Blue Riband run than they had in the mid-1920s, for instance. Indeed the French line would soon launch the *Normandie*. And Cunard was probably financially overstretched anyway. But the main reason for the abandonment of construction was undoubtedly the fast-spreading economic slump. Like the rival White Star and the rest of the merchant fleet, Cunard earned most of its profits from freight, not from passengers, however wealthy they may be. And too many of its ships were losing money because of the collapse in cargo volumes.

And so, just before Christmas 1931, No. 534 was left alone on the yard, a slowly rusting skeleton – a forlorn fate for a vessel intended to be the new flagship of the merchant fleet, Britain's first boat of over a thousand feet in length. More importantly, nearly all her workforce immediately went on the dole in the absence of other meaningful employment on the Clyde. One of the few ships to be launched from Glasgow that year was *Queen of the South*, a mere 260-foot paddle steamer for the London and North Eastern Railway Company that would ferry tourists up and down the Thames, which was not exactly the transatlantic run. The steamer's progress down the Clyde only served to mock the truth: the building of ships was in terminal decline. It was not just the ship-builders – the men who built the hull plate by plate, rivet by rivet – who lost their jobs, but all the down-stream tradesmen too, the painters, joiners, electricians, plumbers, upholsterers and everybody else required to create a great ship, whether they were based in Glasgow or elsewhere. Soon, signs reading 'No Men Wanted' were posted on fences up and down the Clyde. Auden's 'glade of cranes' idled.

Other British ship-builders were also in difficulties. Belfast's Harland & Wolff, which had launched over seventy vessels for Lord Kylsant's White Star line, had no further orders. Construction on White Star's latest, *Oceanic*, another thousand-footer, had been abandoned soon after the Crash; she was broken up and converted into the smaller *Britannic*. And on the Tyne, on England's north-east coast – a centuries-old ship-building hub – smaller yards were closing one by one while the bigger yards competed desperately for business.

Tyneside lived for building ships. In the century so far, an armada of vessels of all sizes and purposes had been farewelled down the river, including the mighty *Mauretania* (the liner that brought Jack Morgan across the Atlantic), oil tankers, freighters, warships, ferries and coastal vessels. Just one firm, Palmers of Jarrow on the river's south bank, had single-handedly launched nearly nine hundred ships in its lifetime, starting with an iron-paddle tug almost eighty years earlier. Most of the population of Jarrow lived within sight and sound of this 'harsh and noisy universe' that had supported them for generations. The menfolk – and in times of extreme urgency such as war, some-times the womenfolk – had helped fashion some of Britain's greatest warships. But now the clanging and banging was falling quiet as orders were cancelled and men were laid off. The nearby Palmers steel works had shut down in 1931 and the shipyard had no further orders for merchant vessels after the tanker *Appalachee* was launched for Anglo-American Oil. There would be no further commissions of any kind, not even warships, after the destroyer HMS *Duchess* went down the slipway a few months later.

Further down the east coast, Sunderland's yards were also in seri-ous trouble. The proud Gray's shipyard had launched its thousandth ship in 1929 only to shut down a year later. Locals still gathered regu-larly at the yard in the hope of picking up scraps of work. Nearby yards had no choice but to follow suit. Some, like Priestman's, would never reopen; others would not launch a ship for five years. Before long, ship production throughout Britain had collapsed by 90 per cent in a dis-astrous decline in economic activity that had awful consequences for those giant staple industries (coal and steel in particular) whose prof-its depended on the construction of sea-going vessels.

A strange phenomenon now occurred. Instead of ships being launched and steaming off over the horizon, the reverse was happen-ing. Rivers and harbours began to fill up with vessels of all kinds. They steamed up the river and dropped anchor, and their crews secured the hatches and rowed ashore, never to return. Soon the waterways of Britain were host to a ghostly line of unmanned freighters and pas-senger ships, swinging to and fro with the current, rusting on their moorings. And these scenes were repeated all over the world, in harbours, rivers, lakes and inlets from the Mississippi to Yokohama. Vessels were being laid up in their thousands and their crews paid off. There was no work for them, no cargo to carry. Every nation's merchant fleet was affected by this creeping paralysis of the great trade routes of the world. Even the mighty *Reina del Pacifico* owned by Britain's Pacific Steam Navigation Company's – a vessel that had reduced the run from Liverpool to Valparaiso in Chile by eighteen days – was laid up for lack of passengers and freight.

The chief culprit for the calamity befalling the global shipping industry was American protectionism in the form of the Smoot-Hawley law that had raised tariff barriers to fatally high levels. Although the protection of American-made goods from foreign competition (agriculture in particular) was very much on the political agenda before 1929, as we have seen, it is unthinkable that a proposal as punitive and hostile as that devised by Utah senator Reed Smoot and Congressman Charles Hawley would have got through the Senate in the years before the Crash. It was only in the months immediately afterwards that the law attracted the essential extra votes, and now it was spreading America's economic contagion around the world. Although academics still debate the extent of the contamination caused by Smoot-Hawley, it is increasingly seen as the first and probably the biggest of a series of blunders that turned an essentially local event, America's stockmarket crash, into a worldwide calamity.

In principle and intention, the act was a fortress. The lifting of rates on dutiable imports into the United States to the highest levels in more than a century effectively erected a blockade around the home markets. Given the size of the increases, it could hardly have done anything else. Measured as a percentage of the value of the imported product, tariffs on chemicals jumped to 36 per cent, sugar to 77 per cent, agricultural products to 35 per cent, cottons to 46 per cent, and wool and silks to 60 per cent. Even these figures understate the case because the tariffs were fixed in monetary terms, at so many dollars a ton. But as the value of the declining volume of goods passing across America's wharves fell because of the general collapse in trade, the rates stayed the same; there was no compensating reduction in the dollar sums payable. In this way the ratio of import duties collected to the value of imports, which is what matters in the end, nearly doubled in size to 60 per cent. The Smoot-Hawley tariff law was throttling the world's biggest business, namely trade.

The evidence is overwhelming. Overall, trade within Europe fell by 18 per cent in the first year after the Crash. Between 1931 and 1932, it fell by a calamitous third. Thereafter, volumes continued to drift down for the next three to five years, the steepness of the drift depending on the country. Measured as an index in dollar terms, the global volume of trade between 1929 and 1934 fell by a ruinous two thirds. No kind of cargo was immune from the contagion. Foodstuffs, live animals, raw materials, commodities, automobiles and other wholly manufactured products – they all plummeted in volumes.

As buyers disappeared, prices inevitably dropped too. The fall in commodity prices was particularly disastrous for the world's vast agricultural sector. Within the first year alone, average global prices for wheat declined by 19 per cent, cotton by 27 per cent, wool by 42 per cent, silk by 30 per cent, tin by 29 per cent, rubber by 42 per cent, sugar by 20 per cent, coffee by 43 per cent, and copper by 26 per cent. And, just as inevitably, production of most products dropped in tandem with demand. Between 1930 and 1933, industrial production in Europe (including Britain) fell by an average 15 per cent a year; global production fell by a third. For the first time since the birth of industrialisation, economic growth hurtled into headlong retreat as entire economies slowed down, like huge locomotives running out of steam. The buying and selling of products around the world, a commerce that had allowed nations to prosper beyond people's wildest imaginations, was drying up with appalling effect.

The nub of the problem was that Smoot-Hawley triggered a wave of copycat protectionism around the world. Fearing ruin after the world's greatest economy virtually shut down its ports to trade, one country after another rushed to defend its industries by erecting its own blockades. In the stampede, wiser counsel was ignored. Just days after the Crash, Britain's president of the Board of Trade, Willie Graham, pleaded at the League of Nations for all countries to freeze tariffs for two years to provide a kind of breathing-space that might encourage mature reflection. All too clearly, he could see what was coming. A freeze would have provided a respite from the panic in which a phased programme of trade-stimulating tariff reductions might have been formulated. However, in the wake of Smoot-Hawley, countries did the opposite in a general knee-jerk response to voters' demand. Australia, for example, quickly raised the duty on a large basket of goods. Soon, no fewer than sixty countries had passed retaliatory, beggar-thy-neighbour protective legislation against foreign-made goods. In a heartbeat, economically speaking, a wall of death had been erected around national boundaries.

Different nations employed different methods, but they added up to the same result. In Europe, France was in the vanguard, forcing domestic importers to buy from a restrictive list of specified goods drawn up by bureaucrats. As the blockade grew ever wider and higher, long-established, friendly and mutually profitable trading arrangements between individuals, industries and nations were obliterated all over Europe and replaced by a hotch-potch of bilateral deals that attempted in ham-fisted, commercially stupid ways to achieve a strict balance between what one country sold and bought from another. Some of these deals actually reverted to barter, a commerce barely seen since medieval times. (The United States, the author of this catastrophe, continued to demand hard currency to support its gold standard and refused to accept goods in exchange for debt.)

In the general race for protection, it became impossible for a nation to stay aloof. For instance, the Netherlands, whose economy crucially depended on cross-border commerce, tried to keep its frontiers open but eventually had to concede defeat and pass similar, if feeble, laws, like the one that required merchants to add a certain amount of local product to every sack of imported corn. 'In brief, there grew up all over Europe governmental control of foreign trade,' noted the magisterial *Economic History of Europe*. 'This was a state of affairs which was reminiscent of First World War days and in the minds of many presaged a new Armageddon.'

It certainly looked like Armageddon in far-off New Zealand, a nation that survived by trade. Although its business with the United States was just about invisible, Smoot-Hawley, acting like a bludgeon, treated this nation of just one and a half million people as though it were a major threat to American farmers. Overnight, New Zealand's exports of wool, butter, meat, skins, leather and even onions, infinitesimal as they were, were shut out. New Zealand's modest duty on American-grown onions of thirty shillings a ton, for instance, was swamped by Smoot-Hawley's totally irrational £9 a ton on New Zealand-grown ones. Scandalised as well as fearful, the nation's business leaders called for hefty retaliatory tariffs on practically everything that was made in America, including timber, paper, machinery, oil and Henry Ford's Model Ts.

But Smoot-Hawley was also backfiring on the United States. In late September 1932, an editorial in the *New York Times* bemoaned a 70 per cent collapse in the value of American exports to Germany – once the United States' third largest customer. The point of the article was to illustrate how these tariff blockades were hurting America. However, the paper was complaining about other countries' blockades, not its own. The *New York Times* believed that it was up to America's major trading partners to lower *their* tariff barriers to boost trade rather than the other way around. (If Germany's new Chancellor, the hapless Franz von Papen, read the editorial, he did not take the advice. Instead he took a leaf out of Senator Smoot's book and raised tariffs and quotas to 'prohibitive levels'.)

The damage caused by the blockades was being heaped on America's farmers – the very people the law was intended to protect. In one of the biggest ironies, especially for farm boy Hawley, agricultural exports were the hardest hit, especially wheat, cotton, tobacco and lumber. Wheat exports, for example, fell by half in volume terms. As their incomes collapsed, many farmers were forced to default on loans to small rural banks. As elsewhere, the collapse in buyers produced a matching decline in prices, and soon the cost of shipping wheat amounted to several times its market value. Across the Canadian border in Calgary, wheat farmers learned in despair that sawdust was selling for more per ton than wheat. And across the Pacific, the economy of the sugar-crop-dependent Hawaii islands collapsed, throwing a quarter of the working population out of a job.

The implosion of trade inevitably rolled into industry, and soon businesses were failing even faster than banks. According to that chronicle of bankrupt businesses Dun & Co, almost forty thousand

concerns folded in 1932. Admittedly most of these were small businesses – 'mom and pop' enterprises – but big business was also
devastated. Heavy industry, the sector that had so excited investors in
the roaring twenties, was practically moribund. Steel production
slumped to an incredible 12 per cent of capacity. Building construction
stood at 48 per cent of its level of 1931, which had been a bad year
anyway. Railroad car loadings, a useful measure of trade activity, fell to
70 per cent. As for auto production, it collapsed by more than half.

Unavoidably, the once mighty New York Stock Exchange reflected
the general collapse in domestic and international trade. Having
drifted mostly downward since the Crash, sporadically sparking false
hope with illusory rallies, the Dow Jones Industrial Average closed on
8 July 1932 at 41.22. The index that had long been the bellwether of the
sharemarkets was down by an unspeakable 89 per cent from its peak
– the lowest reading since the 1800s – and would take another twenty-
one years to regain the levels of 1929. In short, all those people who
had been so inspired by vice-president Richard Whitney's theatrical
demonstration of faith that they had retained their investments were
now staring in horror at an average 11 per cent of their original value.
'Anyone who bought stocks in mid-1929 and held on to them saw
most of his adult life pass by before getting back to even,' pointed out
one economic historian.

Before the Crash, the town of Wichita, Kansas, was the unlikely hub of
America's glamorous new aircraft manufacturing industry. Indeed
with some justification the city advertised itself as the air capital of the
world. Nobody argued with the line anyway, for in the roaring twenties
no fewer than twenty-nine aircraft manufacturers had established
themselves there. 'For men who had a lot of money, aviation was the
thing to get into,' remembered local aeronautical historian Walt
House. Private sales of aircraft boomed, their owners inspired by the
exploits of pioneering aviators such as Charles Lindbergh, the hero of
the industry and one of the favoured investors on J. P. Morgan & Co's
preferred list. Some of the founding companies in aviation had taken
off in a golden period before the Crash, among them Grumman,

Seversky, Curtiss-Wright, Fairchild, North American Aviation, Lockheed and Northrop, most of them piloted by leatherneck aviators with oil on their overalls.

And now most of them had come down to earth. One of the first to close the hangar doors was Travel Air, the biggest aircraft manufacturer in Wichita. A few months after posting record sales, and turning out more than three planes a day, the firm cut production as orders evaporated within days of the Crash. Thereafter other aircraft manufacturers, many of them hopelessly under-capitalised, crashed and burned one by one, dragging engine-makers and other suppliers with them. As local historians recorded, even before the end of 1930 the roll-call of closures included Associated Aircraft, Air Capital Manufacturing, Bowlby Airplane, Continental Aircraft, Wichita Imblum Aero, Knoll Aircraft, Metal Aircraft, C. M. Mulkins, Okay Airplane, Poyer Motor, Quick Air Motors, Roydon Aircraft, Red Bird Aircraft, Self Aircraft, Swift Aircraft, Vanos Aircraft, Wichita Airplane Manufacturing and Yellow Air Cab. Others struggled on for a time before eventually bowing to the inevitable and closing their doors. By the early 1930s, the toll in Wichita alone included Ace, Buckley Aircraft, Hilton, Jayhawk, Lea, Lear, Mooney, Roydon, Sullivan, Watkins and Supreme/Stone Propellor. 'There were vacant buildings everywhere,' remembered a welder who had once been kept busy building airframes.

Henry Ford's aircraft manufacturing division was one of the victims. The industrialist had first entered the industry at the behest of the US government to produce engines for the 1914–18 war, but collapsing sales soon grounded its best-known design, the twelve-passenger 'Tin Goose', so-called because of its corrugated alloy body. It was the last aircraft Ford Airplane produced. Within twelve months most of America's pioneering aviation businesses had been wiped out, although the most resourceful owners did what they could to survive. Clyde Cessna and his son Eldon stayed in the business by building one-off racing planes, while Stearman ceased production but maintained a skeleton staff.

Whether factories were producing aircraft, autos or anything else – even radios, which probably survived the Depression better than any other consumer durable – the collapse in output eroded the government's tax revenue in multiple ways. Washington was deprived of taxes on profits and wages, reducing its own ability to spend for the public good. Wages that would have stimulated the economy were lost. And the decline in export income deprived Washington of valuable foreign exchange that would have underpinned the value of the dollar.

Although there is no evidence that Senator Smoot ever visited a Chrysler factory, he would have learned a lot if he had. Blocked from overseas markets that had accounted for nearly 14 per cent of total sales, Chrysler practically shut down export production. As a result, its 3800-strong overseas dealer network shed sales, profits and staff in a cut-and-dried demonstration of the harm rendered by the law Smoot had so ignorantly championed. By the early 1930s, Chrysler's export sales had more than halved, and as orders dried up, the parent company laid off assembly-line workers from its domestic plants.

But the man who had put his name to the Chrysler Building had found the nerve to find a way out of the slump. With the help of his inner circle of executives, Walter Chrysler devised the Plymouth, probably the car of the Depression. Here was a low-priced vehicle with mid-priced refinements such as the novelty of an electrical fuel gauge and the comfort of hydraulic shocks. While most other manufacturers were caught flat-footed, bereft of ideas other than the instinctive one of pell-mell retrenchment, Chrysler rolled out attractive new variations of its life-saving model such as the 'floating ride' Plymouth that appeared in July 1931 when things were fast heading downhill. So-named because of a radical system for mounting the engine, the automobile was a hit. A master salesman, Chrysler adroitly promoted the Plymouth in ways that satisfied consumer desire for advanced technology despite the hard times ('the smoothness of an eight, the economy of a four'). As the model began to claim market share off GM's Chevrolet and Ford, he cheekily added the slogan, 'It is my opinion that any new car without Patented Floating Power is obsolete.' Soon the company was re-hiring the workers it had laid off and turning out eight hundred cars a day from its main Plymouth plant in Detroit. Within two years, Chrysler's overall sales would be back to pre-Depression levels, four years ahead of GM and seventeen years ahead of an incompetent Ford. By the mid-1930s, Chrysler would wrest the number two spot from Ford in the American automobile market.

But not even Chrysler could surmount the tariff blockades, and its export sales stayed in the doldrums, like those of other American manufacturers. The Smoot-Hawley law was certainly not wholly responsible for the Depression, but there was no doubt it helped propagate it. Monstrosities of economic ignorance, the tariff blockades wreaked havoc on the United States and the rest of the world.

Perhaps the most baffling aspect of these early years of the Depression was that hardly anybody seemed to know what was going on – certainly not President Hoover, who had signed Smoot-Hawley into law, ignoring a mass recommendation by economists to set an example to the world – and to do America a favour – by lowering America's tariffs rather than raise them. Hoover insisted on blaming Europe. The president thought the bank failures of 1931 in Austria and Germany did most of the damage and the collapse of the gold standard did most of the rest. While he certainly had his qualms about Smoot-Hawley, he did not see it as the root of the trouble.

The average American was also bewildered, as well he might be. 'Basically, at the time, people hadn't a clue what had caused the Depression,' argued one historian. After all, it was not as though every American had plunged wildly into the sharemarket in a nationwide orgy of greed, as Treasury Secretary Andrew Mellon and many like-minded, influential people still believed. Of a total population of 123 million, there were never more than about nine hundred thousand speculators, even at the peak of the boom; and there were never more than 1.5 million shareholders. So it could hardly be said that the collapse of the Wall Street boom was solely responsible for plunging the nation into ruin.

Congress never understood either. When European nations including Britain asked in these parlous circumstances for relief from long-standing war debts to the United States, arguing that the collapse in trade had effectively destroyed so much of their income that they simply could not pay the money back, bellicose Congressmen rejected the pleas out of hand. Incredibly, the same representatives who had pushed through the Smoot-Hawley act now urged Hoover, who was sympathetic to Europe's pleas for a deal, to take even sterner trade measures. The insularity of America had become a huge stumbling block to a coordinated solution that might have slowed, stopped or to some extent mitigated the damage wrought by the slump.

One of the few to get the picture – and one of the least likely – was the elderly isolationist senator William Borah, another farm boy who hailed from Idaho. Despite never having left America's shores, he was considered an authority on foreign relations. In common with Senator Smoot, he was a fierce opponent of the League of Nations and practically anything else that might obligate the United States to play a role in the wider world. However, even this monument of jingoism was not so blinkered that he was unable to see what was happening: 'The result [of interference in economic laws] is all about us – disorganized and disrupted monetary systems, closed markets, trade and commerce dwindling year by year, millions of shipping tonnage laid up and shipbuilding practically at an end. If civilization is to be saved, markets must be restored, monetary systems re-established, trade and commerce rehabilitated.' Here was a man who, despite everything, had a feeling for how trade worked and had somehow managed to divine the heart of the problem.

As he spoke, United States trade with the rest of the world was falling to just 18 per cent of the level pertaining in the year of the Crash. Put another way, its commercial dealings with other nations was down by 82 per cent.

Out of legitimate self-interest, Britain was entitled to do something in these threatening circumstances. Some in the National government, including Prime Minister Ramsay MacDonald, genuinely feared the Armageddon. After the departure of an increasingly suffering Snowden to the House of Lords as Viscount Snowden of Ickornshaw in November 1931, the new Chancellor of the Exchequer in 1932 was Neville Chamberlain, a member of a legendary political and business family from Birmingham who took office with the priority of repairing Britain's disastrous losses in trade. And like his father Sir Joseph, he believed in a policy of judicious protection. A low-tariff nation for most of the last hundred years, Britain had to change course, in the new Chancellor's view. 'If we do not think imperially, we shall have to think continentally,' he had argued even before the Crash. Now he was absolutely certain it was time to think imperially. Thus in February 1932, Chamberlain counted it as 'the great day in my life' when he was able to introduce a general tariff of 10 per cent while protecting Empire-produced goods. Unlike his predecessor Snowden, Chamberlain at least had a plan, and it was for an Empire-based sterling area. Imperial preference, in short.

The abandonment of the gold standard had forced Britain into this position. With the Bank of England's reserves still in mortal danger, the City was warned to heavily reduce overseas lending, and a strict embargo on all non-Empire loans was introduced. Britain needed sterling, and the best way to get it in the era of Smoot-Hawley, it seemed to the National government, was by trading with other sterling-based nations, and especially with those of the Empire. Thus the sterling area was born – another child of the Depression. Maynard Keynes, still battling the dogma of the liquidationists, was enthusiastic about the concept, probably *faute de mieux*; indeed he had urged the Labour government to form a sterling bloc after Britain came off gold.

The sterling bloc knocked together a group of countries that traded heavily with Britain, not just Empire nations. In a way there had been a sterling area for at least half a century. According to the theory at the time, the bloc boasted three main categories. One category was connected through currency, holding all official international assets as sterling balances or in sterling-based securities. Into this group came a potpourri of nations such as Eire, Siam, the British colonies except Hong Kong, British Honduras and British Malaya, and the British Mandates such as Palestine, most of which had a long history of commercial dealing with Britain to various extents. Another more heavily involved category included nations with strong commercial ties to Britain: British Malaya, Denmark, Egypt, Estonia, Hong Kong, India and Burma, Iraq, Latvia, Lithuania, New Zealand, Portugal and South Africa. All these held considerable sterling reserves but felt free to switch in and out of other currencies. The third category – Argentina, Finland, Norway, Sweden – pegged their currencies to the pound while holding official gold and/or other currency reserves as well as sterling reserves.

With such a diverse family of nations, it is just about impossible to achieve a precise definition of the sterling area, except to say it was a body of countries tied to Britain by trade, currency, emotion, or all three. If a country raised money in Britain – and improvident Empire countries such as Australia were practically using the City as an over-draft facility – it fell naturally into the sterling bloc. Such countries became members of the bloc by default. No less than 54 per cent of total Australian trade was with the mother country, while New Zealand's, with its infant economy, was 86 per cent. Neither of these countries had anywhere else to go. Highly dependent on Britain, they fixed their own currencies to the pound and held some or all of their reserves in sterling in London, to the huge benefit of the Bank of England and the enormous relief of a now recovered Sir Montagu Norman. They were therefore the most natural members of the new arrangement 'because of a heavy dependence on British trade, or British credit, or both', according to Henry Clay, an adviser to the Bank of England and an enthusiast for Empire trade who argued that the suspension of gold payments 'brought out the true nature of the sterling area'.

Britain naturally assumed it would run the sterling area. As one colonial historian had argued, 'Britain still aspired, and with considerable success, to maintain a high degree of financial authority within the sterling camp. Tariffs and trade were negotiable matters, but the British always took it for granted that finance was too important a matter to be left to mere colonials, even white ones.' Colonial governments routinely complained about 'dictatorship from Downing Street'. As Sir Otto Niemeyer's contentious visit to Australia had demonstrated, most British governments had a paternalistic view of the Empire whose 'unspectacular function was to grow food and produce raw materials for the inhabitants of the UK, who will in turn supply them with manufactured products'.

The Bank of England's Sir Josiah Stamp had put it neatly. Stamp, who had the ear of everybody who mattered, summarised in what can be regarded as a founding document of the sterling area that the Dominions 'must join with Britain as custodians of the validity of sterling values'.[7] In this arrangement there was no question of the Empire's central banks having any more than token independence. It was expected the Dominion banks would 'hold large in London', thus boosting the pound. In short, what the Bank of England wanted, and expected, was pretty much total and transparent cooperation in the maintenance of sterling values, especially now that Britain was off gold and the pound was running free; it did not anticipate any 'action in the dark' that might compromise the floating pound. And although Stamp insisted, as we have seen, that the Bank of England would not behave like a dictator, it 'did assume a right to leadership and did its best via advice, the recommendation of personnel and other means, to influence financiers in the Dominions to its own way of thinking'. Reasonable as this sounds – and the Bank of England was the obvious candidate to do the job of leadership – these observations bore all the hallmarks of 'a latter-day financial imperialism'. Mummy, in the form of the Old Lady of Threadneedle Street, knew best and, as Niemeyer had already made clear, she was reluctant to let her children grow up.

In July 1932, Chamberlain sailed for Canada with half the Cabinet to take the next step in imperial preference – the formalisation of an interlocking, mutually beneficial system that would favour Empire-made products over others. After much arm-twisting and backroom negotiation – several of the Empire premiers proved lukewarm at first – Britain got protection. When Chamberlain sailed back home, British-made pottery, cutlery, typewriters, woollens, cottons, paper, gloves, bottles, cameras, electrical goods, radio parts and many other products were hidden behind duties of up to 50 per cent. And soon 'the great bulk of British industry was protected', to the annoyance of America's Congress, which still wanted trade with the Empire and thought it had every right to have it. Within months it became practically impossible for many Empire countries to import their manufactured products – cars or anything else – from anywhere but Britain.

But not even imperial preference, nor any of the other hastily improvised trade arrangements, could refloat the world's merchant fleet. The damage had been done.

As freight tonnages plummeted, Britain's merchant marine, the biggest in the world, was the hardest hit. 'It is obvious that shipping is experiencing a far more deep-rooted depression than ever before,' observed Lord Essendon of the White Star line. Another of the maritime nobility who ruled the waves, he had taken over White Star after its collapse. Deploring the government's inaction, its apparent willingness to leave the surviving contenders to fight to the death, as 'a crude policy', Essendon demanded that something be done, probably along the lines of Italy, where Mussolini had launched a ship-building industry. But nothing was done, and the Tyne and other British waterways became a graveyard for ships.

The shipwreck of White Star and the cancellation of its orders with Harland & Wolff came as a terrible blow to Britain. It was the first and biggest commercial casualty following the Crash. Not least, there was general dismay because its chairman, Lord Kylsant, was regarded as a figurehead of the nation's flagship industry.

A giant physically as well as commercially, Kylsant stood six feet seven inches in his socks and always dressed as though for the captain's table. He favoured fine suits, stiff collars, diamond-studded ties and silk hats. Before acquiring White Star two years before the Crash, Kylsant had built Royal Mail Steam Packet into the world's biggest merchant fleet, a privately owned navy that was the envy of all other sea-faring nations. The 'Lord of the Seven Seas', as the newspapers dubbed Kylsant, was the recipient of an unusual and remarkably greedy form of recompense for his efforts. He did not take a salary, dividends or even a percentage of the profit, any of which might be considered normal. Instead, he paid himself according to a fixed ratio of gross revenue, an arrangement that rewarded size rather than surplus. In effect, he paid himself by the tonnage. Even for the maritime nobility, this was a daringly generous arrangement.

He was forgiven for his greed because, by means of intricate cross-shareholdings, Kylsant had made himself the admiral of a conglomeration of 2.6 million merchant tons that delivered mail, cargo and passengers, often in exquisite luxury, around the world. But the fleet had grown rapidly, and mainly on borrowed money in the form of fixed-rate debentures, a means of financing which some City institutions regarded dubiously. Debentures were unsecured bonds backed by the credit standing of the issuer rather than by more concrete collateral, and thus left the lender somewhat exposed. And the City was correct in its misgivings. Behind the scenes the company had been accumulating substantial losses even before Wall Street imploded, and the Crash served to expose the deception. When the company failed to pay its normal dividend, it alarmed lenders in the City as well as thousands of small investors. The shares crashed as hard as any of those on Wall Street, in part (the company said) because of its investments in heavy industry rather than because of any problems in shipping. Whatever the reason, the small investors became the first heavy British casualties of the Crash, losing the best part of their money. More importantly from the government's viewpoint, Kylsant's empire was unable to meet repayments on earlier ship-building loans made to it by the Treasury. As a result, Sir Montagu Norman quickly dispatched auditors from the Bank of England to look into the books. They soon discovered that Kylsant had dressed up the accounts to paint a far rosier picture than was the case. The giant firm's prospectus was suspect in essentially the same way as Clarence Hatry's companies had been.

Because of the public shareholdings, the government had no choice but to initiate a criminal prosecution, a sensational event that threw a rare light on how a title and a grand manner can dazzle investors. It transpired that the ocean empire's juicy dividends had not been paid out of current earnings, as implied in its filings, but from a cache of abnormally high earnings banked as a result of generous government contracts during the 1914–18 war. Kylsant had profited mightily from the conflict. It also emerged that the finances of the world's biggest merchant fleet had long been full of leaks; most of Kylsant's ships were mortgaged to the hilt against bank loans. The lord's private navy was sunk.

Thus, in a deviation from the City's time-honoured practice of burying its scandals if at all possible, Kylsant was convicted of making false statements in a financial prospectus for the purpose of raising money. It was a heinous crime for a peer heading a shipping line that bore the charter of Queen Victoria, and Kylsant was sent for a year to Wormwood Scrubs, one of England's grimmest prisons. The sentence should have been much longer – after all, Hatry got fourteen years plus two on hard labour – but it is likely that Kylsant's donations to the

Church of England and other good causes helped soften the sentence. The 'Napoleon of the Seas' (another newspaper sobriquet) made a noblesse oblige-like departure for the 'soot-blackened pile overlooking railway yards and a bleak, 200-acre common', as a magazine described the prison. Even in his ignominy, he preserved his sangfroid. 'My good men, I am ready to go with you,' the disgraced magnate told his warders. He was not, however, ready to be treated like any common criminal at The Scrubs. Although Kylsant got the same-sized cell as his fellow inmates, all his meals were prepared by an outside caterer and delivered by hand.

While Lord Kylsant of Camarthen stewed in prison, his empire disintegrated, and in 1931 he was declared bankrupt. The mighty fleet was broken up and the individual lines were distributed among Britain's shipping grandees – which was how Lord Essendon ended up with White Star.

The British lines could probably have done more than they did to save themselves from the onslaught of the Depression. Proudly independent for decades, most of them were controlled by the nobility, some of them self-made, and they seemed to be attracted to the world stage provided by merchant shipping as well as by a sense of patriotism. The maritime magnates believed they were playing an important role in the Empire. Most of them were enormously wealthy and influential, owning large estates, holding important appointments in government, and maintaining close ties with the City as chairmen of banks. They were inclined by upbringing, attitude and personality to dominating empires and were averse to losing them through rationalisation, however necessary that may have seemed. Unlike other merchant fleets in Italy, Germany, Japan and the United States, many of which hastily merged to achieve vital economies of scale that at least gave them a shot at survival, most British owners were temperamentally unwilling to follow suit and continued to wage a war fought with egos as much as with ships. One of the few lines able to stay in the black was the Peninsula & Oriental Steam Navigation, the world's oldest steamship company, which continued to dominate the Empire route to India, the Far East and Australasia. Otherwise few of the magnates would survive the Depression with their empires intact.

Other commercial empires, even whole industries, were

unravelling, especially those involved in heavy engineering. Although some of these businesses had struggled before the Crash, they would probably have survived in different circumstances. Just one of these was the sprawling Glasgow-based manufacturing works of William Beardmore Jr, later Lord Invernairn. Metallurgist, chemist and mathematician, this bushy-bearded tycoon was the scion of a family of entrepreneurial engineers and a fearless acquirer who had by the 1920s amassed steel mills and coal mines as well as ship-building yards. By the late 1920s he was even trying his hand at producing aircraft, motor cars and motorcycles. Financially stretched before the Depression, Invernairn's unwieldy conglomeration soon ran into trouble after the Crash. Lacking proper funding (and perhaps proper management), it slowly ran down until there was practically nothing left by the mid-1930s.

While Scotland's big business suffered heavily, many smaller enterprises proved surprisingly resilient. Probably because their products cost a few pence rather than many thousands of pounds, the food and drink industries survived, and even prospered. Just up the road from the shipyards of the Clyde, firms such as City Bakeries actually expanded, converting itself into the second biggest retail baker in Britain during the hard years, while Paterson's Camp Coffee (actually an essence of coffee) became one of the treasured brands of the period. Even so, as Scotland continued to suffer from the collapse of trade and as its people fled across the border into England, or indeed anywhere they could, writer George Malcolm Thomson concluded grimly that his nation was 'eclipsed' and the Scots were 'a dying race'.

———

The economic dislocations that had stranded proud ships on their moorings were so deep-seated they were changing the world of trade for good.

The Hooghly river was one of the filthiest in the Empire, at least along the twenty-mile stretch where it passed through Calcutta. It flowed sluggishly, dark and stinking from the waste and sludge emptied into it by the scores of jute mills lining both sides of its banks. In some places, particularly on the bends of the river, mills were jammed almost side by side. Established by Scots who had learned their trade in Dundee alongside the river Tay, the jute industry had practically taken command of this part of the Hooghly. By the early 1930s, mills occupied Birlapur, Uluberia, Shibpur, the industrial town of Howrah on the opposite side of the river to Calcutta, Bally, Barrackpur, Shamnagar, Halishahar, Bansberia and other locations. Most of the jute workers, poor and illiterate country people enticed to the city by the lure of higher wages, lived in hovels in sprawling *bustees* (slums) that stretched for miles over every available yard of ground. Swampy, fetid and noisome because of a hopelessly inadequate sewage system designed and built by the British for a city of six hundred thousand – a fraction of its size now – Calcutta had altered very much for the worse since Rudyard Kipling wrote in 'A Tale of Two Cities',

> *Where the cholera, the cyclone and the Crow*
> *Come and go;*
> *Where the merchant deals in indigo and tea,*
> *Hides and ghi [ghee] . . .*

India had entered the Depression as something of a dumping ground for British-made goods, but among other industries the jute mills were profiting from the upheavals in trade to turn the tables. Ships were steaming up the Hooghly to tie up alongside rickety wharves where they were loaded up with jute – the world's cheapest packing cloth – for freighting all over the world, but particularly to Britain. Exports from Calcutta to Britain would rise by 375 per cent during the Depression, ripping the rug out from underneath Dundee. The Hooghly was rapidly replacing the Scottish city as the jute capital of the world, albeit with the aid of home-grown expertise. According to Gordon Stewart in *Jute and Empire*, about nine hundred of the senior mill staff there hailed from Dundee. Indeed one of the events of the year in Calcutta, at least for expatriates, was the St Andrew's Day dinner where the Scottish contribution to the local jute industry was routinely celebrated with drams of imported whisky.

But as jute from the Hooghly eroded their profits and further threatened their fading power, Dundee's jute barons warned of the 'complete extinction' of their business. They mobilised MPs on both sides of the political fence to protest against Calcutta's alleged dumping of their production surplus, and representatives such as Florence Horsbrugh, the Conservative MP for the city, sprang to their defence. 'There has come upon the workers in the jute trade a new terror, that their work may be taken away, that the mills and factories may be closed down, and that the area may become an absolutely derelict area,' she tear-jerkingly informed the House of Commons. Horsbrugh was in fact notorious among the factory workers of Dundee for (so the story went) advising hungry families to share soup bones between them. Although thousands of Dundee mill workers were certainly being thrown out of work, the terror was probably mostly in the minds of the jute barons whose magnificent houses lined the esplanades of Broughty Ferry, a safe distance from the muck of the mills, and the high ground above the city.

There was nothing the barons could do about Calcutta jute anyway. Like other Empire-made goods pouring into Britain, jute was the beneficiary of the Ottawa trade agreement, the Empire's answer to Smoot-Hawley. Along with jute, a gigantic basket of Indian-made goods was finding its way into Britain – tea, linseed oil, rice, pig iron, even semi-manufactured steel. By the mid-1930s Indian trade was breaking all records, and the jute wallahs pumped as much packaging material down this heaven-sent pipeline as they could. The favourable treatment of these goods was designed, British officials noted po-faced, as 'a development of greatest importance in binding the economic interests of the two countries still closer'. The jute barons begged to differ of course, and their response was to drive the Dundee workforce harder in a ferocious battle of economies of scale in which there could only be one victor. The industry was also under threat from other commercial forces such as the new heavy-duty industrial paper, which was already being used to bag cement, and from bulk freight, which did not need jute or industrial paper.

For fifty years, the jute barons had based the economics of the industry on cheap labour, especially women, children and Irish immigrants. Dundee had long been notorious for employing more women and children than any other manufacturing hub in Britain. As a result, profits had historically been inordinately high. It was not unusual for a mill's owning partners, numbering perhaps three, to share among themselves the same amount they paid in wages to their entire workforce, numbering a thousand or more. When business got tough and profits shrank from sometimes high levels, the barons had usually resorted to the same strategy: to import even cheaper labour from abroad. With a ready source of supply of hands from elsewhere, it was difficult to impossible for jute workers to win a decent wage for themselves. As early as 1886, a senior manager for Baxter Brothers had argued that 'the importation of workpeople from the northern countries of Europe' was the most efficient method of maintaining profits – in short, desperate workers from the Baltic states who would work for even lower rates than Dundonians. Thus the intake from other countries, especially nearby Ireland, had been enormous over the years. 'Whenever there was a want of hand, [the workers] informed their friends over the Channel and a new importation occurred,' recorded the *Dundee Advertiser*, generally a friend of the barons. 'Thus there was always an abundant supply of that class of labour and the wages of the preparing hands never rose in proportion to that of the spinners.'

Some jute barons had a sense of philanthropy, like Sir James Caird, who bought rest homes for the city, helped launch Ernest Shackleton's Antarctic expedition, and funded a fleet of ambulances in the Balkan wars. But most preferred to splash their profits on themselves and on showcase projects such as libraries rather than improve the wages and conditions of their employees.

Mill work was uncomfortable, tiring and dangerous, with all kinds of occupational hazards such as boils under the nails as a result of infection from the dyes. Accidents were common. 'You often heard screams when women got their hair caught in the yarn and ripped out,' recalled one long-time worker. Blindings by flying bobbins were not infrequent; there were numerous one-eyed women among the workforce. And the hours were long, sometimes up to twelve hours without a single break, and were rigidly enforced by mill managers answerable directly to the owners, of whom they were generally in fear, or at least in awe.

The low pay rates were reflected in Dundee's notorious tenements, rivalling those of the Gorbals for lack of sanitation, privacy and warmth. Despite some new housing provided in the 1920s, some of it gifted by Dundee-born merchant banker Robert Fleming, jute workers still lived 'in the most incredible misery' in the 1930s, Labour MP Tom Johnston told the Commons. From this gritty matrix emerged a special brand of female workers – highly independent because they had their own income, pitiful as that might be, opinionated, foul-mouthed and fun-loving. After hours, they rejoiced in shocking the more respectable classes with their sense of abandon and *joie de vivre*. According to the records, these 'witches of Dundee' pushed the social boundaries to the limit, probably getting drunker and having more sex (as measured by the record number of illegitimate children in the city) than any other group of women in Britain. They were also more militant, like the young communist Mary Brooksbank, who whiled away a three-month sentence in prison for 'inciting a riot' – the standard offence for complaining in public about alleged abuses by employers or other leaders of the community – by writing poetry about her work as an underage employee in the mills:

> *Oh, dear me, the mill's gaein fast,*
> *The puir wee shifters canna get a rest,*
> *Shiftin' bobbins coorse and fine,*
> *They fairly mak'ye work for yer ten and nine.*[8]

But many of these women were laid off as the Hooghly commandeered the remnants of Dundee's once-mighty jute industry. In a relatively small city, some twenty-six thousand were out of work. Dundee had become a place of 'singular desolation', wrote journalist James Cameron.

The Hooghly imported the Scottish city's derisory pay rates and general indifference towards its workers. Indeed, shortly before the Depression the crusading parliamentarian Tom Johnston sailed all the way to Calcutta to conduct his own investigation of the indignities visited on the *bustee* dwellers by an industry that was still dominated by expatriate Scots. To his horror, he found a situation considerably worse than back home. Some eighty-five mills employed a quarter of a million men, about fifty-three thousand women in lower-paid and lower-skilled work, and around twenty thousand children. As historian Samita Sen noted, the mill-owners 'refused to pay for training and settling an "efficient" workforce; and they expected their labour force to be manipulable, deployable at will and for such short- or long-term periods as suited them'. In short, Dundee relocated to the banks of the Hooghly.

The occupants of the *bustees* were not entirely meek and submissive – they regularly launched protest strikes or go-slows – but there can be no doubt they were shamelessly exploited. The Hooghly labour force was probably the worst paid in the world, and one of the worst treated. Having dredged the evidence painstakingly, social historian Dipesh Chakrabarty unearthed a working environment of 'low wages, racist supervisors, split families and demanding working conditions'. Some of the jute wallahs achieved enormous profits even during the Depression, paying themselves dividends of up to 70 per cent.

But in other ways the Depression was liberating India. Now self-governing and breaking some of its economic shackles with Britain, the newly independent nation was importing a lot more goods from elsewhere, in particular South Africa and Asia. Indeed the mother country would soon rank only third in the pecking order of suppliers of India's imports. And like the jute wallahs, India's manufacturers were getting into their stride. This was a rude economic shock Chancellor Neville Chamberlain had not anticipated in the Ottawa agreement. As an official economic report noted, 'Indian public men, both politicians and industrialists, seem to be imbued with the conviction that the more domestic production is substituted for imports until the latter are gradually extinguished, the more prosperous the country will become . . .' And maybe they were right.

Economically speaking, India had long been run by Westminster, and very much in the mother country's interests. This was especially true in the highly emotive matter of the upholding of 'British credit' through a strong pound. 'Overlords in London allowed Indian policy-makers little autonomy,' wrote economist Gopalan Balachandran. 'For example, they overruled Delhi to peg the rupee to the sterling when the latter left gold in September 1931.' Those overlords were principally the India Office, the Treasury and the Bank of England, and certainly the pegging of the rupee to the pound was very much in Britain's interests rather than India's. The bank desperately needed the support of a high rupee as its usual sources of capital declined. 'An Indian default would have had catastrophic consequences for sterling,' added Balachandran. Indian gold also provided a God-given lifeline in sterling's hour of need. As it poured into Britain, attracted by the higher price there for the yellow metal, the National government heaved a huge sigh of relief. Neville Chamberlain was relieved and thrilled, writing to his sister that 'the astonishing gold mine we have discovered in India has put us in clover. The French can take their [gold] balances away without our flinching. We can accumulate credits for the repayment of our £80m loan and we can safely lower the bank rate. So there is great rejoicing in the City.'

Another Asian nation rising ominously on the back of the Depression was Japan. Indeed it was turning itself into an economic powerhouse with militaristic, empire-building ambitions. Much more nimble-footed than the United States, Britain or Europe in reacting to the collapse in its old markets, the Japanese government quickly formed a partnership with its industrialists to scour the world for sales. And just as quickly, the effort paid off. Within a couple of years these new markets were buying about a quarter of all Japanese exports, some of them exciting new products such as rayon but also staples such as steel, machinery, foodstuffs, chemicals, finely worked instruments and, of course, cotton, in a direct threat to the Lancashire industry. Almost overnight, the old 'silk' economy emerged as a major threat to the established exporting powers.

The mastermind of Japan's rapid recovery, albeit from a higher economic level than in some other nations, was the extraordinary Korekiyo Takahashi, probably the world's most effective, far-sighted and least likely finance minister of the period. Takahashi was 'one of Japan's greatest financial statesmen' according to biographer Richard Smethurst. He was now in the middle of the fifth of his seven terms as finance minister. Taking over the job in late 1931, Takahashi immediately abandoned the balanced sound-finance budget of orthodoxy, borrowing heavily to boost industrial production on the back of a programme of public works that included heavy military spending and generous subsidies for shipping – exactly what Lord Essendon of the White Star line was advocating in Britain around the same time.

Takahashi was a self-taught, commonsensical economist, the illegitimate son of a court artist and a fifteen-year-old domestic maid. Five years before Keynes published his groundbreaking *General Theory of Employment, Interest and Money* – a tome universally accepted as the manual for Depression-busting economics – Takahashi had already worked out the general principles for himself. As early as November 1929, he had explained in quaint terms the fundamental truth of the importance of spending – basically, the theory of the velocity of money – as the basis of a buoyant economy. Echoing Keynes's famous appeal to the housewives of Britain to go out and, in effect, shop till they dropped, Takahashi expressed the multiplier effect in terms of a geisha house. The analogy was so perfectly expressed it bears quotation in full:

> If someone goes to a geisha house and calls a geisha, eats luxurious food, and spends 2000 yen, we disapprove morally. But if we analyse how that money is used, we find that the part that paid for food helps support the chef's salary, and is used to pay for fish, meat, vegetables, and seasoning, or the costs of transporting it. The farmers, fishermen, and merchants who receive the money then buy clothes, food, and shelter. And the geisha uses the money she receives to buy food, clothes, cosmetics, and to pay taxes. If this hypothetical man does not go to a geisha house and saves his 2000 yen, bank deposits will grow, but the efficacy of his money will be lessened. But he goes to a geisha house and his money is transferred to the hands of farmers, artisans, and fishermen. It goes in turn to various other producers and works twenty or thirty times over. From the individual's point of view, it would be good to save his 2000 yen, but when seen from the vantage point of the national economy, because the money works twenty or thirty times over, spending is better.

Takahashi appears to have had no formal schooling at all. He learned fluent colloquial English from American missionaries. By the age of twelve he was an errand boy for a Scots banker, then briefly a house boy in San Francisco, before returning to Japan at the age of fourteen where he would help translate into Japanese Alfred Marshall's *The Pure Theory of Modern Trade* for the benefit of the government. An omnivorous student, Takahashi was familiar with hundreds of important English-language books on economics, society and related subjects. Unusually outward-looking in an introverted nation, he built up a network of important and useful acquaintances, bankers in particular, throughout Britain and America that stood him in good stead. Jack Morgan became acquainted with Takahashi after Morgan, Grenfell helped raise several large Japanese loans in the 1920s.

Starting from this unpromising background, Takahashi rose steadily up the ranks of bureaucracy under the emperors through sheer doggedness and talent. His high reputation in the capital markets of the west saved Japan more than once. He financed Japan's nearly ruinous 1904–05 war with Russia by raising the money in Europe with the help of the Rothschilds (the famous banking family spent a portion of their enormous fees on a sumptuous dinner at the Savoy Hotel as a mark of respect for the little Japanese central banker). Having rescued his country once, Takahashi did so again in six inspired weeks during another financial crisis in 1927. Now, in his late seventies, he was once again performing miracles.

Unlike many cloistered economists in the west, Takahashi saw his economic constituency as the general population, certainly not the ruling classes and absolutely not the military. He had learned, Smethurst noted, 'the importance of insuring that "rich country" (fukoku) meant rich people and that "strong army" (kohei) did not get out of hand'. As a result, the Depression was essentially over in Japan within little more than a year.

Unfortunately, Takahashi did not live to see all the fruits of his work. Having revived the economy, he began to draw the reins lest everything be put in jeopardy. Thus he reduced the military budget at a time when empire-builders were demanding ships, planes and unlimited supplies of weapons of war. A committed democrat who had resigned his ennoblements – he had been made viscount by a grateful emperor – Takahashi believed an economy should serve the needs of all rather than the ambitions of a few. In a country where assassinations were almost routine, he knew the risks he was running; 'I am prepared to die now,' he once confided to a friend. On 26 February 1936, he was brutally murdered by army officers.

China was also changing fast during the slump. Its emboldened cotton industry had competed with the Lancashire-based mills before the Depression, provoking a commercial attaché in the British embassy to mourn in a 1929 report for London that it was 'quite impossible for Lancashire to successfully compete with the eastern mills in some lines'. A year later, another report warned that 'the days of large profits in old-established lines of trade are gone' and the only way for Britain to win the market back was through 'the closest co-operation between the manufacturer and the agent or merchant here ...' Another two years after that, it was clear the old coolie economy was gone and the boot was on the other foot. Almost overnight, it seemed, China's much more robust and confident manufacturing class could afford to buy British-made machinery, threatening the total ruin of Lancashire. 'It must therefore be in the ultimate interest of Great Britain to co-operate with the Chinese in the establishment of industries calculated to meet the needs of the masses,' observed an embassy report. This was especially the case because Germany, desperate for export income, was engaging in what the British regarded as an unsporting barter trade with China in heavy machinery.

China, which based its currency on silver rather than gold, sailed through the Depression. But in Europe, as the slump intensified and wrought havoc on the lives of many millions, a furious and fundamental debate was developing at street level. People demanded to know why this was happening, why there was such an enormous disparity between the rich and the poor. Within contaminated nations, they started to challenge long-established orthodoxies about the role of government, about the attitude of their employers, in general about those who held power over them who, they believed, had plunged them into this misery. Their patience fraying, they questioned the fairness of the entire social order and in particular the system of capitalism that seemed to work for a few rather than for the majority. If the existing system could not provide a fairer life for them, they would find another one that could.

The rumble of revolution was in the air in Europe, Britain and even within the Empire.

9

———

Fall of the 'Big Fella'

Among the most resentful victims of the Depression in Australia were the veterans of the 1914–18 war. After the horrors of conflict in Gallipoli and on the Western Front, the 'diggers' had returned home in anticipation of a quiet and reasonably prosperous life. Instead, within little more than a decade many found themselves out of a job and fighting to put food on the table. Their numbers were increased by ex-servicemen who had been settled on land after the war, mainly in the Riverina district, a pastoral community in south-west New South Wales bordered by Victoria, but who had failed to make a go of farming and drifted back to the cities, disappointed and embittered. Over 37,500 soldiers had taken up land under the scheme but more than half had given up before the start of the Depression and were now looking for work that was no longer there.

A massive wave of government-assisted immigration from Britain exacerbated the situation. Dreaming of a new life, some 212,000 Britons had taken ship to Australia in the 1920s and many had also tried their hand at farming, with similarly disastrous results. They were now competing with the ex-servicemen for jobs in the cities, Sydney and Melbourne in particular, and causing resentment among the diggers who could not understand why there was no honest toil for them in the nation for whose freedom they had fought. By mid-1932, nearly 32 per cent of Australians were out of work – an incredible percentage with predictably cancerous social results. As historian Wendy Lowen-

stein recorded, people stooped as low as necessary to survive:[9] 'In thousands and thousands of homes fathers deserted the family and went on
the track [road], or perhaps took to drink. Grown sons sat in the kitchen
day after day, playing cards, studying the horses and trying to scrounge
enough for a threepenny bet, or engaged in petty crime. Mothers
cohabited with male boarders who were in work and who might support the family. Daughters attempted some amateur prostitution, and
children were in trouble with the police.'

But nothing made working-class people – veterans in particular –
angrier than the threat of eviction from their homes for inability to pay rent
or mortgage. When returned servicemen believed their places of residence were at risk, they reverted to their military training. Using trench
warfare techniques learned at the front, they barricaded their cottages with
barbed wire, sandbags, wooden planks and anything else to hand. The
communist-led Unemployed Workers Movement, which aided and abet-
ted them, usually pitched in with weapons, publicity and extra numbers.
Then, armed with 'bricks, iron bars, sticks and pick-handles', as a contemporary report put it, they waited for the arrival of the despised and feared
bailiff, landlord or police (or often all three), ready to repel all comers.

In general, the authorities backed the landlords to the hilt, sending
in contingents of police to throw the veterans out of their homes and
turning a blind eye to the bailiffs' use of sledgehammers. Rarely did
local councils or other bodies intervene to assist the unfortunate
tenants, for instance by providing interest-free loans to tide them over
the hard times. The War Services Homes Commission was, as one
commentator noted, 'as ruthless as the banks in evicting those unable
to keep up their rent payments'. As for the police, they did not shy
away from a fight and seemed to take the barricades as an insult to
their duty to maintain law and order. Contingents of uniformed and
armed men regularly stormed homes, kicking in doors, smashing
windows and, in at least one case, firing shots at the defenders.
Vicious as they were, most of these incidents were skirmishes, but
some amounted to full-scale confrontations as thousands of working-
class sympathisers pelted the police with stones and bottles. 'At
Tighes Hill in Newcastle, 200 men battled 60 police for over an hour
with weapons including a sledgehammer,' noted one report. 'It was a
miracle perhaps that nobody was killed.'[10]

A breathless account in the *Sydney Morning Herald* of one furious stoush in the suburb of Newton in June 1931 gives an idea of how rapidly the divisions in the city's society were growing. According to the paper, 'the most sensational battle Sydney has ever known' was waged between forty policemen and eighteen communists. The defenders 'rained stones weighing several pounds from the top of the building on to the heads of the attacking police'. When police finally broke into the house, faces covered in blood, the crowd of many thousands hooted and jeered. Weight of numbers almost always prevailed, and after the battle was won veterans' entire families would generally end up on the footpath outside their picket-fenced cottages, their belongings and furniture beside them, hoping for charity but probably destined to join the migrant shanty towns in suburbs such as Blacktown, Sans Souci and La Perouse. The courts were rarely merciful and many of the protesters were sentenced to jail terms. It was only in the third year of the Depression that commonsense prevailed and the diggers were allowed to stay in their homes, pending better times. But for the intervention of the Unemployed Workers, there would certainly have been many more evictions.

These heavy-handed tactics had general support in New South Wales, a state that still bore some of the dichotomous characteristics of its founding by transported felons and their overseers. The nation had never been scarred by civil war, and Australians liked it that way. They were frightened by overt resistance to authority, even if it was provoked by legitimate grievance, and they could see Sydney was turning all too quickly into one of the most violent cities in the Empire. Thus the local police chief, Glasgow-born William MacKay, who had somehow escaped any responsibility for the riots in Rothbury in 1929, won public backing for his rudimentary notion of policing – or as he put it, 'belting some bloody heads off'.

In other cities, too, a dangerous resentment was simmering just below the surface as a result of the indignities ushered in by the Depression and worsened by the ineptitude of the authorities. The distribution of federal grants for the unemployed was bungled or delayed, or the money was simply misused: some local councils diverted it to boost the wages of existing staff. Itinerant job-hunters – the ones who were in fact making the most determined attempt to find work – were often excluded under ill-considered residency qualifications. And like the National government in Britain, Prime Minister Scullin had little faith in a public works programme, arguing with Chancellor Snowden that any such scheme must at least produce enough profit to meet interest payments.[11] Most of the work that was generated was back-breaking manual labour on road works.

However, Scullin was prepared to back the plan of his own treasurer, Edward Theodore, for a modest boost to the economy. But here the federal government fell foul once again of the obdurate Scot Sir Robert Gibson, who as chairman of the Commonwealth Bank effectively controlled Australia's money supply. When Theodore approached Gibson with his proposal to increase the amount of coins and notes in circulation to tide the nation over the downturn, the banker flatly refused. Gibson believed in saving, not spending. Like most of Australia's senior bankers, he expected the government to purge the economy with the standard dose of bitter medicine through cuts in wages and government spending, including welfare and pensions (he did not, however, propose a cut in lending rates, which would have reduced bank profits). 'National solvency was to take priority over the needs of the poor,' one commentator noted.

While the federal and state governments dithered, the victims of the Depression began to run out of impatience. In Adelaide, unemployed workers measured their iron bars and spiked sticks against police batons in the 'beef riots', so-called because the meat had been allegedly removed from their food rations. In the isolated Northern Territories city of Darwin, fifty unemployed workers stormed the government offices after being refused relief work, inflicting serious injuries on several policemen. In Melbourne, another hotbed of the Unemployed Workers Movement, there were further battles over eviction. In Perth, capital of Western Australia, the unemployed rioted outside the treasury building. At Bulli, south of Sydney, police fired on a detachment of the UWM trying to steal rations from a depot.

Women too began to retaliate against what they saw as unfair treatment, especially when the government of Victoria refused welfare for unemployed females, single or married. A communist newspaper, *Working Women*, was launched, encouraging 'scratching and screaming' women who physically attacked 'scab labour'. Sometimes in defiance of male-dominated unions, which tended to have little regard for the wages and conditions of females, women staged their own strikes. They helped organise anti-eviction protests and intimidated anybody even contemplating the buying of seized furniture. 'You bid for this, you bitch, and I'll tear your bloody hair out,' one woman apparently warned a middle-class housewife at a furniture auction. Others were dragged by policemen through the streets, and were proud of it.

Occupying dangerous ground on one wing of this outburst of female militancy was Adela Pankhurst Walsh, daughter of the legendary British suffragette Emmeline Pankhurst. Once a feminist and communist, the younger Pankhurst had turned a philosophical corner after emigrating to Australia and had launched the anti-communist Women's Guild of Empire in 1929 whose purpose was 'to end the industrial and class strife and to restore industry on a basis of cooperation and goodwill'. Backed by a grateful manufacturers' organisation in New South Wales, this unique body ran what it called 'industrial tea parties' for the wives of unemployed men, and conducted lunch-hour meetings in workplaces where it preached Empire, harmony in the factories and cooperation with the authorities, all to the fury of the militants. Adela Pankhurst became a hated but willing weapon for manufacturers, turning up promptly to help forestall industrial trouble. 'If you want work, come and work like us!' yelled an objector at one factory. 'Twister! How much are you paid for this?'[12] Similar organisations drew closer in the teeth of this shrill hostility, determined to defend traditional values while being characterised as right-wing by the militants. There seemed to be no end of them – the Feminist League, the National Association of Women, the Women's Christian Temperance Union, the Progressive Housewives Association, the women's branch of the Sane Democracy League.

In the same camp as Adela Pankhurst was a respected solicitor named Eric Campbell, a veteran of the 1914–18 war, whose conversion from a soldier with a distinguished war record into a suburban paramilitary who dressed up secretly in Ku Klux Klan robes is only explicable in the context of the times. Here was a man who had served in France, twice been mentioned in dispatches, and won the DSO. As well as a successful lawyer, he was a Rotarian, a member of Sydney's best clubs, a keen golfer and a reputable businessman. Yet he was also the leader of Sydney's New Guard, a fascist paramilitary body claiming forty thousand members at its height. Under the Nazis' swastika flag, its members conducted drills in local parks, sometimes in full view of police and public.

There was no evidence Campbell was inspired by the imminently-to-become-infamous British fascist Oswald Mosley; in fact he became a paramilitary before Mosley became an MP. More an admirer of Mussolini, Campbell appeared to be motivated by the emergence of what he saw as dangerously radical politics. Like his fellow paramilitaries, he saw left-wing bogeys everywhere, and they all threatened Campbell's cherished symbols of throne and Empire. Certainly the communist-led Unemployed Workers Movement was making hay in the conditions: between its formation in early 1930 and late 1931, membership shot up from nothing to thirty-one thousand. The numbers of the New Guard grew in almost direct correlation. It had much tacit support too, maintaining links with the official forces of law and order which seemed to see the fascists almost as allies.

With his dashing good looks and a commanding manner, Campbell was a natural leader. Although the claimed membership was probably an exaggeration, the New Guard's organisation and violence were real enough. Campbell used to send detachments of shock troops by car into working-class suburbs where, reportedly wielding pistols and iron bars, they routinely smashed their way into meetings of left-wingers debating solutions to fast-growing unemployment. Pretty much with impunity, the vigilante group terrorised left-wing discussion groups of the kind that were going on all over Britain in cafés, during dinners at private houses, even at mid-week church gatherings. Plans had even been drawn up to kidnap the New South Wales premier along with the entire state government. Even the notion of such a madcap scheme illustrates how polarised the city had become since 1929.

All the evidence pointed to a nation in mental and economic strife. Indeed, as the stress fractures widened, the nation faced 'imminent collapse' according to economic historian Boris Schedvin.[13] Earlier, economist Lyndhurst Giblin had highlighted the extent of the divide, pointing out that many Australians had grown wealthy in the boom years, as the unemployed could see for themselves in the 'expensive motor cars, two or three to a family; clothes marked up in the shops at extravagant prices; great hotels crowded with visitors who spend more on food for one day than he spends in a week; expensive-looking houses with carefully tended gardens and grounds; thousands of people going off every week to spend hundreds of pounds each sightseeing in Europe'. Yet here they were being told to grin and bear it.

The press overwhelmingly supported the forces of law and order. Nearly every newspaper approved the momentous decision of the Commonwealth Court of Conciliation and Arbitration (the principal jurisdiction for labour disputes) to replace the nearly quarter-century-old principle that the essential needs of the employee should determine the amount of the basic wage, with one that was based on employers' 'capacity to pay'. In the havoc wrought by the Depression, this decision clearly gave carte blanche to employers to pay whatever wages they thought fit to offer.

Like the press barons, the authorities were quick to see the hand of the communists in the anti-eviction riots – and usually they were right. The veterans did, however, find a non-communist ally in Jack Lang, the towering, rabble-rousing premier of New South Wales. The 'big fella' – he stood six feet four inches tall – had swept to power in October 1930 on an electoral bill based on state-sponsored public works, the maintenance of living wages and a decent life for the unemployed. It is highly unlikely Lang would have become premier in a more prosperous era. He owed his popularity to the disaffected working-class districts of Sydney, Australia's biggest and most insubordinate city, as well as to the New South Wales mining districts like Rothbury where the memory of the fatal riot of 1929 was still fresh in locals' minds. Within weeks of taking office, Lang passed laws to combat evictions including a ban on the pernicious practice of selling tenants' furniture to cover back payments of rent. To raise the essential funds to finance a programme of public works, in total contradiction to federal government policy, he launched a state lottery that took a 10 per cent cut off the top of winning bets on the state's racecourses and greyhound tracks. Despite the vilification that would soon be heaped on him, Lang did at least have a plan.

Like many Australian politicians of the era, Lang was the son of immigrants who had worked his way through life in a variety of jobs that made him a kindred spirit – albeit with a completely different accent – to the Red Clydesiders and those members of the Labour Cabinet who had walked out on Ramsay MacDonald in the arguments over the tight-fisted Budget of 1931. His father was in fact Scottish, a watchmaker from Edinburgh, and his mother came from Galway, Ireland. Lang's sympathy for the underdog (and his intense dislike of bankers) was conditioned by his almost Renaissance work experience. He had worked on a poultry farm, driven a horse-drawn bus, sold books, run errands for a firm of accountants, and auctioned houses. It was as a real estate agent that he developed his dramatic electioneering skills. 'His auctioneering produced a crude but effective public speaking style: rasping voice, snarling mouth, flailing hands, sentences and phrases punctuated by long pauses,' wrote biographer Bede Nairn.

Also, like many politicians with complicated backgrounds in terms of birth and upbringing, Lang was full of contradictions, a member of no particular class or cause but an opportunist who did identify with the battlers of the Depression. He had risen in the murky waters of his state's political life by developing a reputation for fighting communism *and* capitalism: the former offended his Catholic upbringing while the latter clashed with his hard-scrabble background. 'Capitalism must go,' he liked to say. Unable to think past their own headlines, Sydney's tabloid newspapers quickly dubbed him the 'Red Terror'.

A deep-dyed Aussie, Lang knew little of Britain, and did not much care about the place (though he was not entirely ignorant of events there: in his election pamphlets he quoted from Keynes's *A Treatise on Money* in support of his programme). Separated by a long sea voyage and centuries of self-reliance, Australia had grown much more independent of the mother country after the 1914–18 war. Australians were proud that they had carved out of raw land whole cities, roads and bridges, an entire and increasingly diverse economy that was one of the world's major food exporters, a way of life, and a highly distinctive culture. They knew what they had done was admirable, even courageous, and it had given them a confidence in their own judgement and endeavours, as well as in an increasingly ingrained opposition to any attempt by London or anybody else to dictate terms. Certainly Lang was having none of it. He was the man who a year earlier had nick-named Sir Otto Niemeyer, the Bank of England's unloved emissary, as 'Sir Rotto' for his recommendation of wage and other cuts to stabilise the economy.

With the Depression worsening, particularly in his own state, the premier proposed the 'Lang plan'. Essentially it was designed to shift the financial burden off the back of Australia and on to the shoulders of the nation's lenders in the London money markets. (Another good reason for this radical solution was that Lang had promised voters more than the state could afford and his government was running out of funds.) Tub-thumping about how the 'money power' held the unemployed of New South Wales to ransom, he argued that bankers should suffer some pain along with everybody else. Thus he wanted a reduction in the rate of interest on his state's loans and a moratorium on repayments until such time as the economy improved and Australia could afford to resume them. And so in March 1931, to the horror of the federal government in Canberra, the Bank of England, the National government and not least Australia's lenders in the City, the 'big fella' repudiated interest payments due on loans raised by his government on the London money market. For the first time anybody could remember, an Australian state reneged on its official loans.

In fact, Lang's proposals had much to recommend them, in particular because the considerable saving in overseas payments could be usefully applied to relief for the unemployed. The saving in payments was equivalent to seventy times the dollop of unemployment relief provided to the states by the federal government the previous year, and would obviously make an enormous difference to the general welfare of the community. It could also be argued that the City had misjudged the state of the economy in making the loans in the first place and that it might consider a temporary reprieve in repayments to be fair in what were clearly exceptional circumstances. In later years it would become accepted banking practice to roll over debt of sovereign governments as well as companies that found themselves in temporary difficulties.

Unsurprisingly, the City did not take this view in 1931. Many of the banks in London had long memories. Some had lent heavily to Australia during the land boom half a century earlier, only to see the money disappear like chaff in the wind as local banks collapsed with the slump in agriculture. It took years for the City, which in reality knew next to nothing about the fragility and cyclical nature of this uniquely different economy, to forgive Australian borrowers, so the reaction to the Lang plan was one of horror. A series of dire consequences was predicted, ranging from irreparable damage to the good standing of Australia in the world's capital markets to a complete freeze on further capital.

As if the reaction in London were not enough, the repudiation of repayments sparked an instant constitutional crisis in Australia as the federal government assumed New South Wales' financial responsibilities in order to maintain good relations with London. The imbroglio split the entire Australian Labor party, with the New South Wales faction firmly on their premier's side and most of the rest implacably on the other, and it helped bring about the downfall of the federal government of Jim Scullin, who had so clearly failed to deliver on his promise to save the nation from the ravages of the Depression. Although Scullin and his government had lost faith in the Niemeyer-dictated deflationary formula, their conversion to state-funded public works and other reflationary programmes had come a couple of years too late.

The government's failure was ably assisted by the intransigence of the Commonwealth Bank's Gibson. To the horror and bafflement of more liberal economists, Scullin had reappointed this guardian of orthodoxy for another seven-year term, but the Scot now proceeded to bite the hand that fed him. Acting like Niemeyer's official representative, he once again flatly refused to print extra money – in effect new credit. Quite the opposite: on 2 April he issued an ultimatum to all Australia's governments that they must reduce their deficits or he would withdraw sterling reserves – a measure which amounted to the same thing. Gibson was behaving like an unofficial Chancellor of the Exchequer. In Britain his high-handedness would have been unthinkable, but it worked in Australia because the federal government did not hold all the purse strings.

It was only under considerable pressure that Gibson relented slightly a month later, graciously agreeing to provide a six-month credit to the government to save some of the more distressed wheat-growers, the people who produced the raw material for the nation's bread. Then, almost as if ashamed of this unexpected burst of largesse, Gibson refused the premiers a modest blanket grant to provide extra relief work. He agreed only to make funds available on an individual basis, and only if the application forms were delivered directly to him by the appropriate local authorities! Out of his rigid convictions of fiscal rectitude, the bank manager had now turned himself into a combination of finance and welfare minister, blocking the policies of the elected representatives of federal and state governments.

As economist Lyndhurst Giblin explained in a Down Under version of Takahashi's geisha metaphor, the entire economy was now hurtling backwards, thanks in part to the hard-headed Scot. As in the case of the Japanese finance minister, the passage merits repeating in full:

> Consider the following argument. A woolgrower receives £900 less income than his average [because of a fall in exports]. He has therefore £900 less to spend. He will reduce his expenditure in those goods and services he can best spare. One third of total consumption is on imports or exportable goods, and we may assume that one third of his reduction of expenditure, £300, will be for such goods, so that the balance of trade will be improved to that extent. The remainder will be for non-exportable goods. Let us suppose he puts off a fencer engaged in improving his property at a cost of £200 per annum; saves £200 on clothing, putting a tailor out of work; and saves another £200 in pleasure traveling, putting a motor mechanic or driver out of work who was previously earning that sum. There is no other income available for employing the fencer, tailor and motor mechanic, and there is therefore a further loss of income of £600, two thirds of the original £900. This £600 of income was also being spent by the fencer, tailor and motor mechanic, one third – or £200 – on imports and exportable goods and two thirds – or £400 – on the landlord and butcher and boot-maker and other Australian workmen. So that there will be an improvement of the balance of trade by £200, and a further loss of Australian income of £400. And so on until, in the end, there has been a reduction in the consumption of imports and exportable goods of £900 in all, and a reduction of Australian income of £2,700, or three times the direct shortage of income of the woolgrower.[14]

As an explanation of the cumulative effect of declining spending, it is hard to beat.

No doubt breathing imprecations against Gibson, Prime Minister Scullin and his government were hurled out of office in a landslide in November 1931, the latest in a long line of administrations around the world that had been capsized by the Depression. The reality was that the luckless prime minister simply did not possess the tools to fight the slump. All his policies had been emasculated by various agencies: by the power of the banks (which essentially controlled the money supply), by dangerously low levels of foreign reserves (which Scullin's government had inherited) – a situation exacerbated by hefty interest payments on public debt amounting to 60 per cent of federal taxes – by conflicts with the upper house, by the obduracy of big employers, by the lack of cooperation of the labour courts, and by no means least, by Niemeyer's wrong-headed economics. (The Bank of England man had thought Scullin 'all at sea'.)

The new prime minister (and former treasurer) was Joseph Aloysius Lyons, a fiscally conservative Empire loyalist later to be revered as 'Honest Joe'. Another self-educated son of Irish immigrants, one of eight brothers and sisters, Lyons' most urgent problem was Premier Lang and a now practically bankrupt New South Wales.

Lyons knew something about reckless financial behaviour. After a series of failed business ventures, his father Michael once bet the remainder of his wealth on horses – more specifically, the 1887 Melbourne Cup – and lost the lot. As a consequence the nine-year-old Lyons had to leave school to work as an errand boy, farm labourer and printer's devil to help put food on the table. Although he later returned to school, the experience taught the lad a lot about the importance of living within one's means, and he never lost his conviction that budgeting should follow rigid principles, both for households and nations. Lyons was adamant that Lang, in defying long-established conventions that required state borrowing to be approved by a special loan council, had clearly gone too far. He promptly passed a law allowing the federal government to recoup the interest paid on behalf of New South Wales from state coffers.

The rebellious premier now found himself in deep trouble. By refusing to pay back the federal government, the 'big fella' had trampled the constitution underfoot, bringing him into confrontation with the governor-general of New South Wales, Sir Philip Game. This British-born professional soldier had fought a running battle with Lang since arriving in Australia in mid-1930 to take over the vice-regal role. Having seen action in the 1914–18 war, rising to the rank of air vice marshal, Game was a good man in a tight spot and he had behaved even-handedly with all parties during the upheavals. Indeed he had warmed to Lang, sympathising with the humanitarian bias of his policies, anti-constitutional as they were. Equally, the premier would have known that Game gave away much of his salary to the needy during the Depression. However, Game had no option but to dismiss the big fella from office, which he did in May 1932, to the enormous relief of Prime Minister Lyons (who was anxious to mend fences with Britain) and London's money markets. Lang's moment had come and gone; thereafter he steadily lost power in state and federal politics, although never his capacity for stirring up trouble.

At the point when Lang suffered the consequences of his intemperance, another state premier was about to start work quietly on a similar programme to the one Niemeyer had practically forbidden. The difference between this politician and the unfortunate Lang was a Scots canniness, a trait he immediately turned to good advantage.

Forgan Smith became premier of Queensland in June 1932, a month after the big fella was dismissed in a general repudiation of radical politics. The new boy soon found himself attending a premiers' conference in Canberra as the only Labour representative there. Smith was surrounded by enthusiastic supporters of Niemeyer's deflationary economics, now back in vogue with the arrival in power of Honest Joe Lyons. Indeed, Lyons proposed a motion specifically endorsing Niemeyer's frugal formula. Somehow Smith contrived to express his misgivings about the motion, craftily moving an amendment that managed to commit the premiers to a programme of reviving industry. Within a few days the Smith amendment won such popular support that it was adopted over Lyons' original motion, much to the latter's irritation.

This astute novice was the son of a gardener who had grown up on a feudal estate at Invergowrie, Perthshire. After a few years on the Clydeside shipyards, he emigrated in his mid-twenties to the burning sun of the far north of Queensland. A painter and decorator by trade, he steadily built a political career as a trade union organiser, finally becoming leader of the Labour party. Forgan Smith was not uneducated by any means. He had briefly attended Dunoon grammar school and was considered bright enough to be a candidate for medical school before opting to earn his living as a tradesman. 'A man of considerable ability – very clear-minded and with a definite purpose,' approved state governor Sir Leslie Wilson in a confidential letter to the secretary of the Dominions Office in London soon after Forgan Smith became premier, chief secretary and treasurer of the state of Queensland. 'He will not accept dictation from his "caucus" and is master of them.'

Smith had his idiosyncrasies, such as adding letters for an honorary doctorate of law after his name in newspaper articles despite having never darkened the door of a university. In a state that notoriously distrusted intellectuals, he also managed to strike a balance between homespun commonsense and high intelligence, 'regularly quoting authors such as Aristotle, Dryden and Maynard Keynes in his public addresses'. He once daringly referred to Nazism as 'Nietzschean in character'. Never mind that this was only true in the sense that Hitler had appropriated a fragment of the great philosopher's huge oeuvre and disgracefully distorted it in the interests of his party, it said something about his reading. Married to Effie, a farmer's daughter from the sugar country around Mackay, north Queensland, Smith genuinely grew to love Australia and in particular Queensland while never quite losing his Scottish accent. He played bowls and golf, went fishing, and liked nothing more than to follow the game of cricket in the glory days of Don Bradman.

After his coup in Canberra, the Scot who had achieved a political eminence in Australia he could not have hoped for back home returned to the state capital of Brisbane on a wave of approval, almost hailed as Australia's economic saviour. Despite the continuing opposition of Gibson, his very different fellow Scot at the Commonwealth Bank, Smith proceeded to launch a public works programme, floating enough loans from various sources to start work on bridges, dams, harbours and highways. As the state steadily prospered against all the odds, the former Clydesider became the uncrowned king of Queensland, which, he liked to say, had 'the highest wage system, the best conditions of labour and the lowest unemployment'. Whether it did or not, the line worked. Whenever the premier returned home from inter-state engagements, his loyal ministers would line up at South Brisbane railway station to welcome back their leader.

The vital difference between Lang and Smith was circumspection. In unstable times the Scot understood it was better not to unsettle an essentially conservative people with inflammatory, rabble-rousing speeches. He was careful to block radicals from rising too high in the party and could be ruthless in arranging their expulsion. He repeatedly warned against extremism, whether communist, fascist or Nazi. He also made sure to work alongside the Australian Workers Union, despite its reputation as one of the toughest of unions. The Queensland branch of this union had no compunction in employing bully-boys to intimidate communists who dared to encroach on its territory, for instance by trying to recruit sugar cane-cutters. Toiling under blazing sun from dawn to dusk, at constant risk of deadly snake bites, they were fertile ground for communists. However, it was a brave communist who went back to the cane fields after a late-night visit from AWU enforcers such as the notorious and burly 'Midnight Joe' Bukowski.

New Zealand had now become one of the most savagely deflationary governments in the Empire. Highly vulnerable because of its agriculture-based economy, the economy was in dire straits. Prime minister and farmer 'Honest George' Forbes had taken a slasher to the economy with the enthusiasm of a man breaking in a few extra acres. Expecting a brief recession, he beheaded practically every government expenditure he could find. Public works was cut by a factor of four, public servants' wages were cut twice, in 1931 and 1932, in line with the fall in the cost of living, and no dole was paid until 1934 when the Depression was almost over as far as New Zealand was concerned. If men wanted work, they had to build playgrounds in the cities, create roads and plant trees on government schemes, often living rough away from their families. The government did not spare even the most vulnerable members of the community: pensions were cut for invalids, widows and the elderly, and family allowances were slashed.

As the situation worsened, with companies collapsing by the hundreds, the government applied a levy on the working economy and gave the proceeds to able-bodied men out of work. Companies were the main contributors to this emergency unemployment fund, paying a penny in the pound on gross profits and on all dividends attributable to overseas shareholders (whose interests obviously did not matter). The workforce also had to play their part for their unemployed brethren: women paid twelve shillings a year out of their wages, men twenty-four shillings, and anybody earning more than £300 a year was levied a penny a pound. Public servants, whom the coalition government hired at a breakneck pace to keep the dole queues as short as possible, suffered the heaviest cuts of all – 30 per cent across the board. Not to be outdone, Governor-general Viscount Bledisloe, an expert on livestock who was proving an extremely popular vice-regal representative, followed suit and cut his stipend by the same amount.

But nothing the government did seemed to work, especially as its most dire predictions were far too optimistic. If all categories of unemployed are counted, the percentage of the total workforce out of a job was close to 30 per cent – far higher than Britain and higher even than the United States. Many went hungry, as the collapse in food sales showed. Even the purchase of staple foods such as potatoes fell by an average of about a third and stayed there for most of the 1930s. Women were making underwear out of sugar sacks and flour bags.

As the situation steadily worsened, the coalition government adopted the desperate measure of reducing repayments on public loans due to the City. For finance minister Downie Stewart, this was anathema and he resigned from office rather than repudiate New Zealand's obligations, as he saw them, to its overseas bankers. Although both he and Forbes were deeply loyal to the Empire, they essentially split on the issue of whether New Zealand or the City came first.

Another Empire loyalist and war hero, the strapping Joseph Coates next took this poisoned chalice but fared, if anything, even worse. In truth there was little New Zealand could do in the circumstances except try and find the funds for make-work schemes.

With its limited public finances, the government could not possibly spend its way out of the Depression. It depended on the City for loans, which were not forthcoming, and it lacked the resources to do much else except wait for things to improve. Inevitably, resentment grew.

Many New Zealanders and especially the powerful farming community blamed the country's mounting misery on the delegation from the Bank of England. For the disgruntled, a book called *The Truth about the Slump* by an intense, crusading journalist named Arthur Field became compulsory reading. As far as Field was concerned, the slump was nothing other than a plot visited on the Empire by Jewish financiers for whom Niemeyer and Gregory were alleged to be agents 'enslaving the Empire with debt'. Hardly any Jewish banker escaped Field's ire, especially if they were Jewish *and* German like Otto Kahn of Kuhn, Loeb on which institution this anti-Semite blamed not only the imminent re-armament of Germany but, to boot, the Russian Revolution. Long after the deputation from the Bank of England had departed New Zealand's shores, they continued to be vilified equally by right-wingers such as Field and left-wingers of the Labour party.

Protests also hit the streets. A demonstration in Auckland organised by the Unemployed Workers Movement turned into a riot after fifteen thousand marchers, angered when police took to their leaders with batons, rampaged up and down the main thoroughfare of Queen Street smashing windows and looting. The outbreak gave the authorities the ammunition they needed to crack down on 'Bolshevists and communists', and one of the organisers received a heavy jail sentence after being beaten up by police.

At the first post-Depression general election, in 1936, the voters punished the government as though it were single-handedly responsible for the slump. Labour had never forgiven the courts for cutting wages by 10 per cent, even though living costs had fallen by 20 per cent, and most workers identified with the sentiments of the anonymous union man who wrote:

O lord above, send down a dove,
With wings as sharp as razors,
To cut the throats
Of Forbes and Coates,
The swine who cut our wages.

Unsurprisingly, a Labour government swept to power in a landslide. It was largely composed of hardcore trade unionists determined to create a paradise for workers. Its new ministers included 'Red Feds' – mainly miners who had fought pitched battles with police and special constables during nationwide strikes, and a couple of navvies and wharfies. Several of them were self-confessed Bolshevists and a few had done time on charges of sedition; four had cooled their heels in Industrial School, a form of borstal for delinquent children. Several were first-generation immigrants from Britain and Ireland. Indeed, some of them had first settled in Australia but had proved too militant even for the coal unions in northern New South Wales, and had fled across the Tasman Sea.

Probably the most radical government in the Empire, it bore a characteristically 'Kiwi' personality. Nearly all of the cabinet were self-taught, hard-knuckled manual labourers who had been brought up the tough way. The prime minister, Michael Savage, had worked as a barrel-washer in a brewery as well as in a wine and spirits shop, as a ditch-digger, a goldminer, a driver of stationary engines, a flax-cutter and a cellarman, while educating himself on writers such as Keir Hardie, the pioneering Scottish socialist. His entire life had given him a natural affinity with employees, and he and his ministers approached the job with a passion for the 'average bloke'.

They were total novices in government. None had held power before and they scraped the bottom of the barrel for talent. For instance, Walter Nash, a former sweet-shop owner from Kidderminster who had twice failed in business in his adopted country, somehow ended up with the finance portfolio. But inexperience did not deter them, and they drove through a flying wedge of laws at the expense of employers. The forty-hour week, compulsory holiday pay, higher basic wages and overtime rates by decree, compulsory union membership, instant pay rises (back paid), restrictions on profits and price limits –

new directives rained down on employers like sleet. Added together, they came dangerously close to abolishing capitalism as it was understood at the time.

The cracks widened in Canada too. As conditions worsened for millions, the seeming unfairness of capitalism came under intense intellectual scrutiny at every level of Canadian society. Had the private ownership of the means of production – the system known as capitalism – run its course? Was there another, better way? In the circumstances these were obvious issues to debate. It was impossible, after all, to argue that capitalism was working for the general good. But allied to these questions was the even more fundamental one of whether or not the nation's institutions had failed the people. Anticapitalist organisations had no doubt that this was the case and were convinced the demise of the established order was nigh. One influential movement in Canada, the harmless-sounding Cooperative Commonwealth Federation, aimed to eradicate capitalism and replace it with a comprehensive programme of socialism that would give all Canadians equal opportunities. Soon this drastic alternative was winning so many votes that it cracked the long-established duopoly of the two main parties.

Communists would win converts right into the late 1930s, especially among immigrant workers. This was achieved with the willing assistance of British communists such as Willie Gallacher, another legendary Red Clydesider who made a rousing coast-to-coast tour of Canada, watched every step of the way by the forces of law and order. He came at the invitation of no fewer than three other Scots holding top positions in the party. Although Gallacher was an MP back home, he did not hesitate to rail against the National government for 'dragging Britain into a new war for the preservation of capitalism'.

As the Canadian communists emerged into the light by mounting protests, visiting factories and generally recruiting more and more members, Prime Minister Richard Bennett started to tighten the noose, cracking down on individuals and organisations seen as a threat to the established order. When a claimed twenty thousand marched during Toronto's May Day celebrations one year to listen to yet another British communist, eighty-year-old Tom Mann, renowned (or infamous) for his role in the 1926 General Strike, it became harder for the Mounties to ignore this rebellious presence in their midst. In due course party leaders, including English-born general secretary Tim Buck, were rounded up and given harsh sentences of five years in the Kingston penitentiary, where Buck was made to serve the full term. Although the blanket ban on the party was removed in 1936, regional governments like the one in Quebec continued to treat communists as pariahs, even passing a Padlock Act that allowed authorities to bolt and shackle any premises that had been used 'for communist purposes'.

And Canada was not even a hotbed of dissent. The vast majority of the population took their hardships on the chin in a spirit of stoicism. 'Some time ago I wrote a letter to you appealing for help or employment,' a certain Charles Grierson addressed the prime minister. 'It is now forty months since I had the pleasure of a pay check. My family are all undernourished, ill-clothed and ill-sheltered and are in need of medical assistance. How long do you think we can carry on under these circumstances?'

Arguably the most stoic people in the entire Empire were the Newfoundlanders, the first colony to win self-government as early as 1855, nearly half a century before Australia and South Africa. This windswept nation on the north Atlantic coast was probably technically bankrupt even before the Depression because of a hugely expensive railway, which the government had been forced to take over from private interests. But it was when the international price for dried cod, a major export, fell by half that the economy promptly collapsed. Measured as a percentage of gross domestic product, the government became probably the most indebted anywhere. Soon more than half of its revenue went towards meeting its public debt, nearly all of it payable overseas.

With its purse empty, the best the government could do for the 25 to 30 per cent of the population that was officially on relief was a payment equivalent to six cents a day for official rations – virtually a starvation diet. Diseases of malnutrition such as scurvy and tuberculosis were rife. With no prospect of the situation improving, the

British government had no option but to intervene for humane reasons, and in February 1934 the government was replaced by a London-appointed commission. This extempore administration continued to run Newfoundland for the next fifteen years, in fact until it was absorbed into Canada.

The dissidents in Canada were not, however, prepared to take it on the chin. They drew their anger from what was transparently an economic tragedy. By 1933, gross national product had slumped by 40 per cent and a third of the workforce was idle. In the wake of Smoot-Hawley, exports collapsed by half. Workers were laid off jobs they had held for years, particularly in the prairie provinces where up to 65 per cent of the population could be on welfare, inadequate as it was. Factories had no option but to lay off workers and reduce working hours for those they could afford to keep on. Even the weather connived with the slump, turning southern Saskatchewan into a dustbowl.

Discontent was especially rife in government-run work camps. Run by the army along military lines, they served only to underline the failure of the existing system. Able-bodied young men were required to toil for twenty cents a day. Inevitably, these boot camps became hotbeds of discontent that soon boiled over into what would become one of the legendary demonstrations of the Depression, when about sixteen hundred young men simply walked out of the federal relief camps one day and headed for Vancouver. It is surprising they had not left earlier, given their circumstances. The 'strikers', as they were called, had made a series of legitimate but futile complaints, asking for proper first-aid equipment, the same basic rights as bona fide employees, the right to vote in federal elections, and certainly more than twenty cents a day. These men were not felons. They had not committed any crime, except to be out of work through no fault of their own, yet they were treated almost as prisoners.

After milling around in Vancouver for two months, the protesters decided to head for the seat of government at Ottawa and confront the prime minister. They jumped aboard freight wagons, cramming inside them, on top of them, and even 'riding the rods' underneath them, and headed east. The 'On to Ottawa' trek had begun.

The protesters disembarked from their precarious positions at Regina, Saskatchewan – a region whose own suffering made the inhabitants highly sympathetic to the new arrivals – and stayed there while eight of their leaders, including communists, went on to Ottawa to meet the prime minister. As an attempt at conciliation it proved disastrous: according to contemporary accounts it turned into a 'shouting match'. The leaders returned to Regina to relay the bad news while a fuming Bennett blamed the communists for stirring up trouble. He was now determined to extinguish what he considered the beginnings of a radical-led revolt against the good offices of the government. It is impossible to believe that the prime minister should not shoulder much of the blame for what was about to unfold.

Regina's Market Square began to fill up on the evening of 1 July 1935 with protesters, trekkers, well-wishers and probably a few troublemakers. Their purpose was to attend a meeting about their grievances and hear speeches by the movement's leaders. Surrounded by Mounties and local police, somewhere between fifteen hundred and two thousand people finally assembled. Oddly enough, most of the trekkers were not present, having opted to stay in the nearby exhibition grounds.

At eight p.m. sharp – a giveaway time that suggested it had all been pre-planned – the forces of law and order charged into the crowd, some on horses, some wielding clubs, others firing shots and throwing tear gas. It was a full-scale, unprovoked assault. By the time it was all over hours later, two were dead – a policeman and a protester – and hundreds injured. The local hospital filled up with Mounties, policemen and trekkers alike. Any trekker found in hospital was arrested in his bed.

A livid state premier dispatched an angry wire to Bennett that roundly condemned the Mounties for fomenting the disaster and insisted on taking the matter out of federal hands. To forestall any further trouble, with both sides now spoiling for another fight, he quickly arranged for the trekkers to be dispatched back home or to the work camps, whichever they wished.

Having bungled the situation from the start, Bennett now proceeded to misread it completely. The government had, he congratulated himself, averted 'a definite revolutionary effort on the part of a group of men to usurp authority and destroy government'. In his own mind the prime minister had somehow managed to convert a march by a column of angry young men from a remote farming community into a full-scale threat to the stability of the entire nation. It was as though he had saved Canada from its own version of the Bolshevik revolution. In fact he had only succeeded in alienating the electorate – he lost the general election of that year in a landslide – while delivering the communists valuable publicity for the radical cause. By shocking many fair-minded Canadians, Bennett also inadvertently created a climate of support for a more organised and fair system of welfare that gradually followed in the wake of the riot. Thus the trekkers got most of what they wanted. More congenial seasonal camps replaced the military-style earlier ones, and wages went up, if only slightly. All along, the trekkers felt they had a good case to make, as their song 'Hold the Fort' had predicted:

> *We're all coming,*
> *Union hearts be strong.*
> *Side by side, we'll battle onward,*
> *Victory will come.*

Bennett's blunder over the trekkers was in fact out of character, probably attributable to his failure to lift Canada out of the slump. In total contrast to Mackenzie King's determinedly laissez-faire style, Bennett had done much to soften the blow. Proclaiming that 'the old order is gone', he had embarked after taking office on a programme of benign intervention that produced a series of well-intentioned laws. It became illegal for banks to foreclose on farm mortgages and to throw families off the land. Over the protests of the banking industry, Bennett established the Bank of Canada that wrested from banks their long-held right to produce their own bank notes at considerable profit. He also prised the banks' gold hoards out of their vaults, forcing them to be deposited with the new central bank. The first steps were taken towards an eight-hour day and a forty-eight-hour working week, a friendlier income tax regime, health insurance, more generous pensions, and grants to farmers, including a huge scheme to restore the southern Saskatchewan dustbowl. Government poured money into welfare, and so did individual ministers, out of their own pockets. One regularly served up a dinner to anybody who knocked on his door, hungry and destitute. Bennett used to return begging letters, but first enclosing a five-dollar bill – a considerable sum. By his own estimate, over a ten-year period in and out of office he gave away well over $2 million.

Neither public nor private generosity sufficed, however. As more Canadians landed on the welfare heap, depending on the public purse for their survival, a frustrated Bennett came to believe his government was powerless. Canada was at the mercy of 'forces which we did not create and which we cannot either regulate or control', he told a colleague. In this, he was perfectly correct. The cross-border trade that had made Canada prosperous had by now slumped to unimaginably low levels and 'recovery in Canada depended on recovery abroad'. The prime minister was also frustrated by Canada's federal system as he constantly ran into trouble over encroachment on regional rights. Further frustrating him, the courts, which preferred to see legal issues at stake rather than human ones, struck down many of his reforms.

In some ways Bennett, the dynamic and somewhat egotistical businessman, was the architect of his own misfortunes. Trusting few to do the job as well as himself, he attempted too much, which caused bottlenecks and delays. The British high commissioner once said that Bennett 'was waiting as usual until he can find time to deal with matters himself'. And Britain's Chancellor Neville Chamberlain had been annoyed by the Canadian prime minister's 'really inadequate preparation' for the trade talks in Ottawa over imperial preference, concluding that he suffered from the absence of a 'professional civil service and no minister whom he trusts'.

As more and more Canadians fell victim to those 'forces which we did not create', he became the nation's scapegoat. Automobiles drawn by horses in the absence of petrol became known as 'Bennett's buggies'. Bennett's government would be voted out of office in late 1935 and replaced by old rival Mackenzie King at the head of the Liberals. Appealing to the owners of 'Bennett's buggies' and other casualties of the Depression, King had shrewdly campaigned on a 'King or chaos' ticket.

Ill with heart disease that surely owed something to the stress of the last four years, Bennett spent most of his final years in Britain. As the fall of one Empire government after another was demonstrating, it was not a good time to be in power.

10

The Woodbine Economy

Cloth-capped men of all ages, buttoned up against the cold, congregate on street corners in towns and cities all over Britain. Some are protected against the cold by belted greatcoats, others only by jackets and waistcoats. Most of them wear ties in an attempt at respectability. As hundreds of photographs taken during the Depression show, some look almost emaciated but most are at least thin and hungry-looking. Drifting on to the street around mid-morning, they stand around for hours on end, often outside grocery shops, or waiting for the pubs to open. Nearly all of them are smoking, generally the cheap Woodbines, the brand with the honeysuckle emblem on the packet, that, strong and unfiltered, is the fag of choice for the unemployed, if they can afford it. At tuppence for five, four pence for ten and eight pence for twenty, they were the right price. Even so, a twenty-packet of Woodbine was something of a rarity. 'Here and there a man would light up a Woodbines from a paper packet of five and take a long slow draw, expanding his chest and holding in the smoke, and blow it out between narrowed lips,' remembered Ralph Glasser in *Growing Up in the Gorbals*. 'A man had to be flush, maybe have backed a winner with the street bookie, or had a birthday, to possess twenty Woodbines.'

The same observation could be made about thousands of suburbs in Britain's big cities. As the staple industries lost dominance in their long-established markets, mass unemployment was becoming the norm in the so-called 'special areas', the euphemism the House of

Lords gave to the worst-afflicted areas, which, by the mid-1930s, encompassed a total population of some four million, nervous of offending the inhabitants or stirring up a political backlash if they used a much more accurate adjective like 'derelict' or 'stricken'. However, in one of the few acts of rebellion available to them, the inhabitants generally insisted on referring to the areas as depressed, distressed or derelict, all of them much more accurate than the peers' characterisation.

There were a lot of special areas, most of them located in places where old industries were winding down and new ones simply did not fit in. The west of Scotland claimed several such areas, including the moribund coal-mining areas of Lanarkshire, Renfrewshire, Dumbarton and northern Ayrshire. There were several in South Wales too, whose steam coal, once the fuel of choice for boilers around the world, was giving way to oil; and several in northern England, including Preston, Cumberland, Durham and Northumberland. But there were plenty of other hard-hit pockets. At peak unemployment in Britain, 34 per cent of coal miners lost their jobs, over 36 per cent of pottery workers, over 43 per cent of cotton machinists, nearly 44 per cent of pig iron workers, nearly 48 per cent of steel workers, and 62 per cent of ship-builders and repairers.

Many of the special areas had been horribly vandalised by the industries that had sustained them, especially the mining towns. Their disfigurement led many to wonder if the price of Britain's now-fading industrial glory had been too high in the first place. An angered J. B. Priestley railed at 'blackened fields, poisoned rivers'. 'The more I thought about it,' he wrote, 'the more this period of England's industrial supremacy began to look like a gigantic dirty trick. At one end of this commercial greatness were a lot of half-starved, bleary-eyed children crawling about among machinery and at the other end were the traders getting natives boozed up with bad gin.' The increasingly incensed dramatist and essayist, though by no means anti-industry, was particularly offended by the havoc wrought on the once-lovely Midlands countryside. 'Industry has ravished it; drunken storm troops have passed this way,' he raged. 'There are signs of atrocities everywhere; the earth has been left gaping and bleeding.' He was equally infuriated by what seemed to him the virtual abandonment of whole communities. Visiting East Durham for the first time, he found a people who had been alienated from the rest of society, indeed from almost everybody but their own kind. They were coal miners living in 'remote, hidden away, mysterious' communities largely ignored by MPs, by the media, by Londoners whose very material well-being had of course depended for so many years on their labours. 'Of the millions in London, how many have ever spent half an hour in a mining village?' Priestley wondered.

There were many dangerous and unhealthy occupations in Britain, but mining coal was by far the most hazardous. Because the provisions of the Mines Safety Act were routinely ignored, roofs frequently collapsed, lung-corroding dust swirled everywhere in the shafts, and explosions were frequent. The statistics tell the story: in the five years to 1931, over five thousand pitmen died while digging out the coal that kept Britain warm, powered its industry, and fired its trains and ships; over eight hundred thousand were injured, often maimed for life. 'There is not a working miner's wife who does not know that her man runs the risk of fatal inrushes of water or gas from old workings,' wrote National Unemployed Workers Movement activist Wal Hannington. In the middle of the Depression, on 22 September 1934, a total of 265 men were entombed in a collapse at Gresford. None survived.

The mining villages were the most miserable places in England. Cottages were blackened by coal dust and soot. Children played in fields smeared with coal, or kicked a ball around narrow, filthy streets. In the village of Shotton in East Durham, kids tobogganed down giant slag tips from which semi-poisonous fumes steadily escaped, hanging like a pall over the houses. 'It's a dirty hole,' wrote miner's wife Phyllis Holcroft about one hovel provided for her by a pit-owner at the village of Denaby in Yorkshire. 'You can never open the window, what with the dust and the stink from the middens.' Although that referred to an earlier, pre-war era, it was shocking that little had changed in fifteen years. Most miners' wives aged before their time, worn out by their environment and worry about their menfolk. Many were adamant their sons would never go down the pit.

Taking thorough notes as he explored the mining area of Wigan, George Orwell was deeply sympathetic to these 'poor drudges underground, blackened to the eyes with their throats full of coal dust, driving their shovels forward with arms and belly muscles of steel'. He had gone down a mine to check for himself, knocking himself cold in the process. 'It brought home to you, at least while you are watching, that it is only because miners sweat their guts out that superior persons can remain superior,' he would write in *The Road to Wigan Pier*.

It seemed that everybody except the mine-owners was shocked by the state of these stricken places. It took the intervention of Archbishop Temple of York to bring to light the situation in the town of Crook, ten miles south-west of Durham, where most miners had been laid off in the early years of the Depression. The archbishop, a militant Churchman who would later be appointed Archbishop of Canterbury, was so scandalised by this that he conducted his own investigation and recorded the findings in *Men Without Work*. What he revealed was far more dire than any government authority had been prepared to admit. Some 71 per cent of the male population had not worked for five years or more.

Jarrow, a town on the south bank of the Tyne river, just a few miles east of Newcastle, was heading in the same direction. With seven thousand unemployed, it was a derelict area by any definition. But what could the new order be? Gazing at what was once a grassy-banked estuary, Priestley saw the 'blackened and ruined' landscape of Jarrow and nearby Hebburn. Had it all been worth it? Foreshadowing the coming battle against industrial pollution, he asked rhetorically, 'What new graces had [the capitalists] added to English life in return for what they had taken away from here?'

On 19 July 1933, after a three-year flurry of work that kept two thousand men in the area employed – a quarter of its full workforce – Palmers Shipyard launched its final vessel, the destroyer HMS *Duchess*. 'There was no ceremony or major publicity . . . There were no more orders and thousands of men in the district were on the dole,' recorded two local historians.[15] The entire workforce was now idle, and it would stay that way. 'If only he had work, just think how wonderful it would be,' the wife of a shipyard worker told BBC Radio. 'In the twelve years since we were married my husband has worked eighteen months. When we were married he was really handsome, but now he's just skin and bones.'

The total shutdown of Palmers, condemning 70 to 80 per cent of the insured workforce to poverty, could have been avoided. At the time a body called the National Shipbuilding Security Trust, composed of leading lights of the industry, was shopping around Britain for struggling shipyards; it then bought them up on the cheap with the intention of mothballing the yards for a forty-year period, which was of course effectively for ever. The purpose of this brutal strategy was to rationalise the industry by removing 'excessive competition'. It may not have been its intention, but the trust was of course pursuing a deliberate policy of putting whole societies out of work. When the trust bought the stricken Palmers yard from the receivers in 1934 and had it dismantled a year later, it effectively consigned Jarrow and Hebburn to a life without a future. In time, this and similar actions would result in a programme of nationalisations by post-war Labour governments, lest anything similar re-occur.

The 'capitalist rulers', as the National Unemployed Workers Movement knew them, then compounded this injustice by refusing the district a lifeline. When a syndicate of steelmakers led by T. Vosper Salt raised sufficient capital to erect a modern steel works in the town – an enterprise that would have delivered some three thousand jobs – approval for the project was submitted to the British Iron and Steel Federation. Working closely with the government, the committee deliberated for the best part of a year – an unconscionably long time in the circumstances – before delivering its decision. The federation would indeed permit the mill to be built, but only on terms that protected the profits of its existing members. One stipulation was that the mill's products must be sold at fifteen shillings a ton *above* those of existing mills. Moreover, any penalty payments for not doing so must be distributed among the federation's nominees.

The terms were so onerous, indeed ridiculous, that they killed the entire project stone dead. In a masterly display of self-contradiction, brick-maker and government adviser Sir Malcolm Stewart would write in a subsequent report on the matter that it was all for the good, an essential sacrifice for the sake of the broader economy: 'The establishment of more economic manufacturing conditions in the future has been sacrificed to procure profits made available by the present good demand influenced by the granting of a materially increased tariff on imported steel and by the defence programme.'

Translated, that meant the government did not want an efficient new mill lest it threaten the profits of an industry now starting to recover behind a rampart of tariffs. In fact the Jarrow mill would probably have strengthened the industry by helping make it more internationally as well as domestically competitive, if only because its prices would have kept the other mills honest. The inescapable conclusion is that the government was firmly in the corner of vested interests.

So, soon after HMS *Duchess* steamed out into the North Sea, the managers at Palmers ship yard simply shut up the offices and left. They did not bother to provide any amenities for an abandoned workforce, which knocked together a social centre of sorts in a couple of old huts, plus a library with a handful of books. Most occupants of 'special areas' could barely scrape a living. The NUWM, which did a thorough job of cataloguing their lot, recorded numerous examples of abject poverty. Most of these examples were eventually corroborated by other sources including council officers, medical officers and general practitioners. By no means the worst case was an ailing Liverpool widow who had four children, one a cripple suffering from tuberculosis, who slept in two beds with old coats and skirts thrown over them. Their food was cooked over an open fire (there was no gas stove or oven) and it had to be prepared in stages because there were not enough cups or small plates to go round, indeed there were no dinner plates at all. One space served as kitchen, dining room and bedroom. Out of her welfare allowance, the widow somehow managed to put nine pence a week into her own funeral fund so that she would not be a burden on her children or relatives when she died.

The NUWM's case studies were described in unemotional terms, providing snapshots of life at the bottom of the heap where up to six girls slept in the same bed, half a dozen families shared an outside privy, rats scurried around ceilings, icy winds blasted through gaps in the masonry, children played in filthy alleys, hygiene was inadequate and parents worried about where the next meal would come from. When a royal commission under Sir Montagu Barlow, a barrister and Conservative member for Salford South, investigated the special areas, its findings verified the research done by the NUWM. So hopeless did the lot of the inhabitants seem that the members of the commission seriously considered the uprooting of entire populations for their own good.

The government did not, however, invite the advice or help in any way of the NUWM. The organisation was regarded as a forcing house for trouble-makers, a threat to the very fabric of society and a running sore in the side of a well-intentioned administration. The NUWM was certainly the former and the latter, but not necessarily the one in the middle. By sidelining the NUWM, an opportunity was lost to engage one of the most spirited and motivated sectors of the community, a body that sought honest work for real wages and believed this seeming miracle could be achieved. Wal Hannington summed it up: 'The unemployed are the victims of a disorder within the economic system which is not beyond human control.'

Given their tribulations, it is surprising how few of the unemployed joined radical organisations such as the NUWM, most preferring to wait patiently for life to improve under the existing system. Certainly the Prince of Wales got a reasonably good reception when he made a much-publicised visit to a distressed area in Glamorgan. Hundreds of cloth-capped, laid-off steel workers came to hear out the future king at the derelict Dowlais steel works in Merthyr Tydfil. They seized every available position, perching alarmingly on old boilers and a twisted mass of pipes, furnaces, railings and corroding towers to hear the prince from his hastily erected platform exhort his audience 'not to lose heart' because their temporary difficulties 'are not forgotten'.

By now, the National government was trying to put both young and old unemployed into voluntary labour camps from where they ventured out to clear forests, dig roads, erect barbed wire fences and install drainage. It was the unemployed youth who were of most concern to the government – 'the most tragic aspect of the special areas and the one fraught with great danger to the State,' observed Sir Malcolm Stewart. Priestley put it more strongly. Seeing able-bodied young men standing idly outside the labour exchanges, he decided they stank of 'defeated humanity'. But the labour camps were hardly a dazzling success. Separated from their families, eating fly-blown food, working long hours, and in some cases barred from going into a nearby village for a night out by the former army officers who were generally their supervisors, the inmates sometimes left the camps more embittered than when they'd entered. Walk-outs and even open rebellions were frequent. 'If there is to be hope for these youths, then training must definitely lead to work,' concluded Sir Malcolm. But there was no work.

The government was unconscionably slow off the mark to retrieve the situation in the special areas. Despite its promises, the commissioners investigating solutions for them were given shoestring budgets and little power. As a result, too little was done too late, and what was achieved often came about through the provision of private money. For the straight-talking Labour MP Nye Bevan, the failure to back the commissioners with a decent budget was a deplorable act of cynicism. 'The whole thing is an idle and empty farce, never intended to do anything,' said the man who had started work in the pits at the age of thirteen and would later become a champion of the National Health Service – a direct outcome of the Depression. A future prime minister and publisher Harold Macmillan, Conservative MP for the down-at-heel constituency of Stockton-on-Tees, was just as alarmed at the consequences of this foot-dragging. 'If research [into the special areas] is pursued too long the time factor will come in, and you may find yourself in the casualty ward while you are still trying to be in the dissecting room,' he warned Parliament.

Many like-minded businessmen, convinced a coordinated national plan was the only hope of averting a social disaster, jumped into the breach. The car magnate Lord Nuffield, the former bicycle mechanic William Morris, was one of several industrialists who backed with his own funds a series of subsistence schemes that provided men with food rather than wages for their labours. Thus, the price of eighteen eggs was one and a half hours' work, of two pounds of lard two hours' work, and so on. The men would have much preferred to do a real job, but vested interests stonewalled numerous government-funded projects. In Wales, for instance, colliery-owners blocked schemes on the grounds they prejudiced their own interests. But at least the subsistence projects allowed men to take food home, and for that reason, as the NUWM duly acknowledged, they could be counted a modest success.

Although he lived a long way from Jarrow, in the much more

pleasant county of Surrey, the businessman and MP Sir John Jarvis
tried to do what he could for the stricken yard. Disgusted at the treatment of the town, he set up a ship-breaking business there in 1934,
which at least provided temporary work. Jarvis also mounted a fund-
raising campaign among his own more affluent constituents to pay
for projects such as a furniture-making works on the old site, and for
wallpaper and paint to spruce up the former workers' homes.

At least private money was trying to make a difference. For the government's part, it seemed that too little was being done too late.

Undoubtedly the most hated government measure in Britain was the
means test, the qualification for welfare relief. The way it was admin-
istered provoked G. K. Chesterton, the liberal Catholic author and
creator of the Father Brown detective stories, to write in an uncharac-
teristic fury, 'It is inhuman. It is horrible ... For the first time within
mortal memory the government and the nation has set out on a definite, deliberate campaign to make the poor poorer ... People who are
already clinging with their teeth and fingernails to the edge of the
chasm are to be formally and legally kicked into the chasm.'

The means test was often enforced under stringent conditions by
zealous and generally hated local officials who sometimes seemed
determined not to approve relief if the applicants still had money in
the bank. For example, when an official discovered that a Lancashire
miner with a wife and six children had had the temerity to retain £15
in an account in the local co-op, he promptly ruled the applicant ineli-
gible. 'Not a case for help so long as this sum is on deposit,' the official
wrote. In short, you had to be penniless to qualifty.

Hundreds of similar cases were quoted by local newspapers, especially in the north of England and Wales, as the strict observance of the
fine print began to be revealed in epidemics of illness. Medical officers
of health started reporting a growing incidence of cases of ill health
and even of slow starvation. 'There is no doubt that large numbers of
children are carrying on today in this country without adequate food,'
warned Dr Kenneth Fraser, the medical officer at a school in Cumberland, one of the special areas. 'The money available for food in very

many homes is not sufficient to buy an adequate mixed diet for the growing child, even on the plainest and simplest lines.' This quickly became a familiar refrain. The medical officer at Preston expressed alarm at the effect of inadequate nutrition on toddlers, who were 'much more prone to rickets than was the case two years ago'. A year later, Dr Fraser in Cumberland noticed 'almost a dramatic increase in the incidence of rickets amongst children of school age'. Liverpool's public health committee became so concerned about the increase in the disease, which can lead to a range of serious ailments as well as permanent disability, that it opened an inquiry. In Newcastle, the medical officer reported that children from poorer families were shorter, lighter and more inclined to serious anaemia than their peers from less impoverished communities. In Durham, alarmed medical authorities discovered an increase in tuberculosis. In the special areas of South Wales, there was an epidemic of severe scarlet fever. In most cases the medical officers were in no doubt about the cause, namely malnutrition.

A committee of the British Medical Association tackled the government on the issue, concluding in a 1933 study that the official estimate of a wage adequate to feed and clothe children was far too low. The study, called 'Food, Health and Income', argued that four shillings a week for food per person – the government's allowance, assuming the recipients passed the means test – was not nearly enough to provide a healthy diet. It listed rickets, anaemia, bad teeth and tuberculosis as the results of this official parsimony. Six shillings a head was barely enough, the BMA's study went on to say. Eight shillings – twice the official estimate – was considered about right. The body's overall conclusion was that, under the means test, 20 to 25 per cent of children in Britain were badly undernourished.

Yet in its determination to save public funds – the reduced unemployment insurance announced by Snowden saved the government £54 million in the two years to October 1933 – the government chose to ignore the evidence of a series of studies such as this on the risks of poverty. In July 1933, health minister Sir E. Hilton Young, assured Parliament there was 'no available medical evidence of any general increase in physical impairment, sickness, or mortality as a result of the economic depression of unemployment'. (After hearing this speech, MPs would probably have repaired to the Members Dining Room, with its magnificent view overlooking the Thames, where the menu would certainly not cause any general increase in physical impairment. For little more than two shillings, they could buy themselves a three-course meal and a bottle of claret.) Backing their minister, officials next engaged in a dispute with the BMA about what exactly constituted an adequate diet, and how much it cost to provide it. While the inhabitants of special areas, in particular children and mothers, grew steadily sicker, the debate came down to percentages of calories. Health ministry officials maintained a man could live on 3,000 calories a day (3,400, said the doctors) and a housewife on 2,600 (2,800).

Several far-sighted employers saw the dangers and moved to avert social disaster, among them a retailer named Spedan Lewis, scion of the family that owned one of the nation's most successful stores. Between his father and founder John, his brother Oswald and himself, they collectively earned more than the rest of the workforce combined. Although this was by no means uncommon in heavy industry – the owners of Dundee jute mills, remember, regularly took in salary a sum equal to what they shared out among a thousand or more employees – the inequality of the division of the spoils of labour troubled the younger Lewis's conscience. He therefore decided to establish a trust that divided the profits among all employees – an act that was considered a commercial heresy.

Outlining his philosophy in a book called *Partnership for All, Fairer Shares*, Lewis's view was that the business should be more a community of colleagues than a formal proprietorship. His motivation was both altruistic and shrewd: Lewis could see that a partnership would involve employees more closely in the performance of the business and hopefully ensure larger and more enduring profits, albeit shared. An immediate result of this turnabout in commercial philosophy was a nine-hole golf course for employees, which the firm opened up in the middle of the Depression. Among other measures, Spedan Lewis went on to provide holiday chalets, albeit rough-and-ready, and encouraged the formation of a choir, reflecting the terms of a constitution that decreed 'partners [the former employees] should not put business too far before pleasure'.

The young Lewis was not alone in his magnanimity. In Bristol, the Wills family practically subsidised the city through the Depression while producing the narcotic that helped take people's minds off it. Sales of the lung-blackening Woodbines rose during the Depression. Far from being a heinous crime, the manufacture of cigarettes was regarded almost as a social good in a nation of smokers. Indeed, the production of Woodbines and other cigarettes was formally measured as an indication of the general health of the economy, and Chancellor Neville Chamberlain would rejoice at the increased consumption of sugar, beer and fags. Britons had 'sweetened their lives' by dispatching 80,000 more tons of the first compared with the previous year, 'washed away their troubles' with 270 million more pints, and, he could have said, inhaled away their tensions with 2,600 million more cigarettes.[16]

Benefactors of the city for a century before the slump, W. D. & H. O. Wills employed thousands of staff, mainly women, right through the Depression as sales of cigarettes soared. To produce enough Bristols, Three Castles, Gold Flakes and Woodbines to keep up with demand, staff worked a long day: up early for a 7.30 a.m. start and knocking off at five p.m., with two breaks totalling one hour and twenty minutes. The Wills were one of the first manufacturers in Britain to provide a staff canteen, medical and dental clinic, and bonus and superannuation schemes. The brisk sale of cigarettes helped fortify Bristol from the Depression. 'The pubs open early; the shops are doing a brisk trade; the wireless and gramophone establishments are grinding out tunes; food of the cheaper sort seems plentiful; and the crowd scene has a hearty eighteenth-century quality,' approved Priestley.

And at the Bourneville estate near Birmingham, the Utopian village conceived by George Cadbury, the chocolate factory's staff enjoyed as good a life as any worker's in Britain. By 1933, Bourneville had grown into a small town with tree-lined roads, open spaces, houses with gardens and a plethora of recreational facilities. An amazed Priestley watched people racing model yachts on a man-made lake, playing games in clubrooms, studying in adult education and general self-improvement classes. Although the writer fretted that Bourneville's inhabitants seemed cosseted and organised, he could not argue with the death rate there: measured per thousand, it was nearly half that of England and Wales. Moreover, Bourneville-raised children were taller and stronger than any others in Britain. Priestley, staring out of the top window of a double-decker tram as it made its way through Birmingham, described the city that had invented the steam engine as 'a parade of mean dinginess'. Compared with Birmingham, which was sinking deeper and deeper into the Depression, Bourneville was indeed Utopia.

As the situation worsened, Prime Minister Ramsay MacDonald adopted a fatalistic attitude. 'So, my friends, we are not on trial; it is the system under which we live,' he told a party conference in the depths of the Depression. 'It has broken down, not only in this little island; it has broken down in Europe, in Asia, in America; it has broken down everywhere as it was bound to break down.' Yet if the system had truly broken, as the prime minister seemingly knew it would, what system did he have in mind as a replacement? And if he had one, why had he not been furiously working on it instead of waiting for the boat to float? Britain's fundamental problem was the special areas, running sores in an otherwise decent society, and it was unlikely they would be rescued from their misery even in the event of a miraculous recovery in international trade.

MacDonald was not, however, totally passive. He sought advice, notably from the dour Scottish mandarin Sir John Anderson. Although by no means an economist, 'Pompous Jock' (as some of his colleagues dubbed him) had the prime minister's ear. When asked for his views on the need for concerted action, Anderson gave it as his firm conviction that unemployment was not nearly as dire as portrayed because of widespread abuse of the dole, despite overwhelming evidence to the contrary. Further, it was a waste of time pouring money into depressed industries while world trade itself was so depressed. And anyway, the 'artificial provision of employment' through public works programmes would hardly make a dent in the dole queues. As such, Anderson's observations amounted to nothing more than a statement of Britain's helplessness before forces over which it had no control, confirming the prevailing view that the only sensible strategy was to sit and hope. Sir John summoned up a nautical metaphor to describe this helplessness. The position of the government, he said, was like that 'of a great ship which has run aground on a falling tide', and thus nothing could be done 'to get the ship afloat until in the course of nature the tide again begins to flow'. In short, Britain was shipwrecked.

The captain of the ship promptly replied, 'Your letter expresses exactly my own frame of mind.'

Predictably, a Treasury report more or less endorsed Anderson's gloomy conclusions that a bigger public works programme could not deliver the desired results – that is, adequate profits to pay for the projects. There were dissenters to this view, such as Vernon Hartshorn, former president of the South Wales miners' union and now Lord Privy Seal. In his contribution to the prime minister's informal brains trust, the veteran politician argued that the old industries were in their twilight and would never again be in a position to rescue the economy; the future now lay with the exciting new industries such as the automobile factories producing cars, trucks and buses. And in the last year of his life, Hartshorn bluntly warned MacDonald that the government could not afford to wait for the tide to lift the vessel of state.

In fact the prime minister did not have far to look – only as far as Sweden, in fact – for evidence that there was an alternative to his docile submission to economic forces. The Scandinavian nation was about to make a miraculous recovery from an economic slump that had been just as severe and dangerous as Britain's. Blood had been spilt on the streets in battles between strikers and strikebreakers. Communists openly held rallies to raise recruits. And although the economy had not collapsed, industrial production fell 10 per cent in double-quick time and unemployment shot up to 12 per cent, higher even than Britain's. In late 1932, a severe winter ruined many farmers and threatened much of the agricultural sector. Yet while MacDonald was lamenting Britain's defencelessness, Sweden was soon on the road to recovery. By the mid-1930s industrial production would be 50 per cent higher than *before* the Depression, and unemployment back to an acceptable 5 per cent. As the situation stabilised, support for communists fell to practically nothing.

How had Sweden achieved its economic miracle? It was remarkably simple. While Britain produced one 'sound finance' Budget after
another, refusing to invest substantially in public projects, Sweden's
coalition government of socialists and farmers adopted the view that
emergency spending – in effect, a crash programme of investment –
would quickly pay for itself after the economy had recovered. Thus,
from late 1932, the government took a deep breath and loosened the
purse strings. In complete contrast to Snowden's infamous Budget of
1931, taxes were cut for average wage-earners, throwing welcome extra
kronor into the economic pot. The minimum wage was raised, with
similar results. A public works programme was launched. The most
vulnerable – the unemployed, the old and the ill – were looked after
with insurance, pensions and medical care. Government subsidised
prices for rural produce, which kept families on the land and slowed
wholesale migration to the cities – a devastating consequence of
unprofitable farming in other countries, and America in particular.
And although the wealthy paid a price through higher taxes, they
could hardly complain because commercial profits were made tax-
free. This was intended not as a sop to the rich but as a stimulus to the
economy, because their profits were reinvested.

While Sweden was providing a model for how to escape the
Depression, and while Prime Minister MacDonald was being fed the
advice he wanted to hear, the intellectual battle was beginning to turn
against the liquidationists. At Harvard University, Joseph Schumpeter
still clung to his purgative theories. According to him, these slumps
'are not simply evils, which we might attempt to suppress, but forms
of something which has to be done, namely, adjustment to change'. If
you interfered with what seemed to him like almost pre-ordained circumstances, you only ended up with a 'sham prosperity so familiar
from European post-war experience' and a much more serious collapse later, rather like a crushing hangover after the party. Thus a
credit-fuelled interference only papered over the cracks, leaving 'an
undigested remnant of maladjustment, new maladjustment of its
own which has to be liquidated in turn, thus threatening business
with another crisis ahead'. It was hardly surprising that Schumpeter's
Harvard colleague J. K. Galbraith, who *did* believe in judicious intervention, held the elegant Austrian's views in some scorn.

In Britain, fellow Austrian Friedrich Hayek had not changed his mind either. He could not see what 'lasting good effects can come from credit expansion' or from some similar artificial stimulus because they only delayed the 'lasting adjustment'. It was best to wait for 'a permanent cure by the slow process of adapting the structure of production'. It was an extraordinarily narrow, unsympathetic, even hard-hearted view, but it had dominated the debate for years.

However, the anti-liquidationists were on the ascendant in Britain. The debate pitted the dry, rumpled Arthur Pigou, an eminent but cloister-bound classical economist from Cambridge University, against the worldly Keynes, also a classically trained economist but one much less rooted in dogma than Pigou, who clung to an almost biblical belief in the tenets of Victorian public finance. By the 1930s, Pigou was something of a recluse. A pacifist, he had driven an ambulance at the front during the 1914–18 war and returned to a life of economics at Cambridge a much-changed, withdrawn man. Although Pigou and Keynes had once collaborated on a book, they were now poles apart. In future publications Keynes would savage him, and Pigou was quite happy to return the compliment when his rival released his otherwise much-admired *General Theory*, a bible for anti-liquidationists. They had already exchanged blows on the famous 'committee of economists' – a turning-point in the debate – summoned earlier by MacDonald to canvass on palliatives for the slump. Others around this table included Hubert Henderson (another open-minded economist), the precocious thirty-two-year-old Professor Lionel Robbins (the only one who had fought in the trenches in the 1914–18 war) and the Bank of England's Sir Josiah Stamp (an expert on the British tax system and the author of seminal books on the subject). One of the joint secretaries was another economist, the little-known but brilliant Richard Kahn, still in his mid-twenties. Usually known as 'Otto', he had studied under Keynes and was probably his closest collaborator. Kahn had been working on his own ideas – soon to be known as the 'multiplier theory' – for five years.

Pigou's works, such as *Book of Money* and *Economics of Welfare*, were diametrically opposed to Keynes's *General Theory*, the book that set the cat among the economic pigeons essentially by arguing that a public spending programme was the way out of the slump. Pigou's review of the *General Theory* was dismissive and even scathing. However, he missed the wood for the trees. As the owner of his local grocery could have told him, the economy needed an injection of liquidity. 'Last October [early in the Depression] I took £19.84 a week for bread,' a shopkeeper told the author of a book called *Hungry Britain*. 'Last week I took £7.33. I now sell forty-eight packets of margarine a week; I used to sell twenty-four a day. I am not selling any cheese at all, nor hardly any tea. I used to sell ninety-six pints of milk a day. Now I sell about one pint a day.' As official figures showed, there had been a collapse in purchasing power, and the decline in the availability of money was casting a pall over the economy. Both foreign and domestic issues of public debt – a standard measure of liquidity – had dropped like a stone under Snowden's chancellorship; between 1930 and 1931 they were down by more than two and a half times, and it would be the mid-1930s before they recovered even to 1930 levels. It was the same over much of the world, except Sweden and a few other more enlightened economies. In France, domestic issues of debt plummeted by more than half between 1930 and 1936. In Germany there weren't any issues at all in 1930 and 1931.

Although Keynes did not originate the multiplier theory, his open mind and basic humanity attracted him to it. And of course he knew all about the velocity of money. As he once said in a BBC Radio address, thriftiness was disastrous in a slump. 'Your saving that five shillings adds to unemployment to the extent of one man for one day, and so on in proportion,' he explained. 'Therefore, oh patriotic housewives of Britain, sally out tomorrow early into the streets and go to the wonderful sales that are everywhere advertised . . .'

The committee of economists had not disagreed about the scale of the problems facing Britain – all had access to the same data – only about the answers. In broad terms, Pigou thought wages were higher than the levels of business justified, especially in the old industries, and would have to come down one way or another. Siding with him, Robbins was against wholesale intervention such as protective tariffs for intra-Empire trade. By contrast, Keynes believed in intervention – 'pump-priming' – to get the economy moving . (Later, Robbins would wish he had backed Keynes. His attitude at the time, Robbins humbly acknowledged, was like 'denying blankets and stimulants to a drunk who has fallen in an icy pond, on the grounds that his original trouble was overheating'.)

Meantime, in the City, most industrialists and big business in general still wanted what they considered sound, practical, well-proven solutions that, they believed, had worked in the past and would work again soon. In practical terms this meant low public debt, low taxes and minimum interference by government which did not, in their view, understand the commercial world. Although by no means indifferent to the fate of the growing army of unemployed, they did not for one moment believe economic policy should be framed for their benefit, for the alleviation of their misery. In this matter Keynes, who once said 'look after unemployment and the budget will look after itself', and other freer-thinking economists were very much on their own.

Jealous of his prerogatives and suspicious of ideas hatched outside the Treasury and its close ally, the Bank of England, Philip Snowden, the Chancellor at the time, believed the prime minister should take advice from him alone. As for Keynes, who was removed from the Chancellor by intellect, upbringing, manner, interests and imagination, Snowden considered him airy-fairy, not nearly practical enough. Although nobody denied that the Chancellor had a firm grasp of the technicalities and the figures, his principal deficiency was an inability to see beyond them, to divine an imaginative solution from the welter of data at his fingertips.

After the report was submitted (and largely ignored), 'Otto' Kahn packed up his papers and went back to Cambridge where he kept working on them. The report made no use of his multiplier theory. He wasn't the only economist working along similar lines, but in Britain he was the theory's parent. Basically the entire concept was constructed on the role of money supply – how the rapid circulation of a pound through wage-earner, shopkeeper, supplier, manufacturer and taxman would invigorate an economy in decline. As Keynes had told the housewives of Britain, thrift served only to paralyse the normal processes of commerce.

The Austrians thought the multiplier theory ridiculous. When the austere Friedrich Hayek visited Cambridge in the middle of the theoretical furore, Kahn buttonholed him and asked him to explain why it would be good for the economy to go out and buy an overcoat. The

Austrian said it would take a long mathematical demonstration to explain why not. For him, the concept was spurious – 'economics of abundance'. Despite their theoretical differences, Kahn and Hayek became good friends.

In the United States, the economist Irving Fisher had bounced back from financial ruin and was doing highly regarded work along similar lines, devising a formula for determining the value of money by the rate at which it is turned over. The irrepressible professor had formed an association to promote the regulation of the money supply which, he argued, would lead to the stabilisation of prices. More specifically, he thought the money supply – essentially the volume of coins and notes circulating in the economy – should be boosted.

In the dying years of his presidency, Hoover was belatedly warming to the idea of a state-funded recovery. Announcing that state-subsidised public works would be a 'new experiment in our economic life' that would provide a 'service to our people', he earmarked $2 billion for projects including the damming of the Colorado river as well as establishing a Reconstruction Finance Corporation with a war chest of $3.8 billion to channel into loans for labour-intensive schemes, whether public or private. The corporation was an instant success. In 1932 alone its emergency infusions of cash had the effect of halving the number of bank failures.

In Britain, however, the National government by and large continued to wait for the tide to turn. 'At its nadir, the Depression was collective insanity,' observed American economic historian J. Bradford DeLong.

> Workers were idle because firms would not hire them to work their machines; firms would not hire workers to work machines because they saw no market for goods; and there was no market for goods because workers had no incomes to spend. [George] Orwell's account of the Depression in Britain, The Road to Wigan Pier, speaks of 'several hundred men risking their lives and several hundred women scrabbling in the mud for hours ... searching eagerly for tiny chips of coal' in slagheaps so they could heat their homes. For this

arduously gained 'free' coal was 'more important almost than food'. All around them the machinery they had previously used to mine in five minutes more than they could gather in a day stood idle.[17]

Had capitalism failed the masses? Some of the best minds in Britain began to question the very system that 'had put the great in Great Britain'. Karl Marx had written *The Communist Manifesto* in 1848 and died nearly half a century before the Depression, but now his revolutionary dialectic was enjoying a second life as communists almost rejoiced in the economic slump, quoting Marx's view that capitalism was on the brink of its third and cataclysmic phase. As he had predicted, production was outracing consumption with devastating results, setting the stage for the workers' takeover of the factories from the debris of the collapse of capitalism, with the discontented masses rallying behind them. If the system could provide a decent life only for most of the population rather than for all, plunging anything between 10 and 30 per cent of people into abject poverty, it was clearly a shaky edifice. Perhaps it was even toppling. Certainly Prime Minister MacDonald believed the system had 'broken down'.

Communists were convinced their hour had finally come. Having gathered secretly for years in backrooms, cafés, local halls, pubs and bars to plot the overthrow of elected governments, they became bolder and emerged into the light, preaching on street corners, handing out leaflets in factories, infiltrating trade unions, mixing with bitter and resentful unemployed, and inciting walk-outs or other disruptions in Henry Ford's Dagenham plant, among other factories. They spread a message that sounded like salvation to people who had lost jobs, assets, self-respect, even a decent meal. In short, they preached revolution.

Following his soul-searing journey through England, J. B. Priestley had his own nostrum: 'We need a rational economic system, not altogether removed from austerity. Without such a system, we shall soon perish. All hands must be on deck.' In short, everybody must share the pain, which they patently were not. The fault lay with 'the shoddy, greedy, profit-grabbing, joint-stock-company industrial system we had allowed to dominate us'. A northerner by birth and a man who preferred people who made things to those 'who deal only in money',

Priestley had become convinced on his extempore bus tour, notebook in hand, that the City had got off more lightly than it deserved compared with the 'shabby, bewildered, unhappy' people of the 'special areas'. 'And I told myself that I would prefer – if somebody must be miserable – to see the people in the City all shabby, bewildered, unhappy,' he savagely observed.

There was no doubt revolution was in the air. At the London School of Economics, political scientist and Labour supporter Harold Laski was holding students spellbound with dangerously original ideas. Often lecturing to standing-room-only audiences, this Manchester-born son of a Jewish cotton-shipper inveighed against what he saw as the inhumanity of the economic system. The suffering of so many was an 'open wound' in British society inflicted by capitalism, he maintained, and there was 'no way of healing it save by bringing the capitalism system to a close'. Laski, who had also taught at Harvard, was furious at the rejection of one palliative after another that might have made the lot of miners, shipyard workers, jute workers and others – everybody in the special areas – a little easier. 'For every serious step which might end this tragedy finds itself thwarted by one or other of the vested interests which flourish under the capitalism system,' he argued, itemising free school meals, the merger of many mines in the interests of higher productivity and higher pay, a shorter working week, paid holidays, company pensions for aged workers, a public works programme and, of course, the government's refusal to relax the means test. 'Each of these founders upon the rock of profit-making,' he charged. Laski was not a communist; he believed capitalism should be overthrown at the ballot box rather than by revolution. However, unless these steps were taken urgently, he 'despaired of the survival of democracy anywhere'.

Whether out of fear of revolution or genuine sympathy, plenty of people normally regarded as moderate also wanted action. Even true-blue Tory MPs such as Lord Wolmer told Parliament, 'We want new legislation [for the special areas] which must be on bolder and broader lines . . . If the government does not rise to the occasion . . . it will find the whole House of Commons against it.' Others were meeting all over London to explore solutions before it was too late. Harold Macmillan, the future prime minister, formed a lunchtime debating group that might tease out the answers. One of the founders of retailer Marks & Spencer, Israel M. Sieff, established a brains trust to explore new methods of political and economic planning to avert similar crises in the future.

Laski's challenging views were published by the Left Book Club, a genuine phenomenon of the Depression. Launched by Victor Gollancz, son of a Jewish wholesaler of jewellery, it gave vent to a whole new wave of thrillingly risky left-wing views. Gollancz had an eye for talent – he'd recruited H. G. Wells for his former employer – a commercial flair and a humanitarian streak. His conscience pricked by the consequences of the slump, he massively enlivened the entire debate by providing a platform for scores of writers, many of whom might not otherwise have found a publisher.

A strong-minded individual, Gollancz had cut his commercial teeth at Ernest Benn's publishing house. 'I spend alternate periods of three months each, hating him and loving him,' Benn would write in his diaries. 'His business ability is tremendous, his energy abnormal, and he has made a great thing of Ernest Benn Ltd. The combination of my finance and his flair has produced the biggest thing in publishing history.' But by the late 1920s, Gollancz was moving to the left, openly supporting the Labour party. Also, he had fallen out intellectually with Benn who had just released his biography, a hymn to unfettered free enterprise called *Confessions of a Capitalist*, the tone of which offended his former protégé in these straitened circumstances.

In short order, Gollancz's new publishing house, begun in 1928, signed up a struggling author called Eric Blair, writing under the nom de plume George Orwell, whom Gollancz identified 'as a coming man in tune with the times', according to Orwell biographer Gordon Bowker. One by one, Gollancz scooped up a huge array of talent desperate to find an audience for daring opinion. Ford Madox Ford was the bohemian writer, editor and publisher who had discovered Ezra Pound and once hired Ernest Hemingway as a sub-editor for the *Transatlantic Review*. Ferner Brockway was a rebel Labour MP and journalist. George Cole was a labour historian and lifelong left-winger.

Out of this first publishing venture of Gollancz's grew the Left Book Club, launched in 1936. By then, Gollancz felt the time was right for a determinedly provocative imprint that could help provide the intellectual foundation for a more sympathetic order. The Left Book Club had two other founders – the iconoclastic Laski and the rebel Labour MP John Strachey, cousin of literary critic Lytton Strachey and a Marxist who had dramatically changed his colours since editing the Conservative *Spectator*. Contrary to its reputation, especially in its early years, the Left Book Club was not entirely a hotbed of revolution, more a commercial venture with a conscience that would attract middle-class readers; indeed it would be 'credited with turning many middle-class people into socialists and even communists'.[18] As the founder wrote, 'the aim of the club is a simple one: it is to help in the struggle for world peace and a better social and economic order and against Fascism by (a) increasing the knowledge of those who already see the importance of this struggle, and (b) adding to their number the very many who, being fundamentally well disposed, hold aloof from the fight by reason of ignorance or apathy'. So although the imprint's goal was to create an intellectual climate for socialism, it was also born of a fear of fascism.

With their yellow or orange covers, the books immediately struck a chord in Britain. A starting membership of ten thousand snapped up the titles on offer, priced at 2/6, with a new title released every month. Gollancz was far too astute to churn out a tedious series of political tracts, choosing instead to release volumes of history, science, fiction and reportage across a universe of subjects. Many of these subjects were too provocative (or serious) for other publishers to touch, but Gollancz fearlessly printed a host of crusading, *engagé* and earnest books, pamphlets and plays written by a unique array of writers. There was *Days of Contempt* by André Malraux, Gaetano Salvemini's *Under the Axe of Fascism*, Clifford Odets' *Waiting for Lefty*, Miles Malleson's *Six Men of Dorset*, and Hyman Fagan's *Why Capitalism Means War, Poems of Freedom*. There was even a *Left Song Book* produced 'with the assistance of members of the Workers Music Association'.

This string of edgy titles suggested a general enthusiasm for charging the barricades. There were numerous favourable tomes on socialism, Karl Marx and the Soviet Union, of which many intellectuals were in awe including the gullible Sidney and Beatrice Webb, who wrote the admiring *Soviet Communism: A New Civilisation?* But even hardcore left-wingers must have struggled with such dismayingly earnest titles as *Freud and Marx – A Dialectical Study*, or G. N. Sere-brennikov's *The Position of Women in the USSR*, or Leon Feuchtwanger's *Moscow 1937: My Visit Described for my Friends*. For a time the Left Book Club flirted dangerously with communism. In the light of the wholesale slaughter of innocents going on there at the time, there were some embarrassingly enthusiastic volumes about Stalin's empire. As it happened, it did not take nearly as long for Gollancz to see through Stalinist propaganda as it did some of his writers, and he would later edit a tome called *The Betrayal of the Left: An Examination and Refutation of Communist Policy*. True to the Left Book Club's goals, Hitler's Germany and fascism in general got short shrift in *Hitler's Conspiracy Against Peace*, *Swastika Night* and *Guilty Germans?*, among others.

Otherwise, the founders' determination to shed light on the dark corners of the Depression largely ignored by the majority of Britons produced disturbing insights into the prevailing inequalities and the width of the social divide. Ellen Wilkinson's *The Town that was Murdered: The Life Story of Jarrow* and Wal Hannington's *The Problem of the Distressed Areas* helped lift the lid on these unfortunate locations. The imprint was also responsible for some of the most thought-provoking literature of the period, such as Harold Laski's *Faith, Reason and Civilisation*. And of course Gollancz had his favourite authors, like Stephen Spender (*Forward from Liberalism* among others), Edgar Snow (*Red Star Over China, Scorched Earth*), Arthur Koestler (*Spanish Testament* and others) and Orwell, the Old Etonian with a penchant for self-debasement (Blair used to dress up as a tramp, although apparently looking nothing like one, and live as a down-and-out). It was Gollancz who took on Orwell's bible of the Depression *The Road to Wigan Pier*, albeit after some unapologetic editing by the publisher whose social conscience rarely got in the way of his nose for what the public wanted.

It says a lot about the mood of the times that the Left Book Club eventually totalled fifty-seven thousand members and spawned some fifteen hundred study groups around Britain, hotbeds of intellectual rebellion meeting regularly to debate a new dialectic for a better world order. Little by little, it turned into much more than a book club, sparking rallies, political and educational classes, stage productions, summer schools and annual rallies attended by thousands. The publisher established such a strong platform for the propagation of socialist ideas that a group of Labour party stalwarts approached Gollancz with an idea for a weekly newspaper. The result was the *Tribune* under the editorship of William Mellor, the former communist and conscientious objector, who promptly hired Orwell to become the literary editor. As left-wing views penetrated more deeply the intellectual consciousness, even poetry became 'tinged with red' in sympathy with the mood. As C. Day Lewis warned, 'It is now or never, the hour of the knife / The break with the past, the major operation'.

Despite the all too evident misery, it would be a mistake to think of Britain as a seething mass of discontent verging on imminent rebellion. Many Britons were blissfully unaware of the Crash, especially the carefree young. Denis Healey, a future Chancellor of the Exchequer, enjoyed a wonderful childhood during this period mainly because his father was in work as a technical school principal (it was a good time to be a civil servant because their pay kept pace with the declining cost of living). As Healey recounts in his memoirs, *The Time of My Life*, he used to cycle among the hills around the village of Riddlesden near the same Yorkshire moors that inspired *Wuthering Heights* taking pictures with his Box Brownie 2A camera, listening on the radio to the dance bands of Jack Payne and Henry Hall, clubbing together with his friends to buy the *Wizard*, the *Rover, Modern Boy* and other weeklies, and causing trouble ('My proudest possession was an air rifle, which I could use to ping the church bell a hundred yards away,' he recalled). As well as the stories, the big attraction of the boys' magazines were the tin cut-outs inside of racing car and aeroplane models. Bearing tuppence in their pockets, boys all over Britain used to rush to the newsagent's on a Friday for their ordered copy.

And the cinemas, spreading like stardust all over Britain, made life more bearable for all but the most impoverished. The first picture house in Glasgow, Green's Playhouse, opened as early as 1927, and within a few years Glasgow could boast over a hundred cinemas with a total seating capacity of 175,000. Even the 'Clydesiders' would soon have a choice of seven. Bearing dream-like, other-worldly names such as La Scala, Rialto and the Regal, the cinemas brought two and a half hours of celluloid escapism to the population, allowing it to forget its travails. Ticket prices were reasonable – just nine pence in Jarrow, three times as much on London's Tottenham Court Road. In an untypically generous gesture, Snowden had cut the tax on entertainment by half, making the cheap seats reasonably affordable. For your pence, you got two or three hours of thundering Wurlitzer organs (at least in the bigger theatres), deep purple carpets, polished brass rails and Arabian-nights lighting. Not everybody could afford the weekly escape, even at a few pence. 'There's no enjoyment comes out of our money,' observed a wife with an unemployed husband. 'No pictures, no papers, no sports. Everything is patched and mended in our house.' But if you had the money, the talkies were a godsend, a safety valve of immense social value. And in 1932, the National government allowed cinemas (though not theatres) to open on the Sabbath. Soon it began to seem that the opiate of the masses was not religion, as Marx had predicted, but the talkies. Certainly the Bishop of Kingston was unhappy about all this entertainment becoming available on a day when the people should be sitting in pews listening to sermons. 'Owing to a commercialism and securalisation [sic] of society, religion was being crowded out,' he regretted.

Although threatened by the cinemas, music halls still survived. In Dudley in the grim heart of the Black Country, Priestley stumbled on one playing *Parisian Follies*. The D'Oyly Carte Opera company was touring the Hippodromes with Gilbert and Sullivan operas. *Sweeney Todd, the Demon Barber of Fleet Street* was doing good business up and down the country, the audience waiting on tenterhooks for the famous line 'I wish the whole world had just one throat, so that I could have the pleasure of slitting it.' Far from the slums of the Gorbals and Jarrow, London's West End flourished. Right through the 1930s, audiences thronged to watch great actors such as Charles Laughton and Flora Robson in *Macbeth*, Noël Coward and Yvonne Printemps in *Conversation Piece*, and Elizabeth Bergner in *Escape Me Never*. And just about everywhere dance halls did good business, even in high-unemployment cities like Dundee where youngsters flocked on Friday nights to Patties, the Palais, the Locarno and the Empress. Similarly, pubs became bolt-holes for millions, noisy and cheerful places where you could drink a few pints and forget about your troubles. Some pubs provided bowling greens just outside, and many hired live bands.

Retailers also came to the rescue of the government as several chains sold cheaper, imported goods that, despite being 'mostly inferior and dubious' had the inestimable merit of affordability. The outstanding retailer of the Depression was Woolworth's. Founded by American Byron Miller, the British branch of the variety store chain adjusted its business to the times. Women thronged the stores, especially on Friday afternoons, which was pay day, to buy practical household items such as zip purses, fruit-preserving jars, tea trays, Marvel rubber soles for their children's school shoes, Johnson's wax polish, table and dessert knives, peroxide ('extra strong') to dye their hair blonde, curtain rails, shoe polish, wooden photo frames and jute wool, all of them for six pence; even little luxuries such as Eclipse vinyl records, metal toys and boiled sweets for the children. Perfumed soap cost only three pence or less. A few items, such as 'Bees' Seeds That Grow', were priced at a penny, making Woolworth's a place where just about anybody, however hard up, could find something to take home.

For many, the chain became an emporium of simple pleasures. By 1932, Woolworth's boasted tea and snack bars at nearly a hundred stores all over Britain. At the flagship store in Oxford Street it was possible to have lunch at a five-hundred-seat self-service cafeteria which offered 'food of the highest quality and the purest obtainable – home-killed meat only, pure butter and lard, no substitutes'. All of it was prepared 'on the premises in hygienic kitchens equipped with the most up-to-date electric stoves, ovens and power machines'. Members of the public were invited to inspect the kitchens, upon request. Even here the sixpenny rule applied: nothing cost more than the chain's top price, not even the English roast beef with Yorkshire pudding, steak and kidney pie, or pork sausages and mashed potato, although a serving of vegetables added another three pence. Most of the 'sweets', such as apple turnover and custard, rich fruit pudding and custard flan, cost three pence.

The British chain became so prosperous as a result of this affordable format that it propped up the original American one founded by Frank Woolworth more than half a century earlier. Although Woolworth's occupied the lower end of the retail market in the United States, in the Depression it was turning out not to be low enough and the dime stores, particularly the red-fronted S. S. Kresge chain and its rival J. J. Newberry, were undercutting them. It did not help that most of them were founded by former employees or suppliers of Woolworth's, these stores owed much to the original dime store chain.

Woolworth's nemesis had been opened by a penny-pinching, God-fearing killjoy named Sebastian Kresge, the son of Swiss immigrants to Bald Mount, Pennsylvania. Although already in his sixties and fabulously rich, Kresge had lost none of this dime-store retailing touch and in the Depression he flooded his stores with cheap goods, turning them into a lifeline for shoppers on the breadline and providing them with a little dignity by offering mass-produced products. The glassware might have been riddled with imperfections in the form of bubbles, dents and ripples, but housewives gladly forgave them their flaws and took home tea sets, punch bowls, candlesticks and dishes of what would become known as 'Depression-ware' for the family dinner table. 'Even in an empty-pocketed era, the glass fitted into most working-class budgets,' wrote one authority.

Although he was wealthy and ahead of his time as an employer, providing paid sick leave, paid holidays, pensions and profit-sharing bonus schemes for staff, Kresge himself lived the dime-store life, proudly claiming that he never spent more than thirty cents on lunch. The story sounds apocryphal, but it's also said that he lined his shoes with paper rather than buy new inner soles. A fabulous benefactor who would give away some $175 million in his lifetime, much of it to anti-drinking, anti-smoking and anti-gambling causes but also to hospitals and universities, Kresge was one of the very few of America's richest men actually to increase his wealth during the Depression. Indeed he might have emerged from it with more money than Jack Morgan himself. Almost tailor-made for the Depression, Kresge stayed true to his dime-store mentality right to the end. In a speech at Harvard University on the august occasion of the dedication of the Kresge Hall, he stood up, remarked, 'I never made a dime talking,' and sat down again.

But if Woolworth's was losing its touch in hardship-hit America, Byron Miller certainly knew how to reach his shoppers in Britain. A prolific advertiser, Woolworth's made sure that every item bore the heart-warming slogan 'British Made'. Everything, apparently, came from Britain: Happy Content darning wool, Chinosplash tap filters,

Marvel rubber soles, the 'best jute' twine, Devon cream toffee, Clock shaving blades, Scourine cleaning powder, even the tea (although more likely from British-owned plantations in Asia).

The government also had reason to be grateful to Woolworth's for the number of staff it hired. The chain found permanent work for sales assistants (usually young and unmarried women), stockroom men, management trainees (always men), cooks (women), managers and merchandisers (men). The stores were located in all the big cities but also the outlying centres such as Southend-on-Sea, Hastings, Bristol, Leicester, Norwich, Doncaster, Southport, Swansea, Edinburgh, Glasgow, Aberdeen and Belfast, among other locations. Career prospects were good, at least for men, because women usually left employment when they got married. The pay varied between thirty shillings and £3 for a five-and-a-half-day week from 8.45 a.m. to 5.30 p.m, much more than it was possible to get on the dole.

In time, the British Woolworth's became one of the most successful Depression-era flotations on the London Stock Exchange. Although only 15 per cent of the company went on offer, reducing the American shareholding from 66 per cent to 51 per cent, it raised so much cash that grateful Woolworth's shareholders in the United States and elsewhere banked a precious exceptional dividend of ninety cents for each dollar invested. The British chain had long since paid back the £50,000 it cost to establish it and now its dividends helped the original company stay afloat during the hard times across the Atlantic. For his sterling work, Byron Miller ended up as the world-wide president; he would note in his diary, 'The child has long since outgrown the parent.' One of Britain's great retailers, Miller kept the 'Better buy British' campaign alive right through the 1930s.

Hour of the Revolution

The men of Germany's Labour Service, the Reicharbeitsdienst, worked hard for their pocket money. In the camps set up by Hitler's new government, they got a few marks a day, plus bed and food. 'Labour service shall be the proud privilege of German youth and shall be service to the entire Volk,' announced the new Chancellor, a firm believer in the health-giving and emotionally uplifting properties of manual labour. Virtual conscripts, the youths were provided with uniforms that conferred on them a special status commensurate with their role, which was practically to rebuild Germany under a public works programme intended to be a monument that announced the recovery of the nation. Performing astonishing feats of large-scale construction in a remarkably short time, they erected stadiums, dykes for flood control, and roads, including the autobahn network of motorways.

The establishment of the Reicharbeitsdienst was the first major initiative of the Hitler government. To the disgust of the increasingly senile President Hindenburg, the former corporal had finally won power in January 1933, largely on a pledge to abolish unemployment. Faced with six million out of work, not counting a further million who were unregistered, and a fast-dwindling public exchequer, speed was of the essence, and the government quickly put all able-bodied men into the service. Trade unions could not object to such summary actions because they had been abolished at the stroke of a pen and some of their leaders imprisoned and tortured or, like the communist leader of the miners' union, murdered. The umberella Labour Front (Deutsche Arbeitsfront) was now the only organisation of workers permitted.

Its head was Robert Ley, a chemist by profession and a fighter pilot in the 1914–18 war, who was now supposedly a drunk. At the stroke of a pen Ley became the head of an organisation of some twenty-five million members – easily the world's largest 'union'. In a textbook exhibition of totalitarian economics, all wages were decided by the Labour Front, which also issued work books in which were recorded every detail of the unionists' employment records. If a worker did not have one of these books, he could not be employed. With nearly all workers under one wing, compulsory deductions were made for income tax. Finance to keep the men of the Labour Front employed on the public works programme was provided by a special business currency. To mop up as many unemployed as possible, Ley refused permission to use labour-saving machinery. As a result, preference in contracts, especially in the construction of autobahns, was given to those companies that relied mainly on pick and shovel. If project managers no longer needed their labour under their employ, they had to seek the special permission of the Deutsche Arbeitsfront to lay them off.

To make the numbers look even better, the government paid many married women a lump sum of a thousand marks to stay at home and concentrate on mothering their children and feeding their men. German schoolboys were also put to work in voluntary labour camps (although it made good sense to volunteer) from where they roamed the countryside planting forests, reclaiming wasteland and repairing riverbanks. Thus most Germans had a sense of involvement in restoring the fortunes of their nation.

Although the workers were virtually press-ganged into the Labour Front, the Nazi government made sure to recognise their contribution in symbolic, eye-catching ways that turned them almost into heroes of the Reich. Uniforms played a huge role in the service. Every recruit was provided with a total of four each – one for parade, one for work, one for exercise and one for sport – all of them bearing a suspiciously close resemblance to official army uniform. Army-like badges bearing swastika symbols were awarded for specific achievements, particularly in sport, and special enamelled stickpins were provided to wear with civilian clothes. No opportunity was missed to underline the significance within the wider community of a member of the Labour Front. A special dagger was provided for ceremonial occasions such as weddings; commemorative medals 'for true service in the Reicharbeitsdienst' were handed out after an approved period of labour; young men were photographed with their families, proudly wearing their uniforms, and were even provided with albums in which they could record their achievements on behalf of the fatherland.

But the ultimate trophy of the Reicharbeitsdienst was the emblematic spade ('your symbol of work and toil') with which all youth were presented when they arrived for their four weeks of preliminary training, which in fact bore a remarkable resemblance to military-style drills. They paraded with the spades, presenting arms as though the spades were rifles. They went from workplace to workplace with the spades slung over their shoulders, singing songs from the Reicharbeitsdienst songbook entitled *Youth, We Love to March*. These spades were never used in anger. Rather, in an obvious apprenticeship for army service, they were kept spotless at all times, neatly stacked in fours, while the workers used less exalted implements to dig, hew and carry.

The new government knew how to motivate its workforce. Under the Strength through Joy (*Kraft durch Freude*) programme which was financed by compulsory deductions from workers' pocket money, the men of the Labour Front were rewarded with cut-price cruises to the Mediterranean aboard custom-built vessels, with bracing tramping holidays in the Bavarian Alps and other exclusive incentives to toil ever harder for the Reich. The coffers of the Strength through Joy organisation, soon overflowing with the contributions of its millions of members, also provided sports facilities such as the stadium in Berlin that became the venue for the 1936 'Nazi Olympics', and allowed for approved forms of entertainment.

Such showcase projects were all part of the Nazis' elaborate, over-arching superstructure for the German people. Robert Ley's organisation made certain to control the workers' leisure time under a blanket programme that rigorously noted exactly how they spent their 3,740 hours a year of free time, and where they spent it. For instance, in the five years between 1933 and 1938, there were 21,146 theatre performances attended by 11,507,432 people, 5,896 hikes, 388 sports events, 20,527 'cultural' events, no fewer than 61,503 improving museum tours and 19,060 propaganda sessions conducted by the German Adult Education Office, among numerous other nation-building activities.

Hitler could not drive, but he certainly appreciated that widespread ownership of the automobile – the most desirable symbol of a nation's affluence in Germany as it was in the United States – would ensure the Nazis' popularity. So the government devised a car-ownership scheme for the masses. But instead of relying on private lenders, as in America, to provide hire-purchase finance, the administration established an arrangement whereby each worker paid five marks a week into a specially designated account. When the account reached 750 marks, the worker became eligible for a car.

There was only one car, the Volkswagen, designed by Ferdinand Porsche with a little help from the Führer, as Hitler would soon be known. Costing 990 marks, the 'People's Car' was a masterpiece of low-cost, four-wheeled transport with a rear, air-cooled engine and light-weight suspension. Miserly with fuel, this Depression-suitable transport could cruise at speeds up to 63mph. The Volkswagen was not the first German attempt to produce a low-cost vehicle – indeed it borrowed heavily from a rival manufacturer – but it would be the most successful. There was one problem with the People's Car – hardly anybody got one and certainly not the thousands of workers who had saved for it. Although it took longer to design, test and produce than planned, Hitler had by then started diverting public funds for war and could not resist the temptation offered by the stockpile of five-mark contributions. He appropriated them and applied the people's savings to the production of weapons. Needless to say, complaints from disappointed Volkswagen owners were few.

After a fashion, Hitler's totalitarian economics worked. Unemployment plummeted, as indeed it was bound to do when nearly every able-bodied person is *forced* to work. However, all that compulsory labour produced extra national revenue, and by 1935 Germany was creating about a million jobs a year and the government was dreaming of full employment. Never mind that the figures were blatantly fudged – the Nazis produced notoriously opaque public accounts to suit their propaganda – or that Jews and women were excluded from unemployment figures – many had been dismissed from the civil service and their places taken by Nazis – or that compulsory military service was soon absorbing young men from 1933, to many observers Germany seemed to be working again and they were duly impressed.

The result was that the new Chancellor was revered as something of an economic genius, within and outside Germany. Books were written about the miracle he had wrought, such as *The Economic Recovery of Germany from 1933 to March 1938* by a highly impressed Dr C. W. Guillebaud. Another economist, C. Bresciani-Turroni, praised Hitler's 'imagination and initiative' and was particularly taken by 'the quick suppression of unemployment' as so many other governments had failed to achieve anything like the same results. The Chancellor also had many admirers in America, among them the aviator Charles Lindbergh and, of course, Henry Ford.

Leaving aside the methods employed, it was true that, while other nations blundered about in search of solutions, this radical German government had discovered what many believed was the long-term solution to possibly systemic unemployment. At that stage no nation had an effective system for handling massed armies of jobless. Attitudes towards the unemployed were still rooted in the fast-disappearing days of agriculture-based economies when much of the food on the average table was grown rather than bought and when it was believed there was always work to do on the land; anyway, in times of dire need neighbours would come to the rescue. But the agrarian economy had steadily been overtaken by the manufacturing-based one with its highly disruptive cycles. Thus, few of the working population now had land to fall back on.

Knowing nothing about economics (he hardly bothered to pretend he did), Hitler simply dished out instructions to his central banker Hjalmar Schacht, and the 'iron man' of German finance (as *Time* once described Schacht) did what he was told. Hitler certainly had bright people around him. Several Nazi economists had long been scornful of the departed Chancellor Bruning's bitter medicine and would claim to be working independently on multiplier theories similar to those of 'Otto' Kahn, now back in Cambridge.

Hitler's government should get some credit for new ideas such as the 'labour creation bills'. These were bank borrowings that kick-started the public building programme – the first plank of Hitler's grand plan – and put wages in people's hands. Most of all, the Führer's admirers gave him full marks for actually doing something, for taking charge of a nearly chaotic situation. Although the price was a command-and-control economy, with practically every activity put under the jackboot, so be it. Prices and wages were fixed. The entire financial sector – foreign exchanges, banks, money and capital – was heavily regulated. Agricultural and industrial production was subject to control. Eventually, most Germans even lost the right to choose their own job, being directed into work at the designation of the state.

As practically the only member of the government with an international reputation, Schacht was of huge assistance in this. Behind the scenes, the head of the Reichsbank negotiated intensively to lighten Germany's enormous burden of debt and succeeded when, in July 1933, a moratorium was declared on all external debt. In effect, Germany stopped paying it back, just as Australia's Jack Lang had tried to do. Instead Schacht introduced complicated arrangements that reserved Germany's foreign exchange for those countries prepared to buy Germany's exports.

Schacht was probably the hardest-headed, most ruthless central banker in the world. He had been centre stage for years and knew everybody who mattered, such as Sir Montagu Norman who was a personal friend. In 1929 he had battled through one reparation negotiation after another in Paris and other capitals, fighting for relief from the annual repayments which were crippling Germany and endangering her recovery. He had not joined the Nazis – 'I wanted to retain my independence,' he once said – but he certainly mixed freely with them after first meeting Hitler and his closest allies in early 1931. He was so impressed with the Nazi hierarchy that he openly supported the party thereafter. Had he not done so, it is unthinkable Hitler would have appointed Schacht to the presidency of the Reichsbank in March 1933.

In economic terms Hitler's timing was perfect, if lucky. Having taken every opportunity he could to lampoon the existing economic

Above In its rise to power, the Nazi party presented itself as the saviour of poverty-stricken farming communities.

Right Present . . . spades! Practically dragooned into labour squads, the men of Hitler's Reicharbeitsdienst were provided with silver spades as a valued token of their commitment to the nation.

A creature of the Depression: New chancellor Hitler addresses the Reichstag in 1933 after crushing all parliamentary opposition.

After 300 miles on the road, the rain-sodden Jarrow marchers enter London in 1936 to protest the town's abandonment by the government.

The ship that saved the Clyde: The *Queen Mary* is launched from the shipyards of John Brown & Co in 1934.

The car that saved Morris: Bicycle apprentice turned automobile magnate Lord Nuffield (*left*) presents the 'Eight' at the Motor Show at Olympia in 1935, with the help of Edward, Prince of Wales.

Master of the 'fireside chat', new president Franklin Delano Roosevelt prepares to explain to the American people how he saved their banking industry from collapse (1933).

Arch-inquisitor Ferdinand Pecora in his New York home in 1933 before interrogating Jack Morgan about the power of J. P. Morgan & Co, the 'house on the corner' of Wall Street.

'So long, it's been good to know ya . . .'. One of millions of refugees from the drought-ridden Dust Bowl states abandons the farm in hope of a better life.

Bewildered depositors gather outside the doors of New York City's American Union Bank, one of thousands of American banks ordered shut. The sign advertises the bank's 'safe deposit vaults'.

The man who brought retribution on Wall Street: Embezzler Richard Whitney, disgraced ex-president of the New York Stock Exchange, leaves Sing Sing prison in 1941 after serving forty months for grand larceny. Barred from Wall Street, he went on to run a dairy farm in Massachusetts.

system, he took power when commercial activity was depressed, unemployment rampant and dissatisfaction at its peak. The German stockmarket was in a tailspin, following roughly the same trajectory as the New York Stock Exchange, and would not stop falling until average share values had collapsed by 74 per cent. This was not as serious as during the hyperinflation of the early twenties when share values had all but disappeared, shedding 98 per cent of their original price and in the process wiping out Germans' equity wealth, but it was grave enough.

Also, the two preceding prime ministers had done their level if unintentional best to hand a deeply disgruntled, increasingly revolution-minded electorate to Hitler on a plate. Bruning's austerity programme had only served to make Germans' lives even more miserable, while his successor, the conniving and ineffectual Franz von Papen, a member of land-owning nobility, had no obvious credentials for the chancellorship except that President Hindenburg seemed to like him. Von Papen knew virtually nothing about the national finances when he took power in July 1932 and probably no more when he left office.

The Americans certainly knew von Papen, though. In 1915, they had expelled him, then a junior military attaché to the German embassy, from Washington in 1915 for trying to buy up all available explosive materials and stockpile them in an effort to prevent the United States from entering the 1914–18 war. And the British certainly remembered him. Von Papen had acted as the go-between in the supply of German arms to Irish rebels for the Easter Rising of 1916 against the British. The French had also formed a firm view of von Papen. According to André François-Poncet, the French ambassador in Berlin, he was not taken seriously by his friends or his enemies, and was 'reputed to be superficial, blundering, untrue, ambitious, vain, crafty and an intriguer'.

Despite this glaring absence of credentials, von Papen had briefly formed a government with the help of the Nazis, who could no longer be excluded. The Nazis had exploited the electoral opportunities offered by the Depression to present itself as a 'movement' (as Hitler characterised it) with a grand plan for economic recovery. By the time von Papen's government failed six months later – to nobody's surprise

– and was replaced by the Nazis, the economy was in a much worse state. In a bitter winter millions of homes lacked any form of heating; children were freezing and even starving. Thus Hitler, promising *Arbeit Und Brot*, became Chancellor. He would for most of the 1930s be seen as a visionary and a poster boy for fascism – the movement that got things working again.

Certainly the Dutch were looking enviously, if nervously, across the border at Germany's economic miracle. They had been the victims of the very kind of purge that Hitler had publicly scorned. Government expenditure in the Netherlands was cut to the bone, including welfare for the poor and unemployed. Exports had collapsed, in large measure because Germany, its biggest customer, had stopped buying Dutch-made products. The nation was financially, administratively and emotionally ill-equipped to deal with an army of unemployed. Non-unionised workers, lacking a temporary income, were treated almost as parasites, forced to report to government agencies twice a day, generally waiting in long queues, submitting to the indignity of home inspections intended to ensure they were not cheating the state of funds. Although they were allowed exemption from the infamous bicycle tax, it was a back-handed form of assistance because it meant they were no longer entitled to carry the appropriate badge on their clothing or bicycles, thus virtually advertising themselves as dependent on the state.

Yet through it all the Dutch remained remarkably stoic, almost submissive. There were actually fewer strikes during the most severe period of the Depression – 1931 to 1937 – than in the relatively benign 1920s. Even token protests such as the rent-strike – a tenant's refusal to pay the landlord – were quickly squashed by the government without much complaint. Indeed, any behaviour that threatened the established order got rough treatment. When the crew of just one ship in the Royal Netherlands Navy refused to work after a cut in their pay, the government's reaction was swift and brutal: it ordered the Dutch army to bomb the offending ship, consigning 22 sailors and fellow members of the armed forces to death. In the face of such a demonstration of discipline, unthinkable in the Royal Navy, the rest of the protesters sensibly and quickly surrendered.

Albeit much less successfully than in Germany, fascists of a different order were also in control in an Austria still suffering the repercussions of the collapse of the Credit-Anstalt bank. The consequent economic slump had opened the door for Engelbert Dollfuss, the devoutly Catholic, diminutive (he stood just four feet eleven inches tall) and decorated former soldier. Dollfuss had become Chancellor in May 1932, heading a government with a negligible majority amid a ruined economy. His chief economic adviser, another liquidationist by the name of Ludwig von Mises, only made the lot of Austrians worse through his classically deflationary policies that also served to totally alienate an increasingly restless and militant socialist movement.

Dollfuss's situation changed for the worse after Hitler came to power across the border. For the next two years he was driven into one corner after another in a vain attempt to escape the domination of Austria by the Nazi party while holding the government together. Italy's dictator Benito Mussolini, who was also concerned about a resurgent Germany, was only too willing to help, promising Austria protection from the Nazis. Thus Dollfuss effectively became a Mussolini-style fascist supported by a paramilitary group known as the Heimwehr, or Home Guard. He banned the Austrian version of the Nazi party in mid-1933, and blacklisted the Socialist party in early 1934, but only after bloody pitched battles in the factory area of Vienna that left hundreds dead including women and children. Compounding this disaster, he also abolished many of the hard-won civil rights of the poorest Austrians. The Vienna massacre provoked American left-wing writer Tillie Olsen to write:

> There is a volume written with three thousand bodies that can
>   never be hidden,
> there is a sentence spelled by the
> grim faces of bereaved women,
> there is a message, inescapable, that

vibrates the air with voices of
heroes who shouted it to the last:
Down with Fascism!
Down with Social Democracy!
Long live our Soviets …

For his pains, Dollfuss was probably the most satirised dictator in Europe. His physical stature earned him a series of pejorative nicknames such as Millimetternich (after the great, much taller Austrian statesman Klemens von Metternich) and 'the jockey'. If you wanted a short black coffee in Vienna, you could order a Dollfuss, albeit surreptitiously. Playwright Bertholt Brecht lampooned him as Ignatius Dullfeet in *The Rise and Rise of Arturo Ui*.

Hitler's brutal foreign policy eventually did for Dollfuss. In July 1934 this unfortunate man was murdered by Austrian Nazis who broke into the chancellery, probably with inside help. Into this precarious position stepped the big-spending fascist Kurt Schuschnigg, a lawyer, a veteran of the 1914–18 war, a Catholic and also a devout anti-Nazi. With about 25 per cent of the working population unemployed – a percentage that was generally fatal to Depression-era governments – he attempted to copy Hitler's economic recipe with a comprehensive construction programme of impressive public buildings and dramatic feats of engineering, particularly in road-building. The Salzburg Festival House remains as a monument to this outburst of infrastructural grandeur, but Austria did not have sufficient funds to finish the entire job, and several of the showcase road projects such as the Grossglockner High Alpine Road remained incomplete. Eventually destabilised by Hitler, who demanded that the Nazi assassination party be released from prison, Schuschnigg resigned and his successor, *faute de mieux*, would in 1928 actually invite the German army into Vienna.

The seizure of Austria, which the Nazis characterised as an alliance, would mark the conclusion of the chain of events launched by the collapse of Credit-Anstalt. One of the occupying forces' first actions was to arrest the Austrian Rothschild, Baron Louis, and throw him into prison for a year, releasing him only after the payment of a substantial ransom by his family. By then, all the assets of his holding company in Austria, S. M. von Rothschild, which the Nazis had put under compulsory administration, had been 'sold' to a Nazi front, the private bank of Merck, Finck & Co, and priceless family valuables looted.

In Britain, Oswald Mosley was perhaps the most attractive politician in Britain and certainly one of the most promising. Square-jawed and dark-haired, with a compelling gaze, he looked like a leading man in one of the romantic talkies showing to packed houses in the cinemas. Women almost routinely fell for him – a fatal attraction that served him well in his career, although not necessarily them. Before his first marriage to Cynthia Curzon, daughter of a former viceroy of India, he had a fling with the older sister, Mary Curzon. After the marriage he somehow contrived to have affairs with the younger sister, Lady Alexandra Metcalfe, as well as with the women's stepmother, American-born Grace Curzon.

Highly intelligent and witty, Mosley was a compelling speaker who in Parliament usually delivered speeches without notes. He had been in politics since 1918, having entered the House at the ridiculously young age of 22 after a distinguished career in the war. First elected as a Conservative, he jumped ship to the Labour party six years later because of the Tories' brutal policy of suppression in Ireland. A member of a well-connected family of landed gentry, he had a highly developed social conscience. Indeed, one reason he became a politician in the first place was to help create a Britain fit for heroes home from the war.

Although young, Mosley had never seen any reason to defer to the warhorses of the Labour party. He brought fresh and interesting ideas to the Labour government, and he worked long hours to try to implement them, slogging his way through tedious committee meetings, producing scores of memoranda, and endlessly debating the problems of the mounting Depression with other socialists. Nor did Mosley defer to the City. He could not, for instance, see why bankers were so happy to lend abroad in these hard times when they could lend more usefully at home. In one typically penetrating memorandum, he asked, 'Why is it so right and proper and desirable that capital should go overseas to equip factories to compete against us, to build roads and railways in the Argentine or in Timbuctoo, to provide employment for people in those countries, while it is supposed to shake the whole basis of our financial strength if anyone dares to suggest the raising of money by the government of this country to provide employment for the people of this country?'

Bit by bit, his thinking led him to support radical and even heretical solutions. For instance, as early as 1925 his pamphlet 'Revolution by Reason' argued for the nationalisation of the banks and their mobilisation for the general good, more specifically for the purpose of putting idle men back in work through the generous application of credit. He was convinced that loans for industry would generate jobs, mopping up the unemployed in double-quick time, and deliver the wages that would boost Britain's buying power.

Like Maynard Keynes and other anti-liquidationists, Mosley believed in a virtuous economic circle. He had long thought the gold standard – the flag in which the City saw fit to wrap itself – a 'gigantic irrelevancy' that worked against the national interest in a period of high unemployment. He would abandon the gold standard and let the pound float. In this he was far ahead of his time, as well as totally offside with the Treasury, the Bank of England and all of Britain's financial institutions.

Soaring on from there, Mosley formulated a grand plan to tie the Empire into a huge trade club, which was also highly precocious. Under this arrangement Britain would sell her manufactured products to the Empire which would in return sell its agricultural goods to the mother country; an 'Empire bank' well stocked with funds would oil this complementary system of trade by providing loans, credits and other forms of finance. The arrangement – British-made goods for Empire-produced wool, meat, dairy products, wheat and other harvest of the land – would continue indefinitely, at least until the Empire became industrial exporters in its own right. Although the arrangement, given Britain's steady loss of non-Empire markets, would probably suit the mother country more than the old colonies, it was at least a plan.

A man of action who happened to be a politician, Mosley had worked on these ideas for years, generally with others such as John Strachey, later of the Left Book Club. Mosley was impatient to get things done. As such, he was the complete antithesis of the dilatory Ramsay MacDonald. 'Socialists have talked of progress but have sought it in the endless discussions of talkative committees,' Mosley would soon write. 'They have rejected and derided the great instruments of leadership and decision by which alone things can be done and progress can be achieved. So their talk of progress has ended in chaos and in flight from responsibility.'

The City and most of the business community had long been scornful of Mosley; but by the mid-1930s they were frightened of him. Mosley had become a significant and ominous figure, founder of, first, the breakaway New Party, and when that failed to take off, the British Union of Fascists. He was considered mad, bad and dangerous.

Oddly enough, the man who would quickly become by far Britain's most controversial politician had launched the fascists on a socialist platform. 'Fascism stands for good wages, short hours, good houses, opportunities for culture and recreation for the workers,' he wrote; it also stood for a national slum clearance scheme, which would rid the cities of their 'plague spots' and replace them with new housing, and for the creation of a hundred thousand family farms of 50 to 150 acres, among other worthy goals. All this seemed so reasonable that, at least early on, Mosley won the support of such political stalwarts as Nye Bevan, champion of the working class. And probably thinking of the slums of his own electorate, Harold Macmillan wrote a letter to *The Times* on 27 May 1930, and the *Daily Mail* in support of Mosley's pre-fascist ideas. The socialist writer George Orwell, however, considered him 'a noisy pedlar of "tripe"'.

But nobody remembered Mosley's socialist views by the mid-1930s. He had become a public menace, a raving anti-Semite who led an organisation of some fifty thousand members, staging increasingly violent marches, especially through London, like the notorious one through the Jewish working-class east London area of Cable Street where he was turned back by a stone-throwing barricade of militant Labour-supporting residents. That brought the fascist leader up against the police commissioner, Sir Philip Game, late of the eviction battles of New South Wales, who promptly banned the march.

The descent of a war hero and humanitarian politician into a posturing fascist who achieved none of his goals is one of the more baffling episodes of the Depression. Certainly it had much to do with Mosley's boundless ego and arrogance; but there can be no doubt about the depth of Mosley's plunge into jackboot politics. After the death of Cynthia from peritonitis in 1933, Mosley assuaged his grief by marrying current mistress Diana Guinness, one of the Mitford girls, at a ceremony conducted in the Berlin home of Joseph Goebbels where the star guest was Adolf Hitler, one of the British Union of Fascists' most ardent supporters.

As the British fascists became more threatening, the government banned uniformed parades under the Public Order Act, just as the German government of Heinrich Bruning had tried to do. Eventually Mosley heaped almost universal condemnation on himself, and many of his former political colleagues, such as Nye Bevan, shunned him. Probably worse in his own mind, Mosley became a disappointment to Hitler.

———

For militant labour, the British fascists served as a lightning rod. Despite their well-intentioned origins, they were regarded as the poisonous scourge of the working class. 'The flower of the working-class movement has been defiled by the jackboot of Fascism,' wrote the NUWM's Wal Hannington. For the trade union movement, radicals and moderates alike, Mosley was the deadly foe, almost the military arm of capitalism that sought to exploit unemployment in order to destroy the workers once and for all. To each other they fearfully quoted passages from the *Fascist Quarterly* about the 'final struggle for power' about to be fought on the streets of Britain and how 'fascist success in Italy and Germany followed upon capitalist trade depressions'.

But Britain was also resounding to the tramp of militant labour's much more worn shoes. It was a sodden line that trudged into London in October 1936 in a steady downpour, flanked by equally waterlogged bobbies in capes walking alongside to ensure the four-wide contingent kept in orderly lines, and well to the left of the road. Passing the marchers, tooting their horns more in support than the reverse, were Austin Sevens, Morris Eights, delivery vans and other examples of

Britain's fast-growing newer industries. A few curious bystanders watched from the footpaths.

As the banners borne by the cloth-capped marchers announced, this was the 'Jarrow Crusade', a non-party protest. They were accompanied by a few well-dressed sympathisers in bowlers, while at the head strode Labour MP Ellen Wilkinson, the Methodist and anti-fascist who would write the definitive book about the abandonment of Jarrow. Apart from Wilkinson and half a dozen women, who joined for the final stage into the capital, most of the marchers were middle-aged men, thin, tired, unsmiling but focused.

The Jarrow march had covered three hundred miles since leaving the forsaken town. 'For the poorest of those left behind their diet consisted mainly of potatoes, broth, bread and jam, or simply bread and dripping,' recorded the local historians' account *Palmers of Jarrow*. 'Women tried to make money by taking in washing, or by selling pies and peas or ginger beer from their homes. Men recovered drift wood from the river and attempted to sell it as firewood around the streets.'

The long hike was just one of several similarly arduous journeys of protest during the Depression, most of them ending up in donnybrooks of varying seriousness in Hyde Park when they finally arrived. One of the longest of these marches went all the way from Scotland to London to advertise the unfairness of the means test, along the way urging others to join them and register their protest against capitalism, which sought 'to starve and degrade the workers'. Other marchers bore posters stating 'By imprisonment and baton charges, they have hoped to force the unemployed into subjection, but they have failed'.

As well as the marches, there were numerous mass demonstrations, like the one in South Wales on 3 February 1935 that brought three hundred thousand on to the streets (according to the *Manchester Guardian*) to air their grievances over further cuts in unemployment benefit. Three days later, Sheffield police fought a running two-hour battle against thousands of protesters. 'There was bloody pandemonium, fighting like bloody tigers – and all the bloody town hall officials were out on the bloody balcony watching us,' recalled protester, Herbert Howarth.

As the Jarrow 200 entered the capital, another, bigger and much more threatening march of two thousand NUWM members was descending on London by a different route. Some in the bigger march had started as far north as Aberdeen some 550 miles from London, along the way meeting with hostility and kindness in more or less equal measure. This was the 'hunger march' led by Wal Hannington (among others) to protest against further unemployment cuts in areas that, as Hannington would later put it, 'had been rendered derelict by capitalism'. While they were barred from some workhouse accommodation, a businessman gave the men hundreds of pairs of boots to ease the blisters as their footwear steadily wore out.

The reception the two columns got when they arrived in London says much about the attitude of the National government, now led by Stanley Baldwin, after the resignation of Ramsay MacDonald and his virtual departure from politics. (He had even lost his seat.) Baldwin was determined to crack down on massed dissidents. Jarrow's easily contained non-party march was greeted by a few faithful while the NUWM were met by a welcoming party of police and perhaps half a million supporters. The prime minister was 'too busy' to see Ellen Wilkinson when she arrived at Parliament bearing a petition, contained in an oak box with gilt lettering, on behalf of the Jarrow 200. But the police were ready enough and in the ensuing exchanges, heads were cracked on both sides. As usual, the ringleaders of the hunger march, including Hannington and the veteran communist Tom Mann, in his eighties, ended up in jail for the umpteenth time.

In later years some of the marchers would say they did not achieve a 'ha'porth of good'. If the aim was to destroy capitalism, that is right enough. But the repercussions of such momentous events inevitably reverberate in many hardly measurable ways, and it is likely the marchers did far more good for the downtrodden of the Depression by taking to their feet than if they had stayed behind in the 'special areas' and stewed in their misery. The marchers must have felt at least some satisfaction when welfare allowances were raised the following year.

12

State of the Nation

As the sun went down, the busiest places in New York were the missions. Every night of the week they were overwhelmed by homeless men. Congregating mostly on the East Side but also on Queens, where many middle-class families had lost their cars, furniture and finally their homes in the Crash, they flocked into the Salvation Army, into shelters like the Municipal Lodge House where clothes were taken away to be disinfected and nightshirts handed out, into flop-houses and into twenty-five-cent-a-night hotels and speakeasies where they were grateful to sleep on sawdust. At least it was better there than the pavement. Rough as these locations were, you could sometimes also get a drink. If you bought one drink, that generally guaranteed sleeping space on the floor, sometimes a free lunch and perhaps another shot of cheap liquor around midnight.

A rough census taken in early 1931 established a floating homeless population in New York of about fifteen thousand, including some two hundred women. Crusading journals like the *New Republic* sent journalists downtown to take notes on this human flotsam and jetsam cast overboard by the Depression. 'Say a man in this town goes to the Municipal Lodge House for his first night,' wrote Mary Heaton Vorse in *School for Bums*. 'Until lately, he would have been routed out at five in the morning. Now he can stay until six. He is given breakfast, then he must leave, blizzard or rain. He can go next to a Salvation Army shelter for a handout, and get down to the City Free Employment

Bureau before it opens. Or he can find shelter in subways and mark the Want Ads in a morning paper.'

For most homeless people, the Municipal Lodge House – 'that place of massed misery' – was the last resort. Bursting at the seams, every night it welcomed a hungry contingent of 3300 who fought for the beds, benches and floor space. The Salvation Army did sterling work, even mooring a boat nearby for six hundred homeless seamen. And so too did concerned, well-dressed young women, arriving from the more affluent suburbs to prepare sandwiches for the down-and-out. Some of these volunteers took over stores and turned them into free restaurants for a melange of individuals that comprised 'men with well-brushed clothes, men who looked like old bums, young white-collar men, all engulfing enormous sandwiches, cheese spread with mustard – three sandwiches to a person and coffee'. The Crash had given the professional bums competition for the city's charity.

Legions of bright university graduates could not find a job, or if they could, probably not the ones for which they had studied. As Alfred Hayes, stirring cheap coffee in a Greek-run joint in New York, lamented about his class,

> *The bright boys, where are they now?*
> *Fernando, handsome wop who led us all*
> *The orator in the assembly hall*
> *Arista man the school's big brain.*
> *He's bus boy in an eat-quick joint*
> *At seven per week twelve hours a day.*
> *His eyes are filled with my own pain*
> *His life like mine is thrown away.*
> *Big Jorgensen the honest, blonde, six feet,*
> *And Daniels, cunning, sly, – all, all –*
> *You'll find them reading Sunday's want ad sheet ...*

They were 'all on the bum', scraping a dollar here and there, pestering the agencies for work, wondering if they should take a boxcar west, brooding about their future, perhaps even in their hopelessness thinking they might 'turn on the gas, jump off a bridge'. Cruelly disappointed, they wondered what all that study had been for:

We're salesmen, clerks and civil engineers
We hang diplomas over kitchen sinks
Our toilet walls are stuck with our degrees . . .

In the state of New York alone there were at least seven thousand qualified teachers out of work, unable to earn a livelihood in their chosen profession. Thousands of lawyers were either eking out a bare existence, compelled to work with their hands, or, in the more fortunate cases, engaged in some other business activity 'to keep themselves from becoming objects of charity', as the new president Franklin Delano Roosevelt said. The song 'Rich Man, Poor Man' summed up the abrupt reversal of fortunes of many once-wealthy people:

I've been sitting on a sidewalk
Just begging for a meal.
I once had a million dollars –
Can you imagine how I feel?

Rich man, poor man,
We're all people just the same.
Rich man, poor man,
It's not you I'm trying to blame . . .

Hoover's replacement in the White House had inherited a truly frightening situation. 'Raw materials stand unused, factories stand idle, railroad traffic continues to dwindle, merchants sell less and less, while millions of able-bodied men and women in dire need are clamouring for the opportunity to work,' Roosevelt summarised, without a word of exaggeration. The consequences of the Depression were visible right across the nation, but more so in rural areas where some families were actually starving, especially in the 'droughty country'. The collapse of farm incomes had coincided fatally with record low rainfalls. During a journey through Midwest towns and settlements such as Elbow Lake, Otter Tail County, Elk River, Kandiyohi, Big Stone, Yellow Medicine and Mille Lacs, local writer Meridel Le Sueur painted a horrifying picture of whole families whose ribs showed through their skin, like those of their cattle. As temperatures well over a hundred degrees Fahrenheit burned up the land, there was little water or feed, so the cows were too emaciated to be sold to the stockyards. 'The farmer has been depressed a long time,' she wrote. 'For the last three years he has been going over into the abyss of pauperism by the thousands. This spring after a terrible winter there was no rain. The village where I live has not exchanged money for two years. They have bartered and exchanged their produce. Last year some had nothing to exchange. We cut down trees in the front yard for fuel and tried to live off the miserable crop of potatoes of last year.'

The failure of local banks had indeed forced the inhabitants to resort to barter. A blacksmith accepted payment in potatoes for shoeing a horse, and a doctor saw patients in exchange for bushels of corn. 'We went to the store but we didn't buy things,' remembered Stanley Jensen from Falls City, Nebraska. 'We traded.' In many regions, America's currency simply stopped functioning as a medium of exchange. In its place people resorted to local variations of substitute money such as 'scrip' that had not been in general use since the 1750s.

Tough as nails, the people of the droughty counties had not totally given up. Farmers tried to plant crops in the hope of rain, only to see them ripped away by ferocious winds from the Dakotas that filled the air with dust and seed, ripped leaves off trees and dried up all moisture. The most severe dust storms enveloped whole towns, towering high above the houses and blocking out the sun. Still, communities tried to look after each other, keeping workers on at half the normal wage. Inevitably, children were pulled from school to help grow food for their own survival.

These residents were the victims of a fateful clash of events totally beyond their control and comprehension. The price of produce had collapsed, in part because of smaller and fewer pay packets in the cities where most of it was sold. But then the weather conspired against them too. 'No vegetables now, and worst of all, no milk,' wrote Le Sueur. Stretched beyond their limits and completely helpless, whole communities eventually abandoned hope, shutting themselves behind closed doors and even pulling the blinds. One farmer shot most of his cattle, then himself.

Expressing in a different way exactly what the new president was saying, Le Sueur presaged the end of the American dream: 'You don't starve in America. Everything looks good. There is something around the corner. Everyone has a chance. That's all over now.'

In the spring of 1933, just a month after Roosevelt's inauguration, thousands of farmers in Madison County, north-east Nebraska, marched on the local town hall to demand a freeze on all farm fore-closures. In these hated events, banks seized all the assets of a property to recover loans that were often worth barely a fraction of the land's value. By 1933, farmers had endured four years of sliding prices and many had fallen behind on mortgage payments to the banks, got into debt at local stores or been unable to meet instalments on tractors and other equipment bought on credit in better times. These protests took place across several states, sometimes taking the form of the 'penny auction'. With the encouragement of the fiery 'Mother' Ella Reeve Bloor, the Midwest's main communist organiser, these were coordinated attempts to block forced sales of farms through intimida-tory tactics. Overalled farmers would warn bidders to desist, or to offer derisory sums such as five cents for expensive equipment, often forc-ing the auctioneer to defer the sale in the absence of more realistic bids. Mother Bloor was trying to create a radical wedge of industrial workers and farmers, normally peaceable men who were turning mil-itant as they saw their future being sold out from underneath them.

Soon mortgagee sales would be banned in several states, but, penny auctions or no, others had come to the conclusion that there was no future on the land and were abandoning the droughty counties for greener regions. For millions of Americans who had settled in the 450 counties of the Great Plains extending from the Dakotas through Texas and New Mexico, the Depression was the last straw. Many had moved there over the previous half-century, hoping to make a life on the land. They had enjoyed some good times of decent crops and rea-sonable earnings, but most had found destitution and defeat. 'Men stood by their fences and looked at the ruined corn, drying fast now, only a little green showing through the film of dust,' wrote John Stein-beck in *The Grapes of Wrath*. 'The men were silent and they did not move often. And the women came out of the houses to stand beside their men – to feel whether this time the men would break.' 'Oregon or Bust' read a sign on the back of many a Model T Ford, Buick or Plymouth as whole families as well as single men and women uprooted themselves and headed for the coast and the cities, away from these dust-ridden, eroded, isolated and indebted communities where life had turned into an endless losing battle. It was one of the great spontaneous migrations in American history.

This great departure from the Dust Bowl had actually begun before the Depression, but now it turned into mass flight. Most people took to the roads in hope, some with barely enough money to buy petrol and food, leaving behind unpaid bills and taxes; others simply walked off the land, leaving it in the hands of the banks or city people who had the cash to snap up distressed assets. Woody Guthrie, son of a cattle rancher and real estate salesman from Okemah, Oklahoma, would immortalise the migration in songs like 'Dusty Old Dust' with the famous chorus, 'So long, it's been good to know ya.' Few understood what had really gone wrong, what lay behind the events that had conspired to ruin their dreams.

But first, and most obvious of all, there was the weather. Droughts had long been routine over much of the 450 counties, but a particularly severe one had begun in 1931, probably because of an extreme meteorological phenomenon in the Pacific; it would run for the best part of an entire decade. In the year Roosevelt took office, 1933, no rain at all fell in some areas. Next, the great drought began to spread, moving over much of the Texas and Oklahoma panhandles, south-western Kansas and south-eastern Colorado. The typically high prairie winds scooped up the exposed soil and moved it about willy-nilly, sometimes for miles, until the winds died down, dumping their loads against farm buildings, fence-lines, houses, all over Main Street. Plainspeople learned to dread the 'black blizzards', the invading dirt storms that might rise hundreds of miles away to envelop whole communities, leaving everything under layers of soil, dust and debris.

Adding to the area's woes, prices for farm-grown commodities had collapsed because of global over-production. A pound of cotton was worth only six cents by 1931, six times lower than twenty years before and three times lower than three years before. At that price it hardly mattered if the crop came up or not because there was no profit in it.

The calamitous collapse in farm-gate prices affected nearly all grow-ers, not just those of the Great Plains. The value of America's total agricultural exports was falling fast, in part because of the world's retaliation against the Smoot-Hawley tariff law.

In reality, no corner of America had escaped the general contami-nation as the Depression spread like an unstoppable virus. Even musicians suffered, like the Carter brothers from Hinds County, Mis-sissippi. Variously known as the Sheiks, Mud Steppers, Blacksnakes and Tennessee Shakers, they were hit performers who had taken their party blues style all over the state. But as audiences shrank, the broth-ers could no longer find recording sessions or engagements and had to jump aboard travelling minstrel and medicine shows to keep going. When even that work fell away, the brothers split. Bo Carter fell into poverty, another brother opened a juke joint, and a third eventually found work on a plantation.

Like everybody else, professional sportsmen suffered from falling attendances. After struggling on for years, hoping for better things, local professional baseball teams such as the Birmingham Barons were eventually forced to shut down, laying off players and staff, or to sell out for a fraction of their pre-1929 value. Purses fell so low on the professional golf tour that novice pros like Ben Hogan, soon to be regarded as one of the greatest of all players, could hardly make a living. 'More golf clubs and courses closed their doors and ceased operations than opened them during this bleak interval, and at one famous club north of Manhattan, in the wake of Black Tuesday (by now, the universal description of the day the stockmarkets collapsed), more than one third of the wealthy membership was never seen again,' explained James Dodson in his biography of the great player.[19]

As for the stockmarket, the 'barometer of the economy', it accu-rately reflected the state of the nation. In the four years since the Crash, it had imploded. The Dow index hit rock bottom eight months before Roosevelt's inauguration. On 12 August 1932 it reached 63, the lowest level since its inception in 1896. Trading was desultory, to put it mildly, and the tickers had no trouble at all in keeping up with the buying and selling of shares. The hero of the brief rally of October 1929, Richard Whitney, had been promoted to president of the NYSE, but now he presided over an institution that was a mere shadow of its old self. On some days not even the most trusted blue-chip stocks registered a single trade.

Yet as the quality of life deteriorated across the nation, Americans learned to stand by one another all over again, just as in earlier times. Anybody on the road looking for a job could generally expect a lift to the next town where there might be a few days' work, sometimes even a free meal. With help willingly given, you could survive. Two college boys who went on the road in the depths of the Depression recalled the Sacramento Valley in California being lined with stalls offering the best of foods at giveaway prices – a nickel for three pounds of grapes, and not much more for figs, quinces, peaches, plums, watermelons and cantaloupes. At stopovers they would order for thirty cents enormous breakfasts of eggs on buttered toast. As long as you wore 'unionalls' – the badge of the working man – you were pretty much guaranteed a ride or, if there was no room in the automobile, a precarious few inches of running board, because, with gas at just ten cents a gallon, few automobile-owners begrudged the lift. In a kind of odyssey through a country where most people were scratching for a living, waiting patiently for things to improve, the boys scored rides aboard Studebakers, Pontiacs, '28 Chevvies and, on one occasion, a Whippett coupé, hanging on for dear life as it hurtled through a back road of muddy potholes. As the humorist Will Rogers used to joke, 'We're the first nation in the history of the world to go to the poorhouse in an automobile.'

Later chroniclers of the period would wonder at the resilience and spirit of the people amid these devastating events. Journalist Louis 'Studs' Terkel, who was raised in a rooming house in Chicago during the Depression, interviewed numerous individuals for *Hard Times*, which would be described as 'a huge anthem of praise of the American spirit'. Historian James McGovern's *And a Time for Hope* described a nation determined to weather these wretched years as best it could. Many of the institutions of the nation might have failed the people, but so far, at least, Americans saw no reason why they should meekly succumb. According to McGovern, even the 'Okies' who fled to California in the great migration from the devastated farming communities did not suffer as tragically as the Joad family so miserably portrayed in Steinbeck's *The Grapes of Wrath*. Although many certainly finished the great migration from the Dust Bowl in a bad way – thin, hungry and penniless – and although many were ruthlessly exploited by the canning companies, it is also true that whole families were taken in by earlier migrants from the droughty counties. Now reasonably well established, these earlier arrivals helped the newcomers through the worst of the hard times. Thus it may well be that the soul-searing photograph by Dorothea Lange, 'Destitute Pea Picker in California, Migrant Mother of 6', may not have been entirely typical of the Okie experience.

There can be little doubt that most Americans did what they could for one another, within families and communities alike, in a simpler life. Families shared home-grown, home-cooked food. Having little or no pocket money, children had their fun on the cheap. Whatever the activity, it had to cost nothing, or nearly nothing. Ingenuity became the order of the day as girls contrived doll's houses out of bits of cardboard and lengths of twine while boys fashioned sports equipment from spare lengths of wood. Younger children wore the hand-me-downs of their older brothers and sisters. Indeed nearly everything was passed on from older to younger – clothes and footwear, trolleys and bikes, toys and school books – in a general recycling of family assets. Thrift being obligatory, many women made their clothes and even their underwear out of whatever spare cloth was available. Unable to afford tram, bus or train tickets, many resorted to Shanks's pony and thought themselves better for it. Cobblers were certainly better off: they became some of the busiest tradesmen of the period. Women still went shopping, but generally to the cheaper stores like the Kresge chain that actually expanded to meet the demand for low-priced goods such as the 'Depression ware' that would become something of a collector's item. And because the 1930s was still in the dawn of mass broadcast entertainment, most people could play an instrument and in many homes the piano became the centrepiece of the living room where family and neighbours gathered around for an impromptu sing-along. Concerts were organised in schools and local halls.

In these ways, many communities believed that the hard times retaught them the heartland values of living side by side, sharing a common interest in each other's survival, tolerating individual differences, providing charity for the less fortunate, and generally making time for one another. Uniting against the common enemy of poverty, they would argue they became less selfish, warmer, more human, more resilient. 'Despite widespread misfortunes, this is an era where people everywhere opened their hearts to anyone in need, and learned to enjoy and appreciate the simple things of life, learning to make do, wear it out, or do without,' remembered one writer in America's *Old Schoolhouse* magazine.

And there was always the marvel of radio to take your mind off things. The glamour medium of the day, it played such a huge role in easing the plight of the nation that its contribution is probably immeasurable. Shows like *Amos 'n' Andy*, the picaresque adventures of two ex-farm boys as they struggled to make their way in Chicago, were so successful that they bound Americans together in their common adversity. At its peak *Amos 'n' Andy* attracted audiences of up to forty million people. Even those who were not necessarily fans of the show knew the wisecracks that quickly became almost the dialogue of the Depression. Beautifully crafted, the fifteen-minute programmes were broadcast six nights a week. So popular were they that even movie houses were forced to delay screenings until the latest episode had finished and listeners could finally wrench themselves away from their radios.

By a fortunate coincidence, radio technology made giant advances during the hard times, hugely expanding the medium's range. 'Radios became more affordable with the sale of table-top models,' noted an historian of the medium. Much smaller and less obtrusive than the early monsters that used to dominate living rooms with their net-covered speakers, fat dials and huge knobs, the relatively inexpensive table-tops came in compact handsome cabinets – hence their later name of 'cathedral radios'. The more affluent could still buy mountainous sets such as Philco's Highboy and other 'musical instruments of quality', but the industry's great service to Americans during the Depression was the invention of ever smaller and more affordable sets, albeit while marketing them in ways that presented them as classy. Thus Philco, the dominant manufacturer, launched the knee-high Baby Grand. Quickly dubbed the 'midget', it made the medium available everywhere it was wanted, and especially in barber shops, where it was obligatory, usually perched on a stool in a corner.

Next came 'pee-wee' radios selling for less than ten dollars, then the 'chair-side' Lazyboy, advertised with an elegant woman reclining in an armchair, one ear bent to her handsome new model which rests on a coffee table. Although several radio manufacturers collapsed during the Depression, Philco kept on investing to the extent of establishing a British subsidiary at Greenford in Middlesex in 1932 that was so successful most Britons thought it was a British brand. But perhaps the ultimate radio was the one installed in the automobile, if you could afford it. Pioneered by the Automobile Radio Corporation's Transitone, it was a sprawling piece of technology that occupied half the dashboard, but it was rated the gold badge of affluence.

As more and more people listened to the radio, companies saw the commercial advantage in sponsoring programmes. Most of the entertainment was light music, humour, sponsored shows, big bands and drama: *True Story Hour, Colliers Hour, Soconyland Sketches, Maxwell House Show Boat* that 'rode a river of sentimentality', *First Nighter*, the mysteries of Sherlock Holmes, and the non-stop comedy of Eddie Cantor, who is credited with introducing the live audience on the basis that genuine studio laughter made the jokes funnier. All helped people through their difficulties.

Best of all, radio was free. Although the sale of records plummeted by a factor of fifteen, from $75 million in 1929 to just $5 million in 1933, radio's audience expanded enormously on the back of hit shows, hit programmes and hit numbers. The big hit of the period was the wry, stoic Bing Crosby version of 'Brother, Can You Spare a Dime?', written by E. Y. 'Yip' Harburg, who had first-hand experience of his own lyrics. A partner in a prosperous retailer of electrical appliances – some of the most popular pre-Crash items – he lost the best part of $250,000 on the stockmarket, but, like so many of his compatriots, he took the setback philosophically. As he told Studs Terkel, 'I was relieved when the Crash came. I was released. Being in business was something I detested. When I found that I could sell a song or a poem, I became me, I became alive.'[20] Thus liberated from the headlong scramble for wealth he had not coveted, but still deeply in debt, Harburg responded with the stoicism of the period and wrote 'Brother, Can You Spare a Dime?' in 1932. Much more thoughtful than many of the determinedly cheerful numbers of the period, the song mourns the poverty of a former construction worker of the very kind who helped build the Chrysler skyscraper the tower to the sun, as the lyrics say. Its completion through 'brick and rivet and lime' left him out of work, asking all and sundry whether they could 'spare a dime'. Construction workers were the people who had refashioned the cityscapes of America, casually risking their lives on a daily basis, as attested by the famous photograph of several of them sitting on a steel beam, dangling their legs in the void high above the streets below, while passing around cigarettes, soda pop and sandwiches. With the construction industry in a state of collapse, a dime would have made all the difference for many of them.

Even the brokers on the floors of America's stock exchanges managed to keep their spirits up. With little else to do, they amused themselves with elaborate games such as 'hazing', a form of initiation ceremony which they played on newcomers to the trading floor. A standard amusement was to invent stocks in imaginary companies and manoeuvre the gullible new boy into making disastrous deals in them before coming clean and, in time-honoured fashion, pouring water in his pockets. The brokers weren't making money, but they could still have some fun.

But the nation could hardly be expected to maintain its spirits for ever. The people needed some tangible hope of improved prospects.

Elected on a platform of sweeping reform, Roosevelt arrived in Washington as a saviour. Standing behind a lectern bearing a bald eagle with outstretched wings, about to take flight, the new president painted himself at his inauguration on 4 March 1933 as a man on a mission to rescue the United States from economic peril, a man who would speak the truth come what may, a man on a righteous crusade to put an end to the abuses that had landed his country in this plight. By any standards, his address was inspiring, memorable and, above all, comforting to a distressed nation.

'So, first of all, let me assert my firm belief that the only thing we have to fear is fear itself, nameless unreasoning, unjustified terror which paralyses needed efforts to convert retreat into advance,' he intoned.

With a sombre Hoover sitting in the audience – he had lost office in a landslide – and most of America tuned in on the radios that took pride of place in their living rooms, Roosevelt went on to present himself as the man for the task ahead in one of the most quoted speeches in American history:

> In every dark hour of our national life, a leadership of frankness and vigour has met with that understanding and support of the people themselves, which is essential to victory. I am convinced that you will again give that support to leadership in these critical days. In such a spirit on my part and on yours, we face our common difficulties. They concern, thank God, only material things. Values have shrunken to fantastic levels: taxes have risen, our ability to pay has fallen, government of all kinds is faced by serious curtailment of income, the means of exchange are frozen in the currents of trade, the withered leaves of industrial enterprise lie on every side, farmers find no markets for their produce, the savings of many years in thousands of families are gone. Most importantly, a host of unemployed citizens face the grim problem of existence, and an equally great number toil with little return. Only a foolish optimist can deny the dark realities of the moment.

It was only in the final minutes of this long address that Roosevelt mentioned a 'new deal for the American people'. Later dignified with capital letters, the New Deal would come to define the first phase of his long presidency.

A new deal for the American people: it was a huge promise, virtually an oath, and it would dramatically change American life in ways that are still debated today and that aroused furious dissension at the time. 'Dozens of our most important government agencies and programs, ranging from social security (to assist the elderly and disabled) to federal deposit insurance (to eliminate banking panics) to the Securities and Exchange Commission (to regulate financial activities) were created in the 1930s, each a legacy of the Depression,' explained economic historian Ben Bernanke.[21]

With his noble forehead and nose, patrician accent, clarity of diction and refined accent, the new president was a convincing and accomplished performer. People believed him; indeed they needed to believe him. This was the man Americans had been waiting for since 1929 – long years of a declining quality of life, years in which the nation had lost faith in many of the people and most of the institutions that had once claimed their trust. It had lost faith in Hoover, in banks and bankers, in the town hall, in big business, perhaps even in the American dream. As the new president had warned, this truly was a dangerous time in the United States.

Roosevelt was a virtual cripple, having been struck down by poliomyelitis twelve years earlier while in his thirties. His affliction had not stopped him becoming governor of New York in 1928, and it had not prevented him mounting a vigorous, even vituperative campaign that preached economic salvation. He had arrived on the inauguration platform as the man to deal with the perpetrators of the Depression. 'In my calm judgement, the nation faces today a more grave emergency than in 1917 [United States' entry into the war],' he told a radio audience in New York in April 1932, in an address adroitly aimed at the average American, the 'little fellow'. The order that had brought America to this state was rotten; 'A real economic cure must go to the killing of the bacteria in the system rather than to the treatment of the external symptoms.' Roosevelt liked to point out that two thirds of American industry was concentrated in a few hundred corporations managed by 'not more than five human individuals' and that a handful of banks directed the flow of American capital.

The statement was only half-right: J. P. Morgan & Co, to which he was referring, only had representatives on many boards for the purposes of safeguarding their own interests. Despite this, Roosevelt had waged a campaign against big business, portraying Hoover as a friend of industrialists who favoured large banks and corporations over the average American. 'The $2 billion fund which President Hoover and the Congress have put at the disposal of the big banks, the railroads and the corporations of the nation is not for [the little fellow],' he said. As for the Smoot-Hawley act and earlier protectionist measures, they were unmitigated blunders that had 'compelled the world to build tariff fences so high that world trade is decreasing to vanishing point'.

Everywhere he went on the campaign trail, the candidate had painted a picture of a hard-up America, a country of disappointment,

a people raped by bankers and big business, prey to 'promoters, slo-
ganeers, mushroom millionaires, opportunists, adventurers of all
kinds'. Roosevelt was not one to mince his words. Even the occasion
of receiving an honorary doctorate at Oglethorpe University in May
1932 provided grist to the candidate's mill. Contemptuously dismiss-
ing the foolishness of people who plunged into the stockmarkets, he
derided 'the hieroglyphics called stock quotations which proclaimed
that their wealth was mounting miraculously without any work or
effort on their part'. He rarely missed an opportunity to attack big-city
bankers: 'Many who were called and who are still pleased to call themselves the leaders of finance celebrated and assured us of an eternal
future for this easy-chair mode of living.' They had robbed not only
themselves but 'much of the savings of the thrifty and prudent men
and women, put by for their old age and for the education of their children.' The Depression had not only stripped Americans of the sense
of security to which they were entitled in a land abundantly endowed
with natural resources, it had removed 'the certainty of today's bread
and clothing'. Essentially, Roosevelt's argument was that a relative
handful of individuals were looting the economy. And it was indeed
true that a third of America's wealth lay in the hands of five per cent
of the population. Many impartial observers, such as W. H. Auden,
who would write a poem in 'one of the dives on 52nd Street' (as he put
it), would agree with him. For Auden the Depression had crushed the
soaring optimism of the roaring twenties:

> Into this neutral air
> Where blind skyscrapers use
> Their full height to proclaim
> The strength of Collective Man,
> Each language pours its vain
> Competitive excuse:
> But who can live for long
> In an euphoric dream ...

But now the nation had all too obviously come back down to earth.
Although Roosevelt was not a politician to pull his punches, neither
was he exaggerating as he described a nation that had come back down

to earth with a bump. Although it must barely have seemed possible to many Americans, the situation had worsened during his year-long presidential campaign. The economy had imploded, real output continuing to fall and unemployment continuing to rise (it was nearly 25 per cent, as high as Germany). 'And many of those lucky enough to have a job were able to work only part-time,' pointed out Ben Bernanke, an authority on the Depression.[22] (Coolidge, the inadvertent architect of this calamity, had died two months earlier of a coronary thrombosis at the age of sixty.) The new president could not have arrived at a better time to make his point. Roosevelt took office in the middle of the most serious of a run of banking panics. Almost as he spoke, millions of Americans were lining up to withdraw their cash, desperate to get their hands on notes and coins they could see, touch and store somewhere. Others were converting the cash into gold.

Roosevelt had hardly stepped off the lectern when he set in motion plans to summon Congress to a special session the very next day when a four-day banking holiday was declared – a deeply shocking event in the world's biggest economy. Pending the passing of the Emergency Banking Relief Act, which declared that 'a serious emergency exists and it is imperatively necessary speedily to put into effect remedies of uniform national application', every one of America's banks had to shut its doors. 'Except for what little was in hand, the money came to a full stop,' remembered one historian. 'The United States for practical purposes had no money.'

Unlike Hoover, who had been frustrated by Congressmen voting along local lines instead of putting the broader interests of America first, the new man in Washington made it crystal-clear he would have none of this short-sighted parochialism. Should Congress fail to adopt the measures that 'a stricken nation in the midst of a stricken world may require', he would not evade the clear course of duty that would then confront him. In short, he would bend the constitution and act unilaterally, if necessary. Faced with so blunt a warning, and staring at the collapse of the dollar, an intimidated Congress gave the president sweeping powers by passing laws that provided for a maximum ten years in prison for anybody undertaking any 'transactions in foreign exchange, transfers of credit between or payments by banking institutions as defined by the President, and export, hoarding, melting, or earmarking of gold or silver coin or bullion or currency, by any person within the United States or any place subject to the jurisdiction thereof . . .'

To describe that as a unilateral action hardly does it justice.

This all-encompassing act gave the comptroller of currency the right to shift a 'conservator' – in effect, a protector of deposits – into a bank at short notice and to send in auditors if deemed necessary. Basically, the new laws were designed to give the federal government much more oversight of the banking system to engineer its rehabilitation. It is a measure of the desperation of the situation that it took just thirty-eight minutes of token debate before Congress rammed through the legislation.

In fact the banking 'holiday' only recognised the inevitable because most of the banks were already shut by order of state governors. But at least it gave the beleaguered US Treasury's mint – the Bureau of Engraving and Printing – the time to rush out enough currency to meet the demand for notes and coins to keep the economy going. Incredibly, the mighty American banking industry had come down to that. As the president would say in the first of his famous radio 'fireside chats' delivered late at night from the White House study, 'scarcely a bank in the country was open to do business'. As an indictment of the quality of the supervisory system he had inherited, the 'holiday' spoke volumes.

It was not just the more vulnerable local banks that were in trouble. Right through February, for example, there had been alarming rumours about large institutions teetering on the brink of failure, including the Detroit institutions dominated by Henry Ford and his family. This was known as the Guardian Detroit Group, a conglomeration of banks on whose board Ford's son Edsel sat along with other motor-city magnates who read like a roll-call of the great automobile brands of the 1930s: Hudson's Roy Chapin, Fisher Body's William Fisher, Packard's Alvin Macauley, Reo's Ransom Olds and GM's Charles S. Mott and Fred J. Fisher. Dubbed the 'automobile bank', the institution controlled twenty other institutions in Michigan with half a billion dollars in reserves. Even as he spoke, Roosevelt may not have been aware that the US Treasury was so worried about the Detroit institutions that it had just dispatched assistant secretary Arthur Ballantine there to check on their state of health. And if he had known about Henry Ford's wilful lack of cooperation, something he did not learn until later, America's favourite industrialist might have earned himself an inglorious mention in one of the new president's fireside chats.

As we have seen, bank failures were nothing new in America. Even during the prosperous 1920s they went into 'suspension' – a euphemism for closing their doors for limited periods that often ended in a permanent closure. Most of these suspensions happened in small rural communities where there was often one bank too many anyway. For example, nearly 4200 institutions of all sizes were suspended in the five years between 1924 and 1929, the years of the roaring twenties, when a bank should surely thrive if it was ever going to. Nor did all the closures bring despair and destitution in their wake because the deposits were often passed to a competing bank over the road without undue disruption to the community's fiscal stability.

Further, most of these mortalities involved small institutions. Of the 659 banks that ran into trouble in 1929 – a good year for failures – only sixty-four were classified as 'national' banks, which were the institutions the US Federal Reserve most worried about. Many of the rest were regarded as tin-pot, store-front banks boasting little more than a clerk, a manager and a safe. In the 1920s there was a remarkably high ratio of banks per head of population, for example, one for every thousand people in Nebraska. These modest institutions took in money as deposits and made loans to farmers for tractors and farm equipment as well as to local businesses for stock. While these loans often served as lifelines in troubled times, tiding their borrowers over during downturns in the price of agricultural produce, the federal authorities did not consider them important enough to play a proper role in the nationwide banking community.

Thus even before the Crash, America's banking industry was a somewhat ramshackle frontier system that had developed piecemeal. Far less sophisticated than in Europe, banks in what was easily the world's biggest economy lacked a robust architecture that recognised the fundamental role they played in communities, big or small. Indeed the situation had hardly improved since the early 1900s when a startled German banker named Paul Warburg observed soon after arriving in America, 'The United States is at about the same point that had been reached by Europe at the time of the Medicis', a period some 400 years earlier. All too soon, others would be in full agreement. The United States banking system was 'an archaic structure, which finally crumpled up under the hammer blows of the depression' was the judgement of a city lawyer named Ferdinand Pecora, shortly to become a household name.

By contrast, although the general economy of Canada was just as badly hurt by the Depression, not one bank failed across the border. Dominated by ten major banks boasting between them a network of some three thousand branches, the industry there proved almost shock-proof in the general disintegration. Canadian banks did not experience any of the runs that were routine across the border in America. Although some branches certainly got into trouble, they were quietly closed or merged with stronger ones instead of being allowed to fail. For this, banking theorists give much of the credit to the Canadian Bankers Association, a far more collegial and coopera-tive body than its American counterpart.

The American banking industry had been heading for a systemic failure ever since Black Tuesday. The first panic of the Depression erupted in October 1930, sparked by the Caldwell investment banking group in Nashville, Tennessee that had plunged heavily into real estate. Unfortunately, the group was the parent of the biggest chain of banks in the South; like dominoes, the failures rolled all the way from Missouri, Indiana, Illinois, Iowa, Arkansas and North Carolina right across to other areas of the United States. In November alone, no fewer than 256 banks went down in that first wave, taking $180 mil-lion in deposits with them. And in December, another 352 banks fell over, destroying $370 million in deposits. But it was the collapse of the Bank of the United States, taking with it a further $200 million of its customers' wealth, as well as two hundred smaller banks, that truly shook the faith of depositors everywhere. In that year, no fewer than 1352 banks locked their doors, nearly half of them in just two months, precipitating a crisis of confidence among millions of depositors who had lost their savings.

A second panic started in March 1931, turning more serious later in the year partly as the result of speculators attacking the dollar when Britain went off the gold standard. Fearing a devaluation of the currency, central banks around the world converted huge quantities of dollar-denominated assets into gold in September and October, depleting the Federal Reserve's gold deposits to dangerously low levels. In turn that provoked a rush by American depositors to withdraw their funds and convert them into the yellow metal – a substitute for currency that was increasingly seen as perhaps the only truly safe store of wealth. A later third crisis, according to students of the Depression, was confined principally to the Chicago area. But however many crises there were, the results were uniformly destructive. No fewer than 2294 banks failed in 1931, brought down in the main by the deteriorating finances of their clients. In that year the creaking edifice of the banking system looked to be on the brink of collapse. Many Americans were withdrawing their money and storing it elsewhere – under mattresses, even in coffee tins in the back garden. As in medieval times in Europe, people began to hoard their wealth, and the monetary system – a hallmark of civilised nations – was in danger of complete meltdown.

The Federal Reserve, which was dominated by businessmen obsessed with 'practical' measures, was largely impervious to the development of theoretical solutions that might have worked to good effect in this fast-developing crisis. Nor was the Fed interested in learning how Britain had dealt with broadly similar crises. In fact Britain had been running a stable nationwide banking system for over a hundred years, ever since the Panic of 1825 triggered in the main by the fragility of small, undercapitalised institutions. These were, of course, the very ones collapsing like cards all over America.

The much-maligned Hoover had done his best to pump money into the system. 'The 72nd Congress [between 1931 and 1933] introduced more than 50 bills to increase the money supply,' noted economic historian John H. Wood. Also, the situation inherited by Roosevelt would have been much worse but for the Reconstruction Finance Corporation established by the defeated president in the teeth of fierce opposition from much of the banking industry, which saw no need for it. The RFC, as it was universally known, drew its funds through the US Treasury, which in turn sold bonds to the public to raise money, and employed them to good, if incomplete, effect.

Basically, the US Fed was uninterested in the security of the nation's savings. Instead of shoring up the nation's banks by pumping in funds to boost their reserves – a strategy that would have protected deposits – it opted to preserve the integrity of the greenback instead. 'The Fed decided to ignore the plight of the banking system and to focus only on stopping the loss of gold reserves to protect the dollar,' noted Ben Bernanke.[23] Thus the Fed hiked interest rates abruptly, offering a better return to foreign investors and making the dollar a more attractive currency to hold. The ploy paid off, at least in terms of the currency, and the United States was able to cling to the gold standard for another couple of years until Roosevelt was finally forced to abandon it.

Far from fretting about the loss of many Americans' life savings, half the Fed's officials seemed to think rampant bank failures were a salutary experience. Totally misreading the situation, they subscribed to Andrew Mellon's view that the weeding out of weak banks was an essential stepping-stone to recovery. Anyway, most of these institutions stood outside the Reserve system, and as a result, they hardly figured in the grand scheme of things, namely the defence of the gold standard. As historian Niall Ferguson summarised, 'the banking system was all but left to collapse'.

Still, it is baffling that the US Fed was so laissez-faire about these collapses, so indifferent to the appalling consequences, given that banks were often the repositories for the rewards of a lifetime's labour. 'The unacceptability of failure would perhaps not be so if they were grocery stores or butcher shops, where failure would be disastrous to only a few people at most; but bank failures paralyse the economic life of whole communities, not only through the loss of money accumulations but by the destruction of the deposit currency which is the principal medium of exchange in all businesses,' one authority pointed out at the time. It was an obvious point, yet it was largely ignored.

In close-knit communities united by the daily routines of life, the bush telegraph worked overtime as the number of failures spiralled. 'Horrible rumours spread through West Hill,' wrote Akron resident Ruth McKenney in her diary. 'Bank officials didn't show up at church services and weren't home at one o'clock to eat the usual big Sunday dinner with their families.' The next day, when Akron banks posted notices announcing they would allow depositors only to withdraw their money on a restricted basis, the word spread like wildfire and customers rushed their banks. 'The lobby of the First-Central Trust Company was a madhouse,' she remembered. 'Bewildered grocery store owners and frantic housewives stood in line with their pass-books shrilly demanding their money. Soft-voiced clerks explained, over and over, that "everything was all right".' But of course everything was not all right.

The newspapers generally did their best to calm things down, adopting the bankers' line and assuring customers there was no need for panic and the monetary system was sound. But the people still wanted to withdraw their money and there was never enough in the vaults to meet demand. As is standard practice everywhere, banks did not retain more than a percentage of deposits on hand, instead putting the money out to work in investments. Evidence would later emerge that the big banks were, in fact, quietly hoarding cash to protect them-selves against the risk of a dreaded run. Subsequent research showed that in January 1933 the total excess reserves of Federal Reserve member banks were nearly fourteen times what they had been just before the Crash. Institutions such as First-Central Trust Company were hoarding money, paying out a bare 1 per cent of customer deposits, even if they had just been lodged as wages.

'I didn't get paid this week!' a working man yelled above the din. 'You've got to give me some of my money!' The bank still shut its doors at midday.

When a bank folded, the manager usually hung a one-word sign on the door saying 'Closed', and went home. After the hue and cry died down, most depositors had no option other than to take it stoically. One daughter remembered her father coming home and announcing, 'Well, that means I'll have to work even harder now. Standing there crying isn't going to help.'

The toll on bank managers, who had to face the wrath of their own community, was high. Although there are no reliable figures on the number of suicides resulting from the Depression, the anecdotal evi-dence is that, unable to deal with the harm the closures caused to their neighbours, or the vilification they came to endure, more local bank managers killed themselves than in any other occupation. A joke began to do the rounds: 'One banker in my state attempted to marry a white woman and they lynched him.'

Once regulators got into the system, it would turn out that even large group banks were disgracefully run, of which Henry Ford's institutions were a prime example. Group banks were assumed to be a safe halfway house between independent local banks and the branch banks of nationwide chains, but it would soon become clear that the Ford-run Detroit Bankers company treated depositors and investors like fools. To acquire Detroit Bankers' total resources of $750 million, a dozen men had advanced just $1200 apiece. Against these paltry commitments, an issue of 120 'trustee shares' gave them all the voting rights – in short, total control. But when they were listed on the Detroit Stock Exchange, the shares had taken off, basically on the back of the trustees' huge reputations in the motor city. Just before it got into trouble, the group's stockholders were assured the institution had bravely soldiered through 'the exceptionally trying times'. In truth, it was insolvent.

The management also turned out to be incompetent, and probably in thrall to the directors. Indeed, Edsel, whose name would later grace Ford's biggest flop, would tell a subsequent inquiry into Wall Street and the banking industry that he could not even remember attending any meetings of the board. Regulators were appalled at the laxity they discovered. 'Bad management' was the judgement of Alfred P. Leyburn, Detroit's national bank examiner. 'And when you say bad management you say a mouthful. It would have taken Houdini to open that bank.'

Most of all, though, Roosevelt's regulators were appalled by Henry Ford's behaviour. When the crisis at the Detroit banks first came to light, the RFC offered to throw a lifeline in the form of a substantial loan as a way of averting what would surely turn into a fatal run with the usual serious consequences. A rescue operation might have averted the loss of thousands of individual deposits. As it happened, Ford had substantial deposits ($7 million) of his own in one bank, Union Guardian Trust. The terms of the deal stated that Ford would have to subordinate this $7 million as a pre-condition of the loan. In short, he would lose his money before the individual depositors lost theirs. Ford flatly refused, precipitating the first and probably the most serious crisis of Roosevelt's first presidency.

However, this first-hand experience of the ineptitude and the obstinacy disfiguring the financial industry was an enlightening experience for the new administration, confirming what Roosevelt had suspected, and henceforth it would drive a hard bargain. And so, the nation's banks were permitted to reopen only after an examiner deemed them to be financially secure. Within three days, five thousand banks – roughly half the total – were back in business, and the rest reopened on a rolling basis. The nationwide run had been averted by the kind of coordinated response that would become a feature of the New Deal. 'People will again be glad to have their money where it will be safely taken care of and where they can use it conveniently at any time,' Roosevelt reassured his listeners in his next fireside chat. 'I can assure you that it is safer to keep your money in a reopened bank than under the mattress.'

Predictably, there was a turn of the knife. The politician in the president could not resist laying the blame on his detractors in Wall Street. 'Some of our bankers had shown themselves either incompetent or dishonest in their handling of the people's funds,' Roosevelt said. 'They had used the money entrusted to them in speculations and unwise loans. This was of course not true in the vast majority of our banks but it was true in enough of them to shock the people for a time into a sense of insecurity and to put them into a frame of mind where they did not differentiate, but seemed to assume that the acts of a comparative few had tainted them all.'

It must have taken an effort for Roosevelt not to name Henry Ford in this diatribe. In lambasting the nation's bankers, Roosevelt surely had right on his side. Although the very large majority of Americans had not played the stockmarket, let alone borrowed on margin, many of the banks had made their customers' deposits available for others to do so through city branches or other channels. Thus, although innocent of reckless speculation, America's depositors would eventually lose about $140 billion of their hard-earned money through bank failures – equivalent to about 15 per cent of the nation's combined life savings.

After this immediate emergency was over, Roosevelt came on the radio again to explain that he had been most concerned by the slow and inexorable collapse in the value of America's major assets. Like all his other fireside chats, it was carefully framed for the 'little people' who would always be his main constituency. And, given the raw power of the United States economy, it was as neat a summary as anybody made of the inherently ridiculous situation – the compounded result of one blunder after another that he had inherited:

Two months ago we were facing serious problems. The country was dying by inches. It was dying because trade and commerce had declined to dangerously low levels; prices for basic commodities were such as to destroy the value of the assets of national institutions such as banks, savings banks, insurance companies and others. These institutions, because of their great needs, were foreclosing mortgages, calling loans, refusing credit. Thus there was actually in process the destruction of the property of millions of people who had borrowed money on that property in terms of dollars which had had an entirely different value from the level of March 1933.

The president had been faced with two stark options. One was to allow the foreclosures of the banks to roll onwards, destroying everything in their path like an unstoppable financial tsunami. The other was to take drastic action. As a member of the president's brains trust summed it up, 'The policies which vanquished the bank crisis were thoroughly conservative policies. The sole departure from convention lay in the swiftness and boldness with which they were carried out.' The administration also used the best available tool in the form of Hoover's Reconstruction Finance Corporation, converting it into a band-aid for banks. As the industry teetered on the brink with incalculable consequences, this organisation pumped staggering sums into banking. In total, the RFC assisted 6800 banking institutions, big and small. Also, with a new-found confidence based on Washington's explicit support, the RFC's regulators were free to do what they had long wanted, namely, clear out the Augean stables. Empowered by shareholdings in the banks acquired through the injection of federal funds, they moved on to boards and demanded reductions in the swollen salaries of top management. Sometimes they even insisted on the sacking of incompetent executives.

There can be no doubt that Roosevelt's first intervention was as effective as it was decisive. After years of routine bank failures in the hundreds and even thousands, the American banking system got something new and it was called stability. Starting from April 1933, bank failures declined steadily to increasingly low, almost negligible levels. However, it would be years before Americans regained their faith in the integrity of the banking system as a whole.

13

The New Deal

Having acted swiftly and boldly to stem a nationwide banking collapse, Roosevelt kept right on going into his legendary first hundred days as his administration launched one new government agency after another. Combined, these agencies would be known as the 'alphabet soup'; the best known – or most notorious – was the National Recovery Administration under retired general Hugh S. Johnson. The NRA had almost unlimited powers, and General Johnson revelled in them. As a biographer wrote of the hard-drinking, cigar-smoking, bull-voiced former military man, he was 'an admirer of Mussolini's Nationalist Corporatist system in Italy, and he drew on the Italian experience in formulating the New Deal'. Although the organisation was by no means fascist, there is something in this observation. It is known, for instance, that Johnson brought to the administration's first cabinet meeting a book by Italy's leading fascist theoretician.

To the resentment of big business which believed (rightly) that its freedoms were being usurped, the NRA quickly drew up a blanket code for all labour. It fixed a minimum wage, limited working hours, and forbade child labour. In return for their compliance, all businesses won the right to fly the Blue Eagle symbol over the legend 'We do our part'. Described by Johnson as 'a truce on selfishness and a test of patriotism', the symbol advertised a business's essential morality. As historian Arthur Schlesinger would write, 'The new emblem became the focus of moral and civic pressure. Parades celebrated it; speeches praised it; throughout the land stores put it in their windows and stamped it on their products. For a time it gave the nation almost a sense of wartime unity.'[24] By no means everybody signed up for the Blue Eagle – Henry Ford, for one (indeed, as he grew old and delusional, he became convinced that Roosevelt was in league with General Motors). But nothing if not determined, the general travelled all over America, preaching the message and sometimes waxing lyrical in the process. Quoting Tennyson's 'Maud', he once proclaimed in a speech to the National Association of Manufacturers, 'We have proved we have heart in a cause, we are noble still. And myself have awaked, as it seems, to the better mind: It is better to fight for the good . . .'

Between them, the 'alphabet soup' bodies covered the gamut of American activity. The Federal Emergency Relief Administration parcelled out funds to the droughty counties and other hard-hit areas for the launch of local public works schemes, though the states and municipalities had to contribute more than their fair share: for every three dollars earmarked for relief, Washington chipped in with a dollar.

The Agricultural Adjustment Administration paid out massive sums to farmers in the form of subsidies to stop them over-producing grain, cotton, tobacco, sugar and other commodities as well as livestock. In the autumn of 1933 the government even bought 6 million piglets for slaughtering. Although many Americans were starving, the agriculture secretary justified these unprecedented interventions, because, 'Agriculture cannot survive in a capitalistic society as a philanthropic enterprise.' The policy worked fast. Tobacco farmers, for instance, tripled their total take from the 1934 crop.

Then there was the Public Works Administration, which started pumping staggering sums into job-creation schemes that quickly mopped up four million unemployed, mainly young men. Within months nearly twice as many men had volunteered to work for the PWA as were enlisted in the regular army. Although they were not issued with ceremonial spades like the men of the Reicharbeitsdienst, over the next few years they would build or repair thousands of roads, schools, parks, airports, sewers, flood barriers and other infrastructure.

All kinds of new laws rained down on the people in those first furious hundred days of the New Deal. Congress even authorised the sale of beer in previously dry states, a shrewd, vote-winning move that created new jobs and boosted tax revenues from excise duties.

As these new agencies, especially the NRA, set about their work, they shed an unwelcome light on some of the worst practices of American commerce, especially in the case of the NRA. For instance, sweat shops were exposed all over the nation, many of which had sprung up since the Depression. The cut-throat rag trade was a notorious offender. Gottlieb's sewing factory in York, Pennsylvania, for instance, was paying women three to four dollars a week – well below the statutory rate. In fact, examples abounded in the state. Bernstein's garment factory paid $2.90 for two weeks' work at an average of three cents an hour. Pressers in the LeHigh Valley Shirt Company got cheques for four dollars a week – less than a third of the rate prevailing in 1930. Button sewers at the York Suit Company earned a paltry three to four dollars for a fifty-hour week. One silk mill actually charged women ten dollars for 'teaching them how to become operators', reported the left-wing magazine the *Nation*. In the tobacco trade employment practices were probably even worse; there were reports of $2.50 for a fifty-hour week in one plant and $1.60 for a fifty-four-hour week in another.

Agencies such as the Bureau of Industrial Relations started compiling details about child labour that made the abuses of Britain's industrial revolution look almost humanitarian by comparison. Many parents took their children out of school and put them into work, ill paid though it was, after employers refused to hire adults because of their higher wages. 'Man is the only animal that lives on its young,' observed one dispirited teacher as her pupils left their desks for a life of toil.[25] In one shirt company nearly all the 'girls' really were girls; only three were over the age of fourteen. A boy in another shirt factory told investigators he regularly worked a ten-hour stint from seven a.m. to five p.m. but also had to return to the factory between seven p.m. and three a.m. One garment factory used to hide its child employees in the cellar when state inspectors turned up. Two brothers named Dashefsky, the *Nation* added, paid as little as ninety-six cents for six days of hard labour. Another employer, having been fined by the state for breaches of the laws on workers' compensation insurance, paid the penalty by deducting it from each child's cheque.

Until the New Deal there had been no overall legal architecture to deal with these practices. The result was that in some states such as Pennsylvania, most of the production of cigars and clothing, from top hats to pyjamas, was achieved using child labour. Sensing a circulation-boosting campaign, newspapers and other publications all over America backed the enforcement of the legislation, publishing letters, articles and poems like the following by Tillie Olsen in a journal named *New Masses*:

> *I want you women up north to know*
> *How those dainty children's dresses you buy*
> *At Macy's, Wannaker's, Gimbel's, Marshall Field's,*
> *Are dyed in blood, are stitched in wasting flesh,*
> *Down in San Antonio, 'where sunshine spends the winter'.*

The National Child Labor Committee, another government authority, also uncovered unethical treatment of children in the 'remote' industries that had long escaped the public gaze. For example, in the 'piney woods' states of South Carolina, Alabama, Florida, Mississippi and Louisiana, which were instinctively resistant to Washington edict, the use of child labour was standard employment practice. Ten- to fourteen-year-olds worked in the turpentine camps for routine 12-hour days, clambering up trees and scarring them so the residue bled into pans. For this, they received between three and eight cents an hour. In the busy months, standard hours were 'sun-up to sundown'. Similarly, in the fruit industries children were worked to the bone, ten- and twelve-year-olds hoeing and digging, picking and packing from dawn to dusk. When investigators, coming face to face with youngsters working dangerous and unguarded machinery, asked for details of accident records, there were none.

One of the most obdurate of industries, the coal sector in particular resented the New Deal, even doing its best to block a dam-building programme on the grounds that the nation did not need any more power than the nation's coal mines were already supplying. In terms so hypocritical they are almost entertaining, John D. Battle, executive secretary of the National Coal Association, informed the Senate:

I wish to make it clear that the coal industry is not opposed to the government constructing dams designed to prevent soil erosion; is not opposed to the government erecting dams to control flood waters; neither is it opposed to construction of dams to improve navigation on the rivers of this country. There is just one phase of this program to which we object most seriously, and that is the federal government spending the taxpayers' money for the erection of power plants which, as we feel, are not needed for the very simple reason that generally, throughout the country, there is an abundance of power capacity . . .

At the time power shortages were frequent. His members also disliked the attack on child labour. Under the government's code for the industry, the only stipulation regarding the employment of children under sixteen was that they should not work inside a mine, but there were nearly sixteen thousand under-eighteens who did. The railway industry was also unhappy when Gertrude Folks Zimand, director of research and publicity of the National Child Labor Committee, warned, 'And the railroad tracks are no place for the 5,665 boys under 18 who are working upon them as "labourers".' Similarly, the iron and steel industries did not take kindly to a deadline under which the nation's blast furnaces and rolling mills were told to shed their five thousand employed boys and hire men in their place.

The mining industry's sweat shops were revealed as one of the worst offenders in labour relations. When miners complained at low wages or some other injustice, they could be laid off at the drop of a hat. In struggling coal-mining communities such as Young Township, Indiana County, coal companies routinely forced down wages or hired non-union miners and if miners didn't like it intimidation was provided in the form of a special 'coal and iron' police force. In areas such as Pennsylvania, unemployed miners sometimes resorted to 'bootleg holes' – discreet mines in small veins where they dug out enough coal to keep the house warm and maybe even sell some on the side at lower prices than 'official' coal. 'Many a family was raised on the money earned at these enterprises,' recalled David Kuchta, son of a bootlegger. Because some of the bootleg holes were perforce located in old, flood-prone workings, loss of life was not uncommon.

Unsurprisingly, many of America's toughest trade unionists emerged from the coal mining industry, among them John L. Lewis, who became the president of the United Mining Workers. A passionate supporter of Roosevelt in his first years in office, he worked New Deal legislation to the hilt, pushing the UMW into non-union coal regions. Organisers fanned out across the nation to bring other pitmen into the fold after the 1935 National Industrial Recovery Act granted the right to form unions and bargain collectively with employers. Unofficial patron of the NIRA was the German-born senator Robert Wagner, a veteran of inquiries into big industry, who argued that 'every worker shall be a free man as well as a name'. However, before the New Deal they were mostly just names. For instance there were no unions at US Steel, Ford or General Motors, and Goodyear and US Rubber tolerated only factory-wide unions and even then at not all of their plants.

The NIRA provided a valuable weapon for unions. A well-organised body such as the Pittsburgh Central Labour Union, for example, spent its regular weekly meetings running through lists of offending employers and planning an appropriate programme of enforcement. As union records show, it dealt with scores of issues at a time that kept hundreds of local businesses on their toes. Thus the Buhl Optical Co was placed on the 'Unfair, we do not patronize list' at the request of the local branch of the Optical Workers Union. With the union in the vanguard, in just one month, May 1935, there were strikes, pickets or other actions against, it seems, half the commercial community of Pittsburgh and its environs. Dairy employees were in dispute with the Rieck-McJunkin dairy plant; the Brass Rail restaurant chain was under picket by bakery workers; City Optical company was about to get a visit from the union's executive board over 'unfair wages'; the Teamsters were on strike at the A&P Tea Co; Sperry Candy Co, makers of Denver Sandwich, Tropic Breeze and other lines, had been struck over an alleged refusal to pay union wages to its engineers; at the request of the Pittsburgh Musical Society, Child's restaurant had also made the 'we do not patronize list'; United Garment Workers were unhappy that the Union-Made stores were selling twenty-five-cent underwear stitched up by prisoners; in competition with their unionized plants, members were urged to boycott products from Eagle-Picher Mining; Wilson Packing had been struck; and so on. While most of the weekly business was concerned with throwing bricks, stores that complied with the New Deal legislation also got bouquets as members were urged to patronise this and that business paying full union wages.

Full-fledged communists undoubtedly served on the Pittsburgh Central and other unions, but their official influence was almost negligible. America's first communist presidential candidate, William Zebulon Foster, had run against Roosevelt, although hardly anybody noticed. A former railway car inspector, Foster would never have been more than a footnote in the campaign, but he never had a chance anyway because police were under orders to arrest him just about every time he showed up to speak and booked him on a creative range of charges including 'suspicion of criminal syndicalism'. To his dying day, which occurred in Moscow when he was eighty, Foster kept the faith, refusing to acknowledge the pogroms in the Soviet Union and stubbornly anticipating a worldwide communist takeover. A likeable man, according to most reports, Foster's blue eyes, reckoned a writer for the *Los Angeles Illustrated Daily News* who interviewed him in the middle of his futile campaign, were 'mild, gentle, almost dreamy'. 'Foster, it seems, approaches the religion of communism not in the spirit of a missionary or a Savonarola, but as a priest celebrating its rites before the altar,' C. H. Garrigues elegantly put it. 'When the time is ripe, the worshippers will come. Meanwhile it is his duty to keep the font filled and the altar swept.'

Perhaps it never occurred to the ever-hopeful former railway car inspector that the main reason why the worshippers never came was because the president was doing the job for him through the New Deal. Although the New Deal and Roosevelt's bulldozing methods would arouse furious debate in the context of their constitutional purity, economic efficacy and even judicial appropriateness, they undoubtedly worked for the 'little people' often ignored in the prevailing, high-flown intellectual argument. For instance, as the Supreme Court was ruling on one New Deal-sparked issue after another in a furious bout of appeals, a million undernourished children were tucking into a proper meal for the first time in years. This was under the auspices of yet another body, the Works Progress Administration, which was serving up half a million hot dinners a day in ten thousand schools. To boot, these programmes were run by twelve thousand previously unemployed people.

One of the great successes of the New Deal, the WPA started out with a mission to feed only the children of 'relief families' but soon found itself dishing up nutritious midday meals to youngsters 'irrespective of their financial condition', as assistant administrator Ellen S. Woodward reported. Like other New Deal bodies, the WPA's good works revealed how the land of plenty had become for many a land of near-starvation. For example, the organisation soon learned that milk was a luxury in most communities, for many children the free meal was their only meal of the day, and most had only a 'meagre breakfast' or none at all. Before the free meals were introduced, some children existed on as little as a single home-cooked biscuit covered with a layer of fat, a biscuit and a piece of fried fish, corn bread with molasses, a cold pancake, or a piece of bread that was 'dirty, dry or mouldy'.

The effect of the programme was indisputably helpful. Teachers reported much-improved school attendance records, rapid weight gains and dramatically happier children. In New York, for example, 'Teachers state that pupils, who once exhibited sullen unresponsiveness, have become alert, interested and in many cases above the average in intelligence.' The New Deal brought relief in numerous ways. In hundreds of struggling towns such as the fast-failing mining community of Carbon Hill, Alabama, there was practically no hope. 'If they hadn't had WPA, people would've just gone down to the stores and taken what they needed,' labourer Ben Pair recalled of the time. 'When the kids look an' say, "Daddy, I'm hungry," why, you just got to have food.' Local doctor O. H. Whitney quickly became an unabashed fan of the New Deal. '[The WPA relief workers] filled up all the old abandoned workings that had collapsed and filled with stagnant water, and that's gotten the mosquitoes away from here,' he enthused. 'And putting in curbs and gutters gave us good drainage.' As a result, malaria cases had fallen by two thirds. Beauty shop owner Maude Patterson added, 'I don't know how we would have existed without the WPA payroll.' By then, one in five Carbon Hill residents was getting a WPA pay cheque – that is, they were relief workers. Altogether, they earned roughly as much as the rest of the local industry, which was mainly mining, put together.

Added together, Carbon Hill acquired through the New Deal a much healthier environment, better roads, a new stadium, a library, a swimming pool and extra school rooms. There were some grumbles – apparently, a few locals were less than truthful about the state of their finances in order to get themselves relief cheques – but otherwise approval for the work of the WPA was almost universal.

As the New Deal trampled all over the much-cherished power of unfettered capitalism, big business began to bitterly resent the president.

The vast utilities sector had as much reason as any other area of big business to worry about Roosevelt's determination to rein in its excesses. This was the home of glamour industries delivering public services such as electricity, gas, telephone and telegraph. By the time of the Crash they had attracted $23 billion worth of public investment, and on the campaign trail Roosevelt made no bones that the sector – this 'lusty younger child [of the railroads]' – needed to be put under federal supervision. 'Electricity is no longer a luxury. It is a definite necessity. It lights our homes, our places of work and our streets,' he said. 'It turns the wheels of most of our transportation and our factories. In our homes it serves not only for light, but it can become the willing servant of the family in countless ways. It can relieve the drudgery of the housewife and lift the great burden off the shoulders of the hard-working farmer.' In short, it was a public good, not a tool of the rich. It was high time that government redirected the sector so that it reflected the national interest.

In fact there was a history there. While Roosevelt was governor of the state of New York, the utilities had attacked him for threatening to regulate them. He believed they had done their best 'to get around the common law, to pyramid capital through holding companies and, without restraint of law, to sell billions of dollars of securities which the public have been falsely led into believing were properly supervised by the government itself'. Certainly the power of a handful of individuals was beyond dispute. A report by the Federal Power

Commission showed that forty-eight of the biggest projects under development by publicly listed utilities sat under the umbrella of just ten companies. These all-powerful ten supplied electricity, gas, telephone and telegraph to 12,500 communities with a population of forty-two million. As such, they were the undisputed sovereigns of America's commercial world.

The collapse of the Insull utilities empire – the 'monstrosity', as Roosevelt called it – was grist to the new president's mill. This failure had done more, he argued, to open the eyes of the American public to the nefariousness of big-business practices than any other. And it was all down to an Englishman.

The object of the president's ire was London-born Sam Insull who had emigrated to the United States as a young man and found a job at the right hand of Thomas Edison. At the very dawn of electric power plants, the former clerk became the great inventor's private secretary. It was an ideal position from which to profit from the enormous commercial possibilities unleashed by the spread of power into factories and homes, and Insull made the most of it by eventually launching his own business.

During the twenties Insull created an enormous web of power companies under an umbrella of investment trusts. The parent company, Insull Utilities Investment, steadily acquired huge blocks of the shares in the power-generating businesses, largely through small investors who came to believe the Englishman was a commercial genius. In its heyday the company attracted more than $1.5 billion from mainly 'mom and pop' investors. By the late 1920s, the firm was a darling of the stockmarket, with the share price multiplying year by year. But in 1931 Insull Utilities toppled from the weight of its investments and the creator fled to Greece, leaving behind hundreds of thousands of ruined individuals – Roosevelt's cherished 'little fellows', the 95 per cent of America's population who could lay claim to only two thirds of the country's wealth.

The subsequent post-mortem revealed a web of logarithmic complexity. Sam Insull's holding companies exercised control over hundreds of thousands of operating businesses that had employed highly dubious practices to inflate their value and that of the shares. Vast swathes of debt had been capitalised as though they were genuine

and profitable assets like factories or power plants. Torrents of dividends, which helped attract investors, had been paid out of capital
rather than from earnings. Adding to the abuses, profits from the
sounder companies had been secretly redeployed to shore up the
weaker ones. To support this tottering edifice, the utilities had burdened the public with 'terrific overcharges' for their services.

As far as the president was concerned, the collapse of Insull's
mighty empire totally justified the federal regulation he clamped on
the utilities. As for Insull himself, Roosevelt would soon order his
extradition from Greece to stand trial under new laws designed to
make investment much more transparent – in truth, more honest –
so that ordinary people could understand it. When he was eventually
brought before the courts, the fallen tycoon elegantly if not entirely
truthfully explained his position and, by implication, that of his fellow
buccaneers: 'What I did, when I did it, was honest; now, though,
through changed conditions, what I did may or may not be called
honest. Politics demand, therefore, that I be brought to trial; but what
is really being brought to trial is the system I represented.'

Much to the president's chagrin, Insull was acquitted of all
charges. Thereupon he exiled himself to Paris where he died a few
years later from a heart attack while travelling on the Métro. Before the
body was cold, a passing thief stole his wallet.

The biggest thorn in the side of big business was the NRA. Because
of its highly specific codes for pricing and production and just about
everything else, detractors saw the inspiration of Hitler and Mussolini
behind the organisation. Although many businesses conformed willingly enough, many bigger companies fought General Johnson to the
bitter end.

Violence became more and more common as the lines were drawn
between employers and labour. In the San Francisco general strike of
July 1934, a waterfront-based dispute that eventually involved sixty-five
thousand trade unionists, trucks were burned, tear-gas thrown, and
police and unionists were clubbed, bayoneted and even shot. 'Troops
occupied the waterfront – sentries with steel helmets and gleaming
bayonets, machine-gun nets, and motorized roving patrols,' noted the
Survey Graphic. The remarks of a leading San Francisco industrialist
may not have been typical but they are certainly revealing. According

to the unnamed boss, the strike was 'a marvelous investment' that would solve the labour problem 'for years to come, perhaps for ever'. He went on, 'Mark my words. When this nonsense is out of the way and the men have been driven back to their jobs, we won't have to worry about them any more. They'll have learned their lesson. Not only do I believe we'll never have another general strike but I don't think we'll have a strike of any kind in San Francisco during this generation. Labour is licked.'[26]

Henry Ford, ageing and delusional, opposed practically every New Deal reform, and especially those imposed by the NRA. Not only did he refuse to sign for a Blue Eagle, he became convinced that Roosevelt was in league with General Motors. His legendary assembly line, which had been thoroughly copied and ameliorated by other manufacturers, had turned into a workers' treadmill at his plants. If the line broke down, all pay was stopped until it started up again. If the breakdown lasted longer than two hours, the men had to make up the time at the end of the shift. Smoking was forbidden, conversation discouraged. 'If a man is one minute late he is docked fifteen minutes,' noted the *Nation*. They were paid in their lunch hour, usually standing in line and if they ran out of time they had to come back later in their own time.

The NRA law permitting workers to join outside, industry-wide unions as distinct from company ones, was anathema to Ford and his increasingly unpleasant managers, a position that would lead to one of the most notorious skirmishes of the Depression. This was the Battle of the Overpass on 26 May 1937, when Ford company employees – actually goons working for the internal security service – gave a thumping to United Auto Workers organisers at Gate 4 of the Rouge factory at Dearborn. In full compliance with the law, the unionists had come to mount a protest for a pay-rise. The unionists, who included the UAW's formidable Walter Reuther, were punched, kicked, slammed on to concrete and thrown downstairs so savagely that one suffered a broken back while local police stood by. The violence was documented by forewarned photographers and splashed across the nation's newspapers next day. The incident hurt Ford so badly that he eventually had to accept the UAW into his plant.

In general, however, big business took on the New Deal in the courts, which resulted in a series of landmark judgements in American legal history. In one known as the 'sick chicken case' concerning alleged violations of the poultry code by a kosher butcher in New York City, the NRA was eventually destroyed by a Supreme Court ruling. This was on the seemingly irrelevant grounds that Washington had no right to interfere in intrastate, as distinct from interstate, commerce. In substance, the ruling meant that everything the NRA had done until now was unconstitutional. An immediate consequence was a massive sacking of adults in favour of children in the nation's sweat shops and factories before Washington was able to wrest back control through its own victories in the courts.

One of these victories involved a chambermaid and grandmother named Elsie Parrish. As a demonstration of big business's determination to thwart the labour law reforms, it is highly revealing. Parrish had been employed in 1933 by the Cascadian Hotel in Wenatchee, Washington and was by all accounts an excellent worker. However when her work ended, the hotel offered $17 'for the balance of her services', having underpaid her by $2.50 for her forty-eight-hour week, according to the state's minimum wage laws. She and her husband sued for precisely $216.19 to recover the missing amount. After losing in the county court, Parrish next took the fight to the Washington Supreme Court, where she won. Thereupon the West Coast Hotel company appealed to the Supreme Court, essentially arguing that the minimum wage deprived workers of rights to contract out the labour at whatever rate they might want. After much convoluted argument about minimum wage laws actually discriminating against women and children, which must have bewildered the chambermaid, the chief justices gave her, and Roosevelt, a much-needed victory with the words:

> What can be closer to the public interest than the health of women and their protection from unscrupulous and over-reaching employers. The exploitation of a class of workers who are in an unequal position with respect to bargaining power and are thus relatively defenceless against the denial of a living wage is not only detrimental to their health and well-being but casts a direct burden for their support within the community. What these workers lose in wages

the taxpayers are called upon to pay. The bare cost of living must be met.

The terms of the judgement pretty much reflected what New Dealers had been saying for the last four years: big business had long exploited its workers. But Elsie Parrish was not too concerned about that. 'I'm not sure I understand all the things but I'm glad it's all over,' she said, pocketing an extremely expensive cheque for $216.19. Although the Washington law was not a New Deal law – it had been passed before the 1914–18 war – it certainly reflected the new administration's philosophy and it was now enshrined in the national conscience.

———

After he had rescued the financial sector, Roosevelt set about taming it. As he made witheringly clear in his inaugural speech, the blame for the last three and a half years of headlong decline in Americans' quality of life lay at its door. 'The rules of the exchange of mankind's goods have failed through their own stubbornness and their own incompetence, have admitted their failure, and have abdicated,' the president thundered in an almost biblical denunciation of his country's banking elite. 'Practices of the unscrupulous money changers stand indicted in the court of public opinion, rejected by the heart and minds of men.' Henceforth there would be 'strict supervision' of all banking, credits and investments. He wanted 'an end to speculation with other people's money', a curb on the power of these 'unscrupulous money changers' who had 'fled their high seats in the temple of civilisation'. The essential preliminary to the promised strict supervision was an inquiry conducted by Ferdinand Pecora.

In fact, an inquiry into Wall Street and the banking industry at large had been launched by Hoover in early 1932, but nothing much had come of it. The weight of the financial industry, which hired the best Wall Street lawyers, had crushed no fewer than three investigating counsels before it finally acquired a new chief counsel in Pecora, a scrappy little Italian lawyer with a steel-trap mind and the investigative instincts of a barracuda. Soon the newspapers were calling it the

Pecora Commission as Roosevelt's Savonarola pilloried one Colossus of Wall Street after another, probing for chicanery, malpractice, deceit and outright crookery.

The first reluctant witness was Richard Whitney. The president of the New York Stock Exchange, who had lost none of his hauteur, tried to put the inquiry in its place. 'The exchange's refusal to pay heed to popular demand for reform was simply a manifestation of courage to do those things which are right, regardless of how unpopular they may be for the time being,' he declared with breathtaking arrogance.

Jack Morgan appeared in May 1933, provoking a frenzy of interest in this largely anonymous individual. Astonishing as it may seem, hardly anybody knew what he looked like. Although he had been at the heart of world affairs for more than 20 years, he had rarely been photographed – he once took a cane to a photographer who tried to do so – or been interviewed. He might have been the face of Wall Street but hardly anybody had seen it. Pecora would later write in *Wall Street Under Oath*, his searing indictment of the evidence he unearthed: 'His very features, no less than his opinions and personality, were almost unknown to the millions of his fellow citizens over whose welfare his firm and its allies exerted so extraordinary an influence.' *Time* noted that a 'milling, jostling, sweating crowd choked the corridors of the Senate Office Building. Men in white linen suits, women with hats askew and hair straggling damply into their eyes, fought to get into a stifling room long since jammed to the doors.'

Now semi-retired and pouring much of his wealth into numerous charities, Jack Morgan had at first warmed to the new president. Although indirectly a target of Roosevelt's wrath, he believed the president was 'approaching his problems in the spirit of getting something done, instead of wrestling for a long time with a Congress of wholly uneducated people who have no courage', as he wrote to an acquaintance in England. 'Of course it is quite possible that some of his cures may be the wrong ones but on the whole things were so bad that almost any cure may do some good.'

The world's most famous banker proved quite a hit. The papers chortled over his dry wit and allegedly English expressions. After one senator presumed to give him a full-blooded lecture on finance, Morgan waited patiently until the tirade had stopped before saying, 'I am sorry I started such a hare.' The man demonised by many as the root cause of their financial troubles also proved an impressive witness when he took the stand, accompanied by a brilliant counsel, John W. Davis, who once stood as the Democratic candidate for president and was a former ambassador to Great Britain. Backed by all 20 Morgan partners including Thomas W. Lamont and George Whitney, Jack 'fiddled with a heavy gold watch, [and] beamed upon the committee as the show began', wrote *Time*, which found him an 'easy, pleasant gentleman'.

Certainly Jack Morgan felt no need to apologise for his profession. 'I state without hesitation that I consider the private banker a national asset and not a national danger,' he said. 'As to the theory that he may become too powerful, it must be remembered that any power which he has comes not from the possession of large means, but from the confidence of the people in his character and credit, and that that power, having no force to back it, would disappear at once if people thought that the character had changed or the credit had diminished – not financial credit, but that which comes from the respect and esteem of the community.' This was a clearly rehearsed overture before the tougher questions and the highly sceptical Pecora did not entirely agree. As far as he was concerned, bankers 'were neither a national asset nor a national danger – they were both'. However, he did admire Morgan, 'the undisputed and absolute, though benevolent, monarch of his realm'. At first, Jack Morgan did not repay the compliment. Highly suspicious of immigrant people, particularly of Jews and Catholics, he privately described Pecora as 'a dirty little wop'.

As Morgan's interrogation continued, the carefully cultivated anonymity of J. P. Morgan and Co clearly fascinated the inquisitors.

'Are you listed among the banks?' asked one senator.

'We hope not,' Jack replied. 'We have taken every precaution to prevent it.'

He was quite imperturbable, even when a publicity-hungry midget named Lya Graf from the Ringling Brothers circus somehow broke through the crowd and, with the help of her press agent, leapt on to the startled banker's lap.

'The smallest lady in the world wants to meet the richest man in the world!' the agent shouted.

'Why, I've got a grandson bigger than you,' quipped Morgan, recovering quickly.

'But I'm older,' said Graf.

'How old are you?'

'Twenty.'

'Well, you certainly don't look it. Where do you live?'

'In a tent, sir.'

Jack Morgan was just as imperturbable in the face of Pecora's probing, even when he knew his answers would prove controversial, even inflammatory.

'Did you pay income tax in 1931?' Pecora asked.

'No.'

'In 1932?'

'No.'

It was these revelations – namely, that one of the world's wealthiest men had not paid any taxes – that caused shock throughout the United States. More than anything else, the two negatives served to ruin Jack Morgan's reputation among the wider public. But he had done nothing more than comply with the law. The firm's – and therefore the partners' – losses had been so great in the aftermath of the Depression that under the United States code there were simply no taxes to be paid. And he had in fact paid taxes in England for both 1931 and 1932.

As it happened, the German-speaking banker Otto Kahn had not paid tax in the loss-making years, yet nobody made much of that revelation. Kahn was a senior partner in Kuhn, Loeb, the bank that 'stood in the breach', as Kahn once said, for the insurers when the *Lusitania* was torpedoed by a German submarine during the 1914–18 war. Hoping to revive the markets in late 1929, Kuhn, Loeb had also stood in the breach for a large issue of shunned stock. Kahn also made a good impression on the investigating committee as he explained that the banking business was all about relationships and expertise. 'Just as if you have a suit of clothes to buy, you would have to pay to one tailor much more than you pay to another tailor,' he told the committee in a sartorial metaphor. 'It is the same. The suit keeps you warm if you buy it from a cheap tailor too. But the other tailor puts the experience and the reputation of making good suits into it, and you go to him.'

'Did not private banking firms as well as commercial banks help along the development of that mania by freely making brokers' loans in unprecedented amounts?' Pecora asked him.

'To put it mildly, they certainly did not do sufficient to prevent or stop it,' the great banker replied.

So Kahn's reputation survived the non-payment of taxes while Morgan's did not. The latter was lumped in with those titans of the finance industry who not only did not pay their taxes in the Depression years but avoided doing so in the boom years too. One of these was 'Billion Dollar Charlie' Mitchell who, in the salad days had sold a large number of National City shares to his wife at a paper loss of $2.5 million before deducting the same amount in his income-tax return for the year.

'I sold this stock, frankly, for tax purposes,' he brazenly told an incredulous committee.

'That was to avoid income tax?' asked one stunned senator.

'Throwing my fortune into the breach as I did for the benefit of this institution, Senator Brookhart, in 1929 I had a definite loss in that stock which I was forced to take,' retorted the oily banker.

Unfortunately for Jack Morgan, he became tarred with the same brush as Charles Mitchell. The public and most politicians were not financially literate, and as the hearings went on the parade of people appearing on the stand were dubbed 'banksters' and, as *Time* magazine observed, became 'the favourite object of abuse'.

More than anybody else, though, it was Richard Whitney who brought regulation down upon the New York Stock Exchange and the rest of the stockbroking industry. Highly suspicious of Whitney's high-minded statements, Pecora got his dogged young lawyers to send an exhaustive questionnaire to the exchange that would have required an analysis of about ten million brokers' accounts. Whitney baulked at this intrusion, pointing out the heavy costs of such an exercise when the members were practically broke. However, the exchange had never been exposed to such demands for information, and Whitney must have sensed his roof crashing in. Eventually relenting, Pecora drew up a less onerous but still thorough questionnaire that for the first time would shed a considerable amount of light on the activities of the exchange and its thirty-four sister organisations around the United

States that between them accounted for 90 per cent of all trading.

In the meantime, Roosevelt had his own committee quietly looking into Whitney's kingdom. This team of inquisitors included such sharp-minded and sceptical individuals as Dean Acheson, then under-secretary of the Treasury, and law professor Adolf Berle, a considerable influence on the president. Like the president, Berle distrusted the increasing depth of industrial concentration, predicting that the modern corporation would, unless it was stopped, overtake the power of government and become 'the dominant form of social organiza-tion'. The professor distrusted investment bankers even more, claiming they had risked the entire economy by the 'tremendous issues of securities many of which [were] unsound'.[27]

As it happened, Roosevelt was acquainted with Whitney and had already sought his cooperation. The president had once sat down with the exchange chief to invite his cooperation in the moral reform of Wall Street, which he considered to be something of a casino. As a starter, Roosevelt suggested the exchange might issue an easily under-standable statement of ethics and values. At this, Whitney demurred, but assured the president that members were 'anxious to put the secu-rity business on a higher plane than it has ever been before'.

When the Pecora Commission had digested all the information provided by the exchange's members, it published what the *New York Times* described as 'an armful of raw and bleeding figures' about the profits made by the broking community. As it happened, these profits were somewhat overblown because, probably deliberately, Pecora also in some cases included in his figures the revenue earned by banks that owned some of the broking houses, which were not necessarily bro-kerage profits. The numbers were, however, sufficiently stupendous to help drive the nails deeper into the exchange's coffin. According to the report, brokers had accumulated $906 million in profits 'despite the Depression' – that is the years between 1928 and most of 1933. As *Time* astutely reported, the government had been the beneficiary of some of those profits: 'Mr. Pecora also failed to mention the fact that state and federal transfer taxes during the period yielded more than $360 million, an amount equal to about 40 per cent of brokers' total profits.' Although the counsel could claim the moral high ground, he was more than willing to use propaganda in his witch-hunt.

Whitney was furious at the fudged figures, claiming they had been presented in such a way as to smooth the passage of the Stock Exchange Bill then before Congress, legislation that would finally regulate his precious exchange. He might have added that Wall Street was being kicked while it was down. Hardly any share-trading was being done in what had so recently been the world's biggest share-trading arena. The 'specialists' on the floor were spending half the day playing backgammon or singing songs like 'Wait Till the Sun Shines, Nellie'.

Nevertheless, Pecora got his way and Whitney's mighty New York Stock Exchange came under government regulation. It must have been galling to Wall Streeters when, on 12 June 1933, he had achieved the ultimate accolade of a cover on *Time*; he was photographed smoking a fat cigar. For Pecora, regulation was a time for rejoicing: 'Fighting at every step, [the exchange] finally went the way of all flesh. Like the humblest of us all, even the mighty stock exchange must now recognise the existence and authority of the United States government.'

Pecora would sum it all up in *Wall Street Under Oath*, which served as a scorching reminder to the regulators of the importance of keeping the monster in chains. Having spent seventeen months as the counsel for the Banking and Currency Committee, he wrote that the 'riotous speculative excesses' of 1929 had only been awaiting the moment to resurface, and would have done so but for his inquiry. 'Though repressed for the present, it cannot be doubted that, given a suitable opportunity, [the excesses] would spring back into pernicious activity,' he predicted. 'Frequently we are told that this regulation has been throttling the country's prosperity. Bitterly hostile was Wall Street to the enactment of the regulatory regulation. It now looks forward to the day when it shall, as it hopes, reassume the reins of its former power.' The hubris of the Wall Streeters still seethed. 'Indeed, if you now hearken to the oracles of The Street, you will hear now and then that the money-changers have been much maligned,' he wrote in a biblical vein that echoed the president. 'You will be told that a whole group of high-minded men, innocent of social or economic wrongdoing, were expelled from the temple because of the excesses of a few. You will be assured that they had nothing to do with the misfortunes that overtook the country in 1929–1933; that they were simply scapegoats, sacrificed on the altar of unreasoning public opinion to satisfy the wrath of a howling mob blindly seeking victims.'

From the twelve thousand pages of largely damning evidence of the Pecora Commission emerged the Securities and Exchange Commission. Its first and unlikely head was Joseph P. Kennedy, father of the future president and a Wall Street operator of the first order who regarded Pecora, confusing his origins, as 'an Irish papist'. During the roaring twenties Kennedy had made a fortune wheeling and dealing in the burgeoning movie business, among others. In fact, not long before his appointment he had been named by the Pecora Commission as a member of a highly profitable pool operating in liquor stocks. But this made-good son of Irish immigrants was also a donor to Roosevelt's campaign, and so he got the job. On his appointment Kennedy was quick to tell journalists he had never got deeply into the securities business anyway. 'The days of stock manipulation are in the past now ... You can't rig the market any more ... I'm no sucker,' he said. 'I never did so much in the market although I did pretty good in the motion picture business.' In a later, more formal statement that was probably crafted by one of the president's speech-writers, he had apparently got religion: 'I do not hesitate to employ that word [spiritual] in connection with finance. We are seeking to recreate, rebuild, restore confidence. Confidence is an outgrowth of character. We believe that character exists strongly in the financial world, so we do not have to compel virtue; we seek to prevent vice. Our whole formula is to bar wrongdoers from operating under the aegis of those who feel a sense of ethical responsibility. We are eager to see finance as self-contained as it deserves to be when ruled by honour and responsibility.'

If Whitney heard Kennedy's observations, he did not take them seriously. While proclaiming the importance of self-regulation for the New York Stock Exchange, he had been quietly embezzling money. The frauds only came to light when his brokerage firm collapsed in March 1938 and the Securities and Exchange Commission conducted a fourteen-day investigation that relied on the evidence of fifty-two witnesses. The inquiry revealed that Whitney had appropriated funds from the New York Yacht Club when he was its treasurer, from the New York Stock Exchange when he was its president, and from his own clients including widows and orphans when he was head of the august firm Whitney & Co. Whitney, the man who had done his best to stonewall regulation of the exchange, turned out to be one of the biggest swindlers of the era, and he was imprisoned in Sing Sing. To save the family name, Whitney's brother George was forced to borrow nearly a million dollars from J. P. Morgan & Co so that Richard could make full restitution.

For Pecora, the fall of Whitney 'hastened and decided the battle'. Thus, after 143 years of proud if far from satisfactory self-regulation, the mighty New York Stock Exchange became subject to laws designed to ensure fair play. The alternative, as one witness told the Pecora hearings, was the butchery of the public investor. Self-regulation had been 'like putting a baby [the investor] in a cage with a tiger to regulate the tiger'.

Turn of the Tide

The first of the stubby little Morris Eights appeared on British roads in late 1934 in the depths of the Depression. Priced from £120, it was a marvel of extempore automobile design. With sales of earlier models dropping, William Morris had rushed the car's development, cutting all possible corners to get it into the showrooms. Indeed, in these days before aggressive patenting, the Morris Eight's engine owed much to Henry Ford's Y-type Eight, its biggest competitor in Britain. As an industry historian would observe, 'Any student of automobile history who cares to compare the eight-horsepower Ford engine of the late nineteen-twenties and the Morris 8 engine of the early nineteen-thirties will find a remarkable resemblance.' A true product of the era, the Morris Eight came in two basic colours (all black, or red and black) and could be ordered in three different versions (tourer, saloon and van). Extra equipment available on most models was confined to bumpers and the latest Lucas 'trafficators' – illuminated arrows that popped out of the bodywork to indicate the direction the driver was turning.

Like most automobile manufacturers, Morris Motors had struggled from the early days of the Crash. Locked in competition with Ford, the firm could not afford to cut prices any further than it already had. Morris, a quick learner who had acquired many of his manufacturing skills by studying American methods, desperately needed another runaway success like his Morris Minor, now four years old.

The self-made founder could hardly have been more different from the commercially sclerotic grandees of the old industries. Innovative, outward-looking, resourceful and energetic (he had been a champion racing cyclist in his youth), Morris was the son of a draper and had left school at fifteen to start his working life as an apprentice repairer of bicycles. Just twenty-one years later, in 1913, he was a budding automobile magnate with a highly successful model, the Bullnose Morris, already behind him. In those days he had scores of competitors in addition to foreign ones such as Ford. There were thirty-one British car-manufacturers, down from eighty-eight only seven years earlier but still a lot compared with the forty-four manufacturers in America with its vastly bigger market. Despite all this opposition, Morris, Austin and Singer were carving up the market between them with a combined 75 per cent of total car output, in exactly the same way as General Motors, Ford and Chrysler were doing across the Atlantic.

Morris had stayed afloat despite the terrific rate of attrition in the industry by being nimble-footed. Although profits were dangerously thin, the firm had become the biggest car-manufacturer in Britain (and Europe) through a determined strategy of innovation in every aspect of the business – steel-stamping, painting and bodywork among scores of other areas – that served to speed up production and improve quality. He took opportunities whenever he could, snapping up suppliers and competitors alike, such as engine-supplier Hotchkiss, the Wolseley car company (originally a manufacturer of sheep-shearing equipment) and, later, Riley – all of them iconic marques. This exciting industrialist was also considered one of Britain's best employers, not only providing staff with paid holidays but also distributing a share of the profits among them.

Fortunately, the Eight, when it came out, was an instant success. By mid-1935, just nine months after its release, over fifty thousand had been sold. Beloved of deliverymen everywhere, the five hundred-weight van with its chromium-plated radiator quickly became a ubiquitous feature on British roads. Police used souped-up Eights to chase criminals. With the help of imperial preference, 'Export' versions went all over the world and in particular to New Zealand, which became the Eight's biggest overseas market. Other Empire countries such as Burma, Ceylon and India also fell in love with the model.

According to Morris Eight historian Harry Edwards, even the exiled Emperor Haile Selassie bought an Eight for his son. And the Cunard shipping company, looking for extra income while half its fleet lay idle, got its design division to produce a handsome four-seater drop-head coupé for a Mayfair showroom. Within three years, some 218,000 Eights had been sold and Morris Motors was very much back in business.

Australia also adopted the Eight, but in a different way. Because complete cars were punished by heavy import duties designed to protect Ford, which had built its own plant in Melbourne in the late 1920s, local body-builders imported the Eight in chassis form and converted the '8/40' into racier shapes and hard-working 'utes' – utilities with loading trays. One Australian company, Ruskin Motor Bodies, became famous for its versions of the model. Apparently named after the British aesthete and critic John Ruskin, who once wrote that 'all works of taste must bear a price in proportion to the skill, time and expense and risk attending their invention and manufacture', Ruskin Motor Bodies had a contract with the Oxford firm to supply chassis. These were then converted into vehicles that in some cases looked much more elegant than the original. With their swooping lines, cars like the Ruskin-bodied Morris 12/4 series III coupé not only became collector's items, they paved the way for the distinctively original, home-grown Holdens and Fords. In time the 8/40s became a highly visible symbol of Australia's economic recovery (albeit slow) under 'Honest Joe' Lyons.

The British car industry ran rings around Ford during the Depression, despite the latter's high reputation. Henry Ford was regarded with almost saint-like status in Britain and Europe, unlike in America, where he was admired and derided in equal measure. As one American journalist wrote, the industrialist 'is hated by nearly everyone who has ever worked for him, and at one time worshipped by nearly everyone who has not'. Certainly, Ford was more widely known than Jack Morgan. 'A significant fact which few US citizens realise is that today Ford is the biggest US name in Europe, bigger than Hoover, Edison or Morgan ...' observed *Time* magazine in mid-1930. However, it is to the industrialist's credit that he did not take fright during the Depression and mount a headlong retreat from

Britain and Europe, as did many other American investors, such as L. K. Liggett, the owner of Boots the chemist, who hastily sold his shares back to the public. Instead, Ford maintained plants in France, Germany, Spain, Belgium, Ireland and Denmark. In Britain, he shifted his main European plant from Manchester to rat-infested swampland at Dagenham in 1931.

Ford certainly believed his reputation. In a signed article in the *Spectator*, he once wrote that 'if some English employers are not efficient enough to pay high wages, the sooner they go the better ... You cannot get good work out of poorly paid men.' (Considering that Ford was notorious among unions in America for his less-than-ideal treatment of workers, this was quite some claim.) Although forty per cent of the cost of his new plant at Dagenham had come from British investors, Ford ran the British subsidiary as wilfully as he conducted affairs back at Dearborn, very much as a personal fiefdom. Ford repeatedly countermanded British managers who complained that the American-designed vehicles such as the Model A, which Dearborn insisted on foisting on them, were too big, too heavy, too expensive and too basic for British roads and buyers. 'You are trying to tell me how to design an automobile for the English market?' he once bellowed at a quavering executive.

Yet, his executives were right. For example, the Model AF (the F standing for 'Foreign') sold only five cars in Britain. While his badge steadily lost market share to Morris and Austin, Ford continued to lecture his rivals on the foolishness of producing 'baby cars' such as the Austin 7 with its little motor, especially for the rougher country of the Empire. 'Some English cars have not been suitable to pioneering conditions in your Dominions, and your manufacturers have not attempted to make the type of cars wanted,' Ford said, blithely ignoring the success of the Eight in those very nations. Morris and other domestic automobile-makers needed no advice from the American magnate. Their rapid response to hard times by unveiling nimble, cleverly engineered vehicles caught the US giant flat-footed.

Behind his back, Ford's British engineers mounted a covert and drastic re-engineering of the Model Y, renamed the Popular, to bring it under the £100 barrier and finally provide effective competition for the Morris Eight and the Austins. Puzzlingly in view of the economic devastation in America, where Ford sales had collapsed by up to sixty per cent, forcing him to cut his workforce by up to forty per cent, Henry Ford and his inner ring of managers back home never seem to have mastered Depression-era engineering. They even gave away much of the truck and van market to Morris and Bedford by forcing V8-powered monsters on the new Dagenham works instead of the economical four cylinders Britain's delivery industry demanded.

The agility of the newer, smaller industries could have provided a lesson to the ossified staples. And there were a lot of them: out of a total of 140,000 factories in Britain, 30,000 were classified as small businesses employing fewer than twenty-five people. In the circumstances their performance was inspirational. Employment in car-manufacturing rose steadily, up by 12 per cent in the 1930s, while the electrical industry took on 24 per cent more workers, cycling 22 per cent, chemicals 15 per cent, and man-made fibres and materials 33 per cent. Indeed, Imperial Chemical Industries (ICI) was expanding so rapidly that it could not find enough suitably qualified technicians for its plants.

The progress of the new economy also caught the governments of the early 1930s by surprise. While they had been overwhelmingly preoccupied with the tribulations of the staples, attempting to squeeze the last drop out of them or hoping for a miraculous revival, the new industries had developed with a minimum of government help. The retail industry was a good example. Although spending power declined steadily, shopping chains managed to extend their foothold with aggressive and novel commercial techniques. For instance, Tesco, the store founded by Jack Cohen in a Hackney market, was heading for a pre-war total of a hundred shops while Marks and Spencer was up to 234 stores and Sainsbury 244. Handicapped by a lack of commercial imagination, the staple industries barely budged in the meantime. Coal production continued to fall inexorably and was soon 'in an appalling mess' with hundreds of smaller pits barely making ends meet. Cotton exports sank to half the pre-Crash volumes. Ship-building was marooned in a Sargasso Sea of lost orders, and Dundee's jute industry ceded victory to Calcutta. Sir Montagu Norman's Bankers Industrial Development Company proved a damp squib. After nearly a year of existence, as

National government historian Robert Skidelsky noted, 'only one small scheme had actually been submitted and approved'.

However, Britain was slowly emerging from its long trough to the relief of Chancellor Neville Chamberlain who rejoiced in the steady recovery. In 1933 he pronounced, 'Of all countries passing through these difficult times the one that has stood the test with the greatest measure of success is the United Kingdom.' Never mind that this was a considerable exaggeration, as Sweden could have pointed out. In 1934 Chamberlain, more optimistic again, promised that his Budget, which reduced income tax by six pence in the pound – equivalent to 2.5 per cent – would take Britain from 'Bleak House to Great Expectations'. And in 1935, politicking again, he maintained the 'nation has regained 80 per cent of its prosperity', although without defining precisely how he had measured it. While it was true that Britain had seen off the worst of the Depression, wage rates had barely recovered. Although they bought roughly 10 per cent more than they did before 1929 because of the decline in prices, they would not increase in nominal terms until the late 1930s.

Smashing a bottle of Australian burgundy on the side of the mighty vessel, Queen Mary pressed a button and, slowly at first, it started to move down a slipway already wet from pouring rain. The 'greatest mass ever moved by man from land to water', was on its way into the Clyde. The ship, named after the monarch who launched her, was No. 534.

After sitting for two years and four months on the banks of the river as a half-finished hulk, she had been rescued by a hefty government grant and her hull finished off, ready for fitting out. She could no longer claim to be the world's biggest ship – France's new superliner the *Normandie* was a few feet longer and wider – but she would certainly be the fastest with a top speed of thirty knots. But most importantly for the government and the enormous crowd of a hundred thousand present at the launch, including most of the royal family who had been holidaying at Balmoral, and as many of the residents of Hutchesonton and the Gorbals as could find standing room, the *Queen Mary* was presented with some justification as the symbol of Britain's emergence from the Depression, a triumph of the ship-building craft.

The launch was almost as technical a feat as the ship's creation. Because the vessel was longer than the Clyde was wide, she had to be turned rapidly lest she ran ignominiously aground on the mud on the opposite bank. Tons of chains were draped around her sides to slow her as soon as she hit the water, stern first. At great expense, a tributary of the Clyde had also been dredged and widened to accommodate her bulk. There was also the very real risk of the surge created by 34,000 tons of steel pouring straight over the banks of the Clyde and inundating, or even drowning, some of the spectators. But the launch proved a success, and the *Queen Mary* was anchored to be finished off over the next eighteen months.

Thus, on 26 March 1936, she was ready for sea trials. Screws churning in the muddy waters, the completed vessel was eased into mid-stream, shepherded by a fleet of tugs, as hundreds of shipyard workers hung precariously off cranes to watch her progress. An impressed journalist for the *Glasgow Herald* marvelled at the vessel's 'dignified beauty', the 'fitful sunlight on the water [that] cast a shimmering reflection on the gleaming black hull', observed all the while by awed crowds with 'wonder writ on every face at the masterpiece which has been fashioned by Clyde craftsmen'.

The workforce that had finished off No. 534 was not, however, the same workforce that had started it. In J. B. Priestley's opinion, their world had changed for ever, not just by the experiences they had been through, although these had undoubtedly hardened them, but by the advent of technology, which he believed had liberated them. In his estimation the new industries had launched a social revolution by improving the longterm prospects of the poor. From now on, more Britons would have access to a life previously led only by their betters. For Priestley, the 50mph buses that had transported him around the country had won the class struggle, liberating the masses by ushering them into a more congenial world. 'They offer luxury to all but the most poverty-stricken,' he rejoiced. 'They have annihilated the old distinction between rich and poor travellers.' Henceforth it would be 'the decaying landed country folk, with their rattling old cars, their draughty country houses, their antique bathrooms and cold tubs, who are the Spartans of our time.' In short the people had been liberated without the revolutions that were already raging – or soon would – in Spain, Italy and Germany. If a wide definition is given to 'technology', and if other advances such as retailing, cinemas and Morris Eights are included in it, this observation is true enough.

But it was more than that. Attitudes had also changed. For many, the Depression was the last straw; never again would the British people allow themselves to be treated as the flotsam and jetsam of the economy. In future they would be certain to vote in governments that guaranteed them a fair share of the good life that had for so long eluded them and been the preserve of the few.

Thus capitalism survived in Britain. But it was not the same capitalism preached before the Depression. It was a more inclusive and humane capitalism that, under duress, recognised the contribution of all the workforce. As a result many of the firebrands of the Depression, even people like Wal Hannington, became reasonably content with the way things turned out.

Elsewhere, however, the forces unleashed by the Depression were about to explode. In Germany, the spade-bearers of the Reicharbeitsdienst were now enlisted in the imperial army and training for a war that would set back the progress of this hard-won, more benign capitalism by twenty to thirty years. And in Japan, the militarists who had murdered Korekiyo Takahashi were already planning a conquest of the Pacific.

Even before he made his appearance at the Pecora Commission, Jack Morgan was arranging his retreat from Wall Hall and Britain. Much of his fortune was disappearing in tax increases, declining income and the heavy new death duties imposed under the New Deal. Although he still spent as much time as possible in the village of Aldenham, he had been forced to reduce the payroll by natural attrition, economise on the maintenance of buildings, and stop investing in the farm. As he wrote to his staff at Aldenham, 'I am myself cutting back down as far as possible on all expenditure in my houses, both in England and America, and am doing nothing except that which turns out to be absolutely essential.' Personal possessions went the same way. In quick succession, prized art, some land and the launch *Navette* were sold, while his private yacht, the *Corsair*, was donated to the British Navy.

Long an anonymous donor to many charities, the banker threw himself into unemployment relief in the worst-affected areas of New York City. But he gradually became disillusioned with Roosevelt and took the rare step of writing a letter to the *New York Herald Tribune* that exposed what he believed was the fallacy of the New Deal: 'All this renewed talk about pump-priming overlooks the simple fact, known to every farm boy, that pump-priming accomplishes nothing when the well is dry. You don't even get back the water used for priming.' In private letters to Sir Montagu Norman, he now described Roosevelt as 'a crazy man'.

The House of Morgan's entire business was carved up under the New Deal. Over the protests of the Bankers Association which condemned the act as 'unsound, unscientific, unjust and dangerous', the Glass-Steagall law forced the House of Morgan in common with other investment banks to separate deposit-taking business from investment activities. At first Jack Morgan was outraged at this intrusion into the life and affairs of the bank he had inherited from his father almost as a sacred trust. 'We should very probably have to disband the larger part of our organization and thus should be less able to render in the future that important service in the supply of capital for the development of the country which we have rendered in the past,' he argued. To the very end he saw banking as an influence for good. But the die was cast, and J. P. Morgan & Co chose to become a deposit-taker under the name of Morgan, Stanley & Co.

With the virtual extinction of the House of Morgan, Jack pretty much lost interest in everything but his family and friends and his hobbies, especially the rare books. In his final years he hardly did any banking business at all. And he was utterly dismayed by the conflict that erupted in a Europe whose rehabilitation he had helped finance after the earlier 'war to end all wars'.

He died in Florida on 13 March 1943, of a heart attack followed by a stroke. He was seventy-five, and had outlived his friend and partner Edward Grenfell by nearly eighteen months. Although Jack Morgan had deployed his energies over the years in helping rehabilitate whole economies for the common good, not just for the governments of the day as was often claimed, he was not much mourned outside his family and friends and his enormous range of business acquaintances. Indeed, ignoring his generosity to a host of good causes as well as his love of antique books, the *New Republic* viciously observed that Morgan 'added nothing creative or humanising to American life'. To its discredit, the magazine concluded that 'his passing subtracts nothing'. Perhaps the banker's immense wealth and lifelong distance from ordinary people made it unlikely he would be remembered any differently.

Morgan's fortune had been decimated by the Depression. Although he died with a worth of $16 million, he retained only a third of that after taxes. And of course he was the last of the Morgans to run the bank.

Much of the village he loved still exists, preserved among a high-quality residential development. The old trees, Church Farm cottages, the social club in which Jessie busied herself, the magnificent Saxon church which Morgan's wealth helped maintain: they are all still there. The banker is not buried in the graveyard but many of the villagers he mixed with made it their final resting place, joining their forebears from the previous century, among them the Biddells, Eames, Wilkinsons, Fortnums, Kiffs, Larkins, Ellises, Kings, and one Pythagoras Quarry, an inmate of the Brewers Almshouse. The cricket club is still active, playing on summery Sunday afternoons the game Jack Morgan never quite understood, on a sloping ground in front of the social club. There is, however, little outward evidence of Aldenham's former occupation by the world's richest man, just a street named Morgan Gardens.

Epilogue

Could it all happen again? In the year it took me to write this book, several events have occurred in the global economy that were considered unthinkable when I first put pen to paper. At that time the global economy was merrily expanding, rising house prices in much of the Western world were turning property-owners into paper millionaires on the back of historically low interest rates, banks were reporting colossal profits, specialist buy-out firms such as those in the private-equity sector were cheerfully predicting the $100 million deal, and most governments were highly optimistic about the future. After all, what could possibly go wrong?

Thus it was considered unthinkable that defaults on high-risk mortgages could provide the spark for panic and turmoil in the global financial markets, as they did. Similarly, on the generally accepted principle that the geographic dispersal of debt should have the effect of reducing systemic risk and was therefore a good thing, it was also considered unthinkable that elaborate, highly leveraged packages of loans including these high-risk – or subprime mortgages – could explode around the world like so many randomly laid land mines. As it happened, these packages turned out to be more lethal *because* they were dispersed. Equally, it was unthinkable that the world's banks might lose $500 billion or more (we are unlikely ever to know the exact amount) through reckless lending within a few months.

Likewise, any suggestion that one of America's biggest banks, Bear

Stearns, might be sold in early 2008 for a fraction of its valuation a year earlier would have been laughed out of court. In effect, Bear Stearns was rescued, just like Northern Rock, Britain's fifth-biggest mortgage lender, and other institutions in Germany and other European countries to save them from total collapse with fearful consequences for the rest of the industry.

Unthinkably, for a few fraught months the world's central banks faced the nightmare of a systemic collapse of the financial system. The US Federal Reserve and other central banks around the world were forced to pump torrents of money into the financial markets to prevent them from seizing up, like giant engines without oil. The last time this happened was under the New Deal when President Roosevelt poured vast sums down the pipeline of the Reconstruction Finance Corporation to avert the failure of much of the American banking industry.

The similarities between then and now are striking. When a furious Congress lambasted the banking industry for its irresponsibility, incompetence and greed in the wake of the latest panic, members employed the very same adjectives hurled at bankers in the 1930s. And when some of Wall Street's biggest names were jettisoned for their failure to maintain the integrity, stability and even competence of an industry that underpins the very fabric of society, it recalled the way that Roosevelt's banking supervisors kicked out managers for their ineptitude.

In the firm judgement of a shocked Alan Greenspan, revered former chairman of the Federal Reserve, the world witnessed 'the most wrenching [crisis] since the end of the second world war.' Yet nobody saw this catastrophe coming, just as nobody saw the Depression coming.

Although the financial and stock markets are very different now than they were in the thirties – infinitely bigger, more complex and sophisticated, more interdependent, faster-moving, more volatile, more indebted and much, much more specialised – they still bear comparison in terms of basic principles with today.

Let's take just one of these – the growth of credit. This is the great age of debt, both personal and public. Just about everybody can borrow money, whether for productive purposes or for pure pleasure. The Western world had never accumulated so much debt as a percentage of income as they did in the nineties and early years of the new millennium, whether the loans were for consumer durables, housing and land, investment, public infrastructure from buildings to railways, or even for holidays, something for which nobody could get a loan in the thirties. Indeed, many of us are so indebted that we spend most of our lives working for the banks.

A similar phenomenon occurred during the roaring twenties, probably the first great sustained bout of indebted extravagance. 'In the United States a feature of the expansion [in the 1920s] was abundant supplies of credit,' economic historians Barry Eichengreen and Kris Mitchener have explained. Loans were freely available for practically anything – for sharemarket investment, real estate, and consumer durables from motor cars and sewing machines to radios and pianos. A whole new wave of lending institutions – finance companies of various kinds – sprang up, rolling around the world from America into Britain and several Empire nations, Europe, Scandinavia and Japan. Modelled on the automobile companies' finance divisions, they issued personal debt with unprecedented generosity. Known as the instalment plan in America and as hire purchase in Britain, the principle was the same: buy now, pay later.

One of the results of such easy credit was that at the time of the Crash 80 per cent of Americans had no savings at all. This was partly because their disposable income was relatively low but also because much of what was left went into finance payments. It was the same in Britain and other countries, albeit on a smaller scale because the consumer finance industry had started there from a much lower base.

Another thought-provoking comparison with today is the remarkably low interest rates that prevailed in the twenties. They were so tempting they encouraged lenders to compensate for low real returns by multiplying the volume and size of the debt they issued, a tactic which quickly and inevitably led to financial excesses. This generally happens when, as economists point out, the natural rate of interest (the one more accurately reflecting prevailing conditions) is higher than the market rate (what borrowers are charged).

Just one consequence of this almost desperate lending was a boom in commercial construction projects around the world but particularly in major American cities, most of it financed by banks. Another was an avalanche of farm and residential mortgages, many of them of dubious merit just like today. Mortgage lending multiplied wildly in the run-up to the Crash, more than tripling in the United States. When the bottom fell out of the sharemarkets of the world and entire economies crashed, borrowers were stuck with hefty debt secured against assets of declining value, also like today.

Another noteworthy point of comparison is the level of leverage – the amount of debt piled on top of principal. When money is cheap, levels are historically high. The result is an explosion of credit.

The investment trusts that sprang up in the 1920s were pyramids of debt teetering on a tiny base of capital. These financial structures first made their appearance in England in the late nineteenth century but it was American financiers who souped them up in precisely the same way as today's hedge funds did with their asset-backed paper incorporating layer upon layer of subprime and other forms of debt. By the time of the Crash, the investment trusts had been converted into the financial equivalent of skyscrapers in the hands of Wall Street's operators. As more and more margin – or borrowed money – piled into the investment trusts, they became fatally top-heavy with debt. When they imploded, that debt was multiplied in exactly the same way as the profits had been in better times. Thus, although the US Federal Reserve and other central banks did not print money wildly at the time, constrained as they were by the rules of the gold standard, they were undermined by the rapid expansion of credit in the roaring twenties equivalent of the secondary banking market.

Similarly, central bankers were aghast when they discovered the prevailing levels of leverage in the financial markets in the run-up to the credit crunch of mid-2007. Ratios of ten to one were common in the roaring early years of the new millennium, with reports of a stratospheric 100 to one. When conditions are right, as indeed they had been, these levels massively increase the capacity for profits far above the financial instrument's underlying earnings. But of course the reverse applies when conditions change for the worse. As Warren Buffett, one of the world's richest men and certainly its greatest investor, famously observed, such instruments are 'weapons of mass destruction'. Until mid-2007, many ignored him.

As economists have pointed out for over a century, the rapid expansion of credit always poses risk. As long ago as the 1870s, Henry George established the connection between easy debt and wild speculation. In the thirties Lionel Robbins blamed the Depression on credit growth, as indeed did J.K.Galbraith. Although this is supposedly the age of disciplined regulation of financial, share and other markets – a trend that originated in the thirties – somehow the banks managed to slip the regulators' leash, distributing credit around the world like so much chaff. Casinos were literally better regulated than the banking industry.

So, once again the banking industry is bracing itself for an entirely new and much more forceful era of supervision because of the damage left in the wake of the 'worst crisis since the second world war'. It may work out better this time, it may not.

Meantime, the big question must be: are we in for another Depression? The answer very much depends on the financial condition of the individual or company. A golden rule says that heavy borrowing can work when things are buoyant; but the reverse applies when they go into headlong retreat. 'Investors who are seriously in debt when a price deflation occurs are in big trouble,' explained economic historian Roger W. Garrison in a survey of the causes of the Depression. 'If there are enough such people and they all have to tighten their belts, then aggregate spending falls precipitously and the whole economy is in big trouble – especially the banks. In the face of bad loans and hard times, banks become more conservative. They build up their reserves, which intensifies deflationary pressures. The big trouble gets bigger. This kind of self-aggravating process can turn a 1930 into a 1933.' Record levels of personal indebtedness, a general belt-tightening, fast-slowing growth, banks hoarding capital – we have all these conditions right now.

There is also a human dimension today that bears comparison with the Depression. Although the American economy boomed in the 1920s, much more strongly than the war-devastated European and British ones, the profits were unevenly shared in what amounted to a massive mal-distribution of wealth. In 1929, just 0.1 per cent of

Americans controlled 34 per cent of all savings, according to research by the Brookings Institute. Thus the gains were unevenly distributed, with average disposable income growing by just 9 per cent, many times below the increase in manufacturing output, yet the average disposable income for the top-earning 1 per cent shot up by an incredible 75 per cent. As economic historian Paul Gusmorino III pointed out in the mid-1990s, 'the rewards of the "Coolidge Prosperity" were not shared evenly among all Americans'.

In exactly the same way today, massive profits reaped by a handful of individuals, especially in the primary and secondary banking sectors but also in numerous other industries, have not been passed on. For example, the so-called private equity sector, which typically works on high levels of leverage, has been able to add value to companies through a combination of technical skill and the commitment of thousands of employees, yet the proceeds have not trickled down to the vast majority without whom this would not be possible. More provocatively, the single-digit tax rates paid by the partners on these profits are much lower than those levied on the majority of their employees. These disparities alarm social historians and indeed the more thoughtful members of the wider banking community, some of whom fear a widening split between owners and employees that is already reflected in a growing militancy by unions demanding a bigger share of the cake.

Yet there are good reasons for optimism. Like other industries that were once vital to a nation's economic well-being, the agricultural sector, which collapsed in the United States in the 1930s and greatly exacerbated the plight of many Americans, Australasians, Europeans and other peoples, is not nearly so important in today's much more diversified global economy. The same applies to textiles, coal, steel and other former warhorses of the economy.

Also, we are smarter than we were in the 1930s. The institutions that blundered about then, making one gaffe after another, are now greatly more experienced and knowledgeable. To put it another way, a repeat of the Smoot-Hawley Act is unlikely. As such, institutional intervention should be more effective, as indeed it has proved so far.

Additionally, the manufacturing economy around the world, which is the true engine of growth, is much bigger and more robust than it was (just one happy result is a booming global merchant navy and consequently buoyant ship-building industry). Increasingly affluent nations in Asia and eastern Europe have served to broaden global markets, underpinning manufacturers everywhere. Thus the world economy is more balanced, less dependent on the condition of a handful of nations, and therefore less vulnerable to shocks.

Still, anxieties remain that further unthinkable events may yet occur, like giant earthquakes. The ruptures that appeared from mid-2007 show that the financial system – and people's material wealth – is much more vulnerable than anybody thought.

Endnotes

1 *The Times*, 28 January 1931.
2 Ibid., 12 February 1931.
3 Ibid., 1 August 1931.
4 Ibid., 7 August 1931.
5 Ibid., 24 August 1931.
6 All reported by *The Times*.
7 'Central Banking as an Imperial Factor' (Cust Foundation Lecture, Nottingham University, 1934), pp. 1–17.
8 Quoted in *Dundee: A Short History* by Norman Watson (Black and White Publishing, 2006).
9 *Weevils in the Flour: An Oral Record of the 1930s Depression in Australia* (Scribe, 1998), p. 2.
10 Caleb Williams, curator of the Justice & Police Museum. Exhibition: Tough men, hard times. Policing the Depression.
11 It is interesting to speculate what the state of Britain's roads would be if the Romans had adopted a similar view.
12 *Brazen Hussies and God's Police: Fighting Back in the Depression Years* by Janey Stone (Hecate, 1982), vol. 8, p. 21.
13 *Australia and the Great Depression: A Study of Economic Development and Policy in the 1920s and 1930s* (Sydney University Press, 1988), p. 210.
14 Inaugural lecture as Ritchie Professor of Economics at the University of Melbourne, 28 April 1930.
15 *Palmers of Jarrow* by Jim Cuthbert and Ken Smith (Tyne Bridge Publishing, 2004), p. 40.
16 In a speech in 1935, claiming that Britain had regained '80 per cent of our prosperity'.

17 From chapter 14, 'The Great Crash and the Great Slump', in *Slouching Towards Utopia?: The Economic History of the Twentieth Century* (University of California at Berkeley and NBER, 1997).

18 *George Orwell* by Gordon Bowker (Abacus, 2003), p. 198.

19 *Ben Hogan – The Authorised Biography* (Aurum Press, 2004).

20 Quoted in *Hard Times: An oral history of the Great Depression* by Studs Terkel (The New Press, 2001).

21 'Money, Gold and the Great Depression', the H. Parker Willis lecture in economic policy, 2 March 2004.

22 Ibid.

23 Ibid.

24 From 'The First Hundred Days of the New Deal', essay in the *Aspirin Age: 1919–1941*, pp. 275–96 (Isabel Leighton ed. 1999).

25 Quoted in *Survey Graphic*, 1937. [vol/no.?]

26 Ibid., 1934, vol. 23, no. 9.

27 Quoted in *A Simple Code of Ethics: A History of the Moral Purpose Inspiring Federal Regulation of the Securities Industry* by John H. Walsh, in Hofstra Law Review, vol. 29, 2001.

Picture Credits

P. 1 (*top*) © H. Armstrong Roberts/Corbis (*bottom left*) © Getty Images (*bottom right*) © Getty Images; p. 2 (*top*) © Popperfoto/Getty Images (*bottom*) © MEPL; p. 3 (*top*) © Hulton-Deutsch Collection/Corbis (*bottom left*) © Getty Images (*bottom right*) © Getty Images; p. 4 (*top left*) © Library of Congress (*top right*) © Getty Images (*bottom*) © Getty Images; p. 5 (*top left*) © INTERFOTO Pressebildagentur/Alamy (*top right*) © Library of Congress (*bottom*) © Corbis; p. 6 (*top*) © Getty Images (*bottom left*) © Popperfoto/Getty Images (*bottom right*) © Hulton-Deutsch Collection/Corbis; p. 7 (*top left*) © Corbis (*top right*) © Bettmann/Corbis (*bottom*) © Library of Congress; p. 8 (*top*) © Bettmann/Corbis (*bottom*) © Bettmann/Corbis

Index